India and its Emerging Foreign Policy Challenges

India and its Emerging Foreign Policy Challenges

Editors

Dr. Roshan Khanijo & Dr. Anurag Tripathi

CHRIST
(DEEMED TO BE UNIVERSITY)
BENGALURU · INDIA

**United Service Institution
of India, New Delhi (India)**

**Christ University
Bangaluru (India)**

Vij Books India Pvt Ltd
New Delhi (India)

Published by

Vij Books India Pvt Ltd
(Publishers, Distributors & Importers)
2/19, Ansari Road
Delhi – 110 002
Phones: 91-11-43596460, 91-11-47340674
e-mail: vijbooks@rediffmail.com
web : www.vijbooks.com

First Published in India in 2018

ISBN: 978-93-86457-74-5 (Hardback)
ISBN: 978-93-86457-76-9 (ebook)

Contents

Around The World

Changing World and the Threat

Foreword

USI in collaboration with Christ University is publishing the first book titled "India and its Emerging Foreign Policy Challenges", a collection of articles written by Senior Research Scholars and few select articles written by young interns. This institution has been active in providing internship programmes to graduate/post graduate students coming from across the country. USI is well aware that today's youth, while enterprising and academically orientated, unfortunately lack a medium to express their views. Hence the institution has taken the initiative to encourage the students to pursue research on contemporary issues related to India, and has now made the effort publish their work. USI conducted a month-long internship programme where the students were acquainted with contemporary issues on National/International strategic affairs. Furthermore, they were also given an introduction to research methodology to provide them with the tools required to effectively conduct and pursue research in a disciplined manner. On the basis of their individual topics, the students were assigned to subject experts who provided them with guidance and insight and honed their research skills. This book is the culmination of the collaborative effort put by research scholars and by some of the students, their guides and our team at USI, to pursue novel modalities, and bring fresh research perspectives on current issues.

This is just the beginning and I am sure that the young interns will benefit from this exposure and this publication will help them in their future research careers. This book is the first step that has been made by the students in their pursuit of knowledge and serious research work. Since research is an ongoing process of learning, unlearning and relearning, starting so young will give them time to sharpen and hone their skills with age and experience. I am sure they will continue their journey down their various individual paths and be successful wherever they go from here. We at USI hope that we have been successful in generating interest among the students and helped them in developing the requisite skills to continue their academic pursuits. I wish them all the best and hope that in the future, they continue down this path and find themselves paving the way for a more inclusive and diverse academic environment.

Lt Gen PK Singh
Director
United Service Institution of India

Foreword

As a growing power, India's relationship with the external world is an important matter to study. This book covers various aspects of India's relationships as well as emerging geopolitical scenarios which invariably receive heightened attention among scholars and policy analysts. It is a compilation of scholarly works focusing on different strategic issues of India's concern which include maritime security, geo-economics, ethnic conflict, climate change, cyber security and so on. It is, indeed, a great effort by the Christ University and the United Service Institution of India to bring out a book collecting chapters from both young and emerging scholars and seasoned practitioners together to analyse the issues of India's foreign policy. I congratulate all the contributors for their endeavor to complete this project. I hope this book will help a better understanding in the foreign policy analysis of India.

Fr Jose C C PhD
Director,
Department of International Studies,
Christ University

Abbreviations

AL	Awami League
ARF	ASEAN Regional Forum
BGB	Border Guards Bangladesh
BIDA	Bangladesh Investment Development Authority
BIMSTEC	Bay of Bengal initiative for Multi-Sectoral Technical and Economic Cooperation
BNP	Bangladesh National Party
BSF	Border Security Force
CAR	Central Asia Republic
CBMP	Coordinated Border Management Plan
CBM	Confidence Building Measures
CCCC	China Communication Construction Company
CCS	Cabinet Security Committee
CIJWS	Counter Insurgency and Jungle Warfare School
CRED	Centre for Research on the Epidemiology of diseases
CSIR	Council of Scientific and Industrial Research
EC	European Commission
EGX	Egyptian Exchange
ETIM	East Islamic Turkistan Movement
FICCI	Federation of Indian Chambers of Commerce and Industry
GoI	Government of India
ICP	Integrated Check Posts
IDLG	Independent Directorate of Local Governance
ITEC	India Technical and Economic Cooperation
ICCR	Indian Council for Cultural Relations

IGCC	Indira Gandhi Cultural Centre
IOR	Indian Ocean Region
IOR-ARC	Indian Ocean Rim Association for Regional Cooperation
IPCC	Inter – Governmental Panel on Climate Change
ISIS	Islamic State of Iraq and Syria or the Islamic State of Iraq and al-Sham
IS	Islamic State
ISIL	Islamic State of Iraq and the Levant
IMU	Islamic Movement of Uzbekistan
JCC	Joint Consultative Commission
LBA	Land Boundary Agreement
LCS	Land Customs Stations
LTTE	Liberation Tigers of Tamil Eelam
MEA	Ministry of External Affairs
MHA	Ministry of Home Affairs
MOEF	Ministry of Environment and Forest Affairs
MPMAR	Ministry of Planning, Monitoring and Administrative Reform
MSR	Maritime Silk Road
NDMA	National Disaster Management Authority
NLD	National League for Democracy
ODA	Official Development Assistance
PIWTT	Protocol on Inland Water Trade and Transit
RTD	Registered Traveler Program
SAFTA	South Asian Free Trade Area
SDP	Sustainable Development Projects
SIMBEX	Singapore India Maritime Bilateral Exercise
TIP	Turkestan Islamic Party
UNCLOS	United Nations Convention on the Law of the Sea
XUAR	Xinjiang Uyghur Autonomous Region

Contributors

1. Dr Roshan Khanijo – Senior Research Fellow, USI.

2. Dr Anurag Tripathi - Assistant Professor, Christ University, Bangalore.

3. Dr BinodKumar Singh - Research Associate, Institute for Conflict Management, New Delhi.

4. Dr N. Koiremba Singh - Assistant Professor, Christ University, Bangalore.

5. DrVenu Gopal Menon - Professor, Christ University, Bangalore.

6. Mr. Paul Verghese - Research Assistant, Centre for Development Studies, Trivandrum.

7. Dr Madhumati Deshpande - Assistant Professor in Christ University, Bangalore.

8. Dr JoshyM.Paul - Assistant Professor, Christ University, Bangalore.

9. Dr Sanchita Bhattacharya - Research Fellow, JNU and visiting scholar in Institute for Conflict Management, New Delhi.

10. Cdr Subhasish Sarangi - Senior Research Fellow, USI.

11. Mr Gaurav Kumar - Research Associate, USI.

12. Ms Richa Dohgera - Research Scholar, Christ University and USI.

13. Ms Apoorvi Mishra - Research Scholar, Christ University and USI.

14. Mr Ram Prasad. P - Research Scholar, Christ University and USI.

15. Ms Shivangi Srivastava - Research Scholar, Christ University and USI.

16. Mr R.L.Abishek - Research Scholar, Christ University and USI.

17. Mr ArunTeja. P - Research Scholar, Christ University.

18. Ms SoundaryaJ - Research Scholar, Christ University.

19. Mr Shantanu Roy-Chaudhury – Research Scholar, USI, now doing M.Phil in Oxford University.

20. Ms Bhavya A. G - Research Scholar, Christ University and USI.

21. Mr Aditya G. S - Research Scholar, Christ University and USI.

India and its Emerging Foreign Policy Challenges

Introduction

Dr. Roshan Khanijo & Dr. Anurag Tripathi

This book titled, "India and its Emerging Foreign Policy Challenges", is a joint effort by the Christ (Deemed to be University), Bengaluru, and United Service Institution of India, New Delhi. The book focuses on India's foreign policy challenges, as also the emerging major global threats.

India's endeavour under Prime Minister Modi is to actively interact and cooperate with the international community and to promote India's regional and global objectives. India has tried to deepen her engagements with the South Asian neighbours, as also built important strategic partnerships with U.S, Russia, Korea and Japan. There has been an upward trajectory in India's Act East Policy, in terms of political, economic and defence cooperation, and her engagement with the Southeast Asian and East Asian countries has enlarged. In her Look West Policy, India is simultaneously, trying to balance her relationship with the Gulf nations and Israel. Thus, India is slowly expanded its diplomatic footprint and its outreach, to both, existing as well as new partners.

But as the global environment is dynamic, hence issues like climate change, cyber, terrorism, etc, are challenging the nations. In India's neighbourhood, the nuclear brinkmanship has seen an upward turn both in terms of missile development as well as its diversification. In such an environment, it becomes imperative to understand the global threats as also India's approach to these and other regional and sub regional challenges.

Therefore, this book is divided into three parts. The first part deals with a brief overview of India and its emerging foreign policy, starting with the neighbourhood. The first article in this section is the "Indo-Bangladesh Relations: Scaling New Heights", which is written by Dr. Binod Kumar

Singh. With Bangladesh, India has many broad areas of cooperation but there are contentions also - like sharing of river waters, border management, etc.; these contentious issues may impact Indo-Bangladesh relations. The friendly relations between the two countries cannot continue, if key bilateral issues are not resolved peacefully and equitably. India, as an emerging power, has the responsibility to understand and respect the concerns of small neighbours, and so it needs to take initiative to settle the bilateral issues with sensitivity and common sense. Although, under the present leadership there is tremendous goodwill for Indian people in Bangladesh, but the same may change if there is a change in the leadership, as there are disgruntle elements in Bangladesh, who have a more pro-China approach. Hence there is a need to settle the issues and build a long-lasting relationship with Bangladesh.

Dr. N. Koiremba Singh and Ms. Richa Dohgera in their article, "Security Environment of Afghanistan: Implications for India", discusses the rising vulnerability to Afghan people, from various terror groups. The threat from the Taliban though has lessened to some extent, but it has also led to other terror networks becoming active in Afghanistan, thereby, also overshadowing hopes of reconciliation. The ISIS with the loss of its territories in Iraq and Mosul, are now in search of new breeding grounds and their target is Afghanistan. The authors point out to the anti-Western and anti-American propaganda, that the terrorist organizations have adopted. In 2017 ISIS attacked a hospital in Kabul, killing 38 people. Though, the Americans retaliated by having air raids on the terrorist camps of ISIS, killing at least 35 ISIS militants, but the threat continues. The author believes that a peaceful Afghanistan will play a pivotal role in the security dynamics of the Indian sub-continent.

Dr. Joshy. M. Paul, in his article "India-ASEAN Maritime Cooperation" discusses the importance of India's Maritime Cooperation with the South East Asian nations in facilitating peace and security. He also recommends a Quadrilateral maritime exercise in the territorial waters of the ASEAN countries, and also highlights the significance of India's presence in South East Asia, to counter China's presence in the Indian Ocean region.

Dr. Madhumati Deshpande and Ms. Apoorvi Mishra in their article "The Major Irritants in Sino-Indian Relations: The way Forward", describes, in four phases the relationship between India and China. The article also tracks the growing economic and commercial trajectory between the two countries. The article enunciates that it is imperative for the two countries to solve their political disputes -starting with the border issues,(and the need for a workable solution for the borders). This, in turn may help in building up a conducive environment for economic growth and stability.

Continuing, with a competitive India-China relation in the global sphere, Mr. Ramprasad P in his article, "India and China: Eying Foreign Ports in Sri Lanka", narrates the growing influence of China in Sri Lanka. China's efforts to develop the Hambantota port and the economic hardships and the debt trap of Sri Lanka. He also discusses India's efforts to build infrastructure in Sri Lanka. He lays emphasis on the joint cooperation of India and China in non-traditional security challenges like piracy, natural calamities, etc in the Indian Ocean Region, which may reduce tensions and build confidence. The author suggests the need for an effective long-term strategy to counter China in Sri Lanka.

Ms. Shivangi Shrivastava in her essay "Strategic Importance of Myanmar for India", describes the emergence of Myanmar as a lucrative destination, and also a gateway to South East Asia, for India. Thus, Myanmar is an important country for India's 'Act East Policy'. Myanmar due to its geographical location can also facilitate better security management for the Northeastern states of India, provided, India develops better relationship with Myanmar. China is expanding its trade and transport network with Myanmar, which is a concern for India, as the Northeast region of India, has become highly susceptible to the offensive Chinese economic trade practices; whereby, these territories are made the dumping grounds for Chinese cheap goods. Also, Chinese intrusion into the Indian Territory, which China claims to be theirs, is a cause of concern. The author thus, suggests resolution of existing border problems between the two countries, through creation of smart borders, thereby, decreasing the chances of China's interfere in the Northeastern states of India.

Mr Gaurav Kumar in his article, "The Changing Trajectory of Indo-US Relations", traces the journey of the Indo-US relation, which has seen an upward trajectory for the last few years. The two nations are the strongest supporters of democracy and have witnessed unprecedented bilateral cooperation, which has also led to multilateral cooperation, and is set to shape the global arena in the coming years. In contemporary global settings, the relationship truly appears to be of two natural allies, having common understanding of the threats, and also have similar solutions to those threats.

The current thrust and the tenor of the relationship thus, provides clear indication as to what direction the future holds for these two countries. The author lists the various areas of cooperation and the endeavour is to make the relationship stronger and long lasting.

Cdr Subhasish Sarangi in his article, "India and Japan: Confluence of Strategic Interests", traces the historical relationship between the two countries. Japan's engagement with independent India commenced with the signing of a peace treaty on 09 June 1952. Japan was one of the earliest foreign aid contributors to India with its Overseas Development Assistance (ODA) that commenced in 1958, and has consistently provided financial assistance to India over the decades. The bilateral relationship though suffered a setback in 1998 due to the nuclear explosions undertaken by India; however, the relationship since then has grown tremendously, especially under the leadership of PM Modi and PM Abe. There has been confluence of mutual strategic interests which has led to an all-round development between the two countries.

Mr. R.L Abhishek in the article, "China, Pakistan Nuclear Posture: Challenges for India", narrates the nuclear environment in South Asia. The challenges and compulsions faced by India, to become a Nuclear Weapon State. He also analyses in detail the nuclear doctrines of Pakistan and China and how it may impact India. It gives suggestion as to how India's nuclear doctrine can be strengthened, so that nuclear deterrence is maintained.

The second part of the book deals with some major predicaments that few nations are facing.

Dr. Sanchita Bhattacharya in her article, "Separatism and Struggle for Autonomy in Xinjiang" discusses the Uyghur militancy in Western China. The author talks about the need for an inclusive Chinese policy, where the Muslim population of China is integrated in to the mainstream. The Chinese government needs to develop empathy towards the Uyghur minorities of Xinjiang, if they want to prevent the problem from getting escalated. The social, cultural, economic, condition of Uyghur in Xinjiang needs to be addressed, if political situation needs to improve.

Mr. Arun Teja in his article, "Egypt's Uncertain Future under President Al Sisi's Rule", narrates the past political and economic turmoil in Egypt, and the continuation of the same, should parallel economic developmental programme fails in Egypt. This is because; it would make Egypt highly dependent on foreign nations, due to its growing economic debt. On political front, long term deprivation of rights may result in dissatisfaction amongst the public, though; in near future this may not be a threat, as President Al-Sisi enjoys a positive image amongst the society and media, (due to its propaganda of economic development), resulting in lesser anti – Sisi position. However, things may change and the political turmoil may resume as Egypt has a history of armed revolt.

Ms. Soundarya J in her article, 'Countering China's Legal Warfare in Territorial Disputes: Doklam and South China Sea', discusses the lessons learnt from Doklam dispute. It describes in detail the "Three Warfare" of China and the result of Doklam issue as a new strategy, to counter Chinese brinkmanship. It debates the need for a political will, to not to succumb, to China's Three Warfare strategy.

The final part of the book deals with three major threats, namely, climate change, terrorism and cyber challenge.

Ms. Bhavya AG in her article "The Impact of Climate Change on Natural Disasters in India" narrates the emerging threat of global warming and climate change to India, as also to other nations. There is a need to recognise a nations' ability to prevent, mitigate, respond and recover from these catastrophic events. More and more nations are becoming vulnerable to climate change, and there is a need to address this challenge systematically, because if timely actions are not taken, then the nations may have to divert a large sum of money in disaster management, which can impact the economic growth of the country.

Mr. Shantanu Roy-Chaudhury in his article, "ISIS and India", describes how the Islamic State of Iraq and Syria (ISIS) took the world by storm in 2014, when it managed to capture large tracts of land in Iraq and Syria. By declaring itself a caliphate and through extremely successful online propaganda, the organisation managed to lure thousands from and around the world, to fight for them. What set them apart from other groups was their ability to use social media for recruitment. This success also led to many people being radicalised in other countries and carrying out the attacks planned by ISIS. Although, ISIS began its propaganda in India, the organisation failed to gain a strong foothold in the country, despite the fact that India is a home to the third largest Muslim population in the world. Credit has to be given to the Indian government and its counter terrorism units along with the population, which for the most part has resisted the "caliphate". However, although ISIS has been declining drastically, it should not be written off, as with its method of lone wolf attacks, it may create mayhem, as it has been partially successful in creating terror in Europe and other parts of the world.

Mr. Aditya GS in his article "The Need for Global Cyber Laws", states that the threat of Cyber Law cannot alone be solved through new software or passing of legislation. It is therefore required that there should be a global consensus on the implementation of a universal cyber law, without breaching the state sovereignty. The article also tries to discuss the various global cyber conventions like the Budapest convention, the Tallinn Manual, UN efforts, etc, to highlight the importance of countering cyber challenges.

Thus, this book's endeavour is to give a broad outlay of challenges both global and regional, so that a reader develops a holistic view of India's challenges. These may emerge from its immediate neighbourhood, as also due to global issues like terrorism, climate change and cyber.

Indo–Bangladesh Relations: Scaling New Heights

Dr. Binod Kumar Singh

India and Bangladesh share a unique bond and a special relationship rooted in a common cultural heritage, shared principles and values, and forged by common aspirations and sacrifices of its peoples. India is committed to carry forward the mission of strengthening the historic bonds and impart a vision for the future that is durable and sustainable and conducive for the collective prosperity of the region. (MEA, GoI, 2012) India was the first country to recognize Bangladesh as a separate and independent state and established diplomatic relations with the country immediately after its independence in December 1971. (MEA, GoI, 2016)

Bangladesh emerged on the world scene as an independent Sovereign Republic on December 16, 1971, under the politico-military patronage of India and this set the stage for Indo-Bangladesh relations. India's active assistance in the freedom struggle of Bangladesh contributed to a warm start in Indo-Bangladesh relations. In fact, India played a pivotal role in the liberation of Bangladesh. India proved to be the strongest and closest ally of Bangladesh throughout the war, India sheltered about 10 million refugees from Bangladesh, hosted the Bangladesh government -in-exile and eventually took part in the 1971 war. India thereby earned the friendship of Bangladesh. (Nair, 2008)

India is a significant factor in the domestic politics of Bangladesh. The depth of the relationship with India has become a cliché to define 'independence' of Bangladesh. Insecurities regarding India in strategic and politico-economic context are fathomable but what one fails to understand is the manner in which India is dragged into the political rivalry between the two dominant parties – the Awami League (AL) and Bangladesh Nationalist Party

(BNP). The overwhelming domestic political compulsions in Bangladesh have severely restricted the Indo-Bangladesh relations and have been made both the countries extremely cautious about dealing with each other. Extreme cautiousness especially in the case of Bangladesh's approach to the bilateral issues with India has resulted in a sluggish progress on bilateral issues. (World Focus, 2006)

Thus, India and Bangladesh relations have suffered cyclic phases of highs and lows, largely reflecting the changing governments both in Dhaka and New Delhi.

Indo-Bangladesh relations contain many ideological issues, characterised by political misunderstanding and a perceived sense of economic dominance. The question that has puzzled the minds of policy makers and analysts in both the countries is why the relationship that was marked by the euphoria over India's role in the Liberation War have been one of the difficult relations that India has with the South Asian neighbours. From the Indian point of view, there is a historic sense of hurt and betrayal. Though India played an important role in the creation of Bangladesh it is primarily seen as a threat. India's sheer size, its economic potential has added to its ability to intervene. This is seen by Bangladesh with apprehensions. Extreme sense of distrust, insecurity and perceived domination of India has shaped Bangladesh's foreign policy. (World Affairs, 1999) Therefore, Bangladesh's responses to foreign policy choices have been cautious and measured. It is hesitant and finds it uncomfortable to function under a bilateral parameter. Whether it is trade, export of gas, provision of transit or water issue, it has argued for multilateral arrangements. A divided polity, polarized on ideological line and extremely sensitive political atmosphere has made both the political parties of Bangladesh (AL and BNP) and their relations with India subject to domestic political dynamics. It also has constrained India to take the relations forward and India has been circumspect in its reaction to various statements that emanates from Dhaka. (World Focus, 2006)

However, since 2007, there has been a positive engagement between the two countries. And after the AL assumed power in January 2009, the relationship has scaled a new height. Both countries have witnessed high level visits in the past eight years. The then President of India, Shri Pranab Mukherjee, during a speech on November 19, 2015, said "India-Bangladesh relations are a good example of progress in looking at a shared future. Our relations today are the best ever since 1974. They are based on mutual benefit, equality and respect for sovereignty. India attaches the highest importance to bilateral relations with Bangladesh. We have always believed that strong, stable and prosperous neighbours are in our interest. India and Bangladesh are not just neighbours. We are two nations bound by the threads of history, religion, culture, language and kinship." (President's Secretariat, GoI, 2015)

High Level Visits

There have been regular high-level visits and exchanges between the two countries. There have also been frequent visits at Ministerial level as well as between senior officials on a regular basis. Bilateral relations between India and Bangladesh received a major boost through the landmark State visit by the Prime Minister Mr. Narendra Modi, to Bangladesh from June 6-7, 2015, at the invitation of the Prime Minister Sheikh Hasina. During the visit, 22 bilateral documents were concluded, including the exchange of instrument of ratification for India-Bangladesh Land Boundary Agreement (LBA) and a second Line of Credit (LoC) worth US$ 2 billion. (High Commission of India, Dhaka, 2015)

To participate in the first edition of the Raisina Dialogue being organized by the Ministry of External Affairs and the Observer Research Foundation, H.E. Mr. Abul Hassan Mahmood Ali, Foreign Minister of Bangladesh, visited New Delhi from March 1-3, 2016. On March 2, 2016, Foreign Minister Ali had a bilateral meeting with the Indian counterpart during which the two Ministers reviewed progress on bilateral cooperation initiatives since Prime Minister Modi's visit to Dhaka in June 2015. Applauding the excellent state of relations that currently prevail between India and Bangladesh, they expressed their determination to deepen ties even further. (MEA, GoI, 2016)

As part of regular interaction between the two sides, Foreign Secretary of India Dr. S Jaishankar paid a bilateral visit to Bangladesh from May 11-12, 2016. During the talks, both Foreign Secretaries reviewed progress on decisions and understandings reached during the visit of Hon'ble Prime Minister of India Narendra Modi to Bangladesh in June 2015. Both sides noted with appreciation that there has been excellent implementation of decisions taken, which are evident from the results in all sectors. (MEA, GoI, 2016) At the invitation of the Foreign Secretary of Bangladesh Mr. Md. Shahidul Haque, Dr. S Jaishankar, Foreign Secretary of India, visited Bangladesh from February 23-24, 2017. During his stay, the two Foreign Secretaries reviewed the areas of bilateral cooperation between the two countries. Both Foreign Secretaries also shared their perspectives on regional and international issues of mutual interest. (MEA, GoI, 2017)

Notably, at the invitation of Indian Prime Minister Shri Narendra Modi, Prime Minister of Bangladesh Sheikh Hasina was on a State Visit to India from April 7-10, 2017. During the visit, 36 bilateral documents were concluded in various areas including in high technology areas of Civil Nuclear Energy, Space, Information Technology, Defence, Capacity building etc. A third Line of Credit (LoC) worth US$ 4.5 billion was also extended to Bangladesh. (MEA, GoI, 2017) The two Prime Ministers also decided to mark the year 2018 as the Year of India in Bangladesh, and 2019 as the Year of Bangladesh in India. They also decided to commemorate the 50th anniversary of the Liberation War of Bangladesh in 2021 and 75th anniversary of India's independence from British rule in 2022. (MEA, GoI, 2017)

Further, Indian Finance Minister Mr. Arun Jaitley arrived in Dhaka on October 3, 2017, afternoon on a three-day official visit at the invitation of Bangladesh Finance Minister Mr. AMA Muhith. A 30-member high-level business delegation from the Federation of Indian Chambers of Commerce and Industry (FICCI) also accompanied the Finance Minister of India. Remarkably, on October 4, 2017, after signing a $4.5 billion Line of Credit (LoC), Mr. Arun Jaitley said "India-Bangladesh relations are at their best today and stand out as a model for other countries to emulate. India is fully committed to partner Bangladesh in its economic development. As a longstanding development partner of Bangladesh, we have extended three LoCs worth $8 billion to Bangladesh in recent years." (*Dhaka Tribune*, 2017)

Separately, Indian External Affairs Minister Mrs. Sushma Swaraj visited Bangladesh from October 22-23, 2017, to attend the fourth Bangladesh-India Joint Consultative Commission (JCC) meeting. They discussed the common challenges such as terrorism, extremism and radicalization. They also discussed various aspects of the bilateral relations and reviewed progress on key initiatives and decisions, including those taken during the recent visit of Hon'ble Prime Minister of Bangladesh to India. (MEA, GoI, 2017)

Bilateral institutional mechanisms

There are more than 50 bilateral institutional mechanisms between India and Bangladesh in the areas of security, trade & commerce, power & energy, transport & connectivity, science and technology, defence, rivers & maritime affairs etc. (MEA, GoI, 2017) The principal mechanisms are:

1) **Political and Security Cooperation**

Home Minister level bilateral talks between India and Bangladesh were held in New Delhi on July 28, 2016. The Bangladesh delegation was led by the Home Minister Mr. Asaduzzaman Khan and Indian delegation by Union Home Minister Shri Rajnath Singh. The two Ministers emphasized the need for speedy operationalization of three bilateral memorandum of understandings (MoUs), signed during the visit of the Prime Minister of India to Bangladesh in June 2015. Both sides emphasized the importance of effective implementation of the Coordinated Border Management Plan (CBMP) to enhance cooperation between the border guarding forces of the two countries and to enable them to better monitor the identified vulnerable areas. They also expressed satisfaction over the signing of an addendum to the Bilateral Extradition Treaty of 2013 to further streamline the Treaty and to make it more effective. (MHA, GoI, 2016)

The Fourth meeting of the India-Bangladesh Joint Consultative Commission (JCC) was held in Dhaka when Mrs. Sushma Swaraj, the Minister of External Affairs of India, paid an official visit to Dhaka from October 22-23, 2017. During her visit, she and her counterpart reviewed bilateral ties and discuss ways to further strengthen the relationship. (MEA, GoI, 2017) She also inaugurated 15 Indian-assisted development projects worth about $8.7 million including installation of 11 water treatment plants in the southwestern coastline of Pirozpur, 36 community clinics and reconstruction of Dhaka's historic Ramna Kali Temple destroyed by invading Pakistani troops in the 1971 Liberation War. (*The Hindu*, 2017) The 3rd JCC was held in New Delhi on September 20, 2014. Separately, Indian and Bangladeshi Armies on November 16, 2017, concluded a joint 13-day counter-terrorism exercise in the north eastern Indian state of Mizoram. The training exercise, codenamed "Sampriti 2017", was held at the Counter Insurgency and Jungle Warfare School (CIJWS) at Vairengte in Mizoram. It was the seventh exercise in the Sampriti series. The exercise was aimed at strengthening and broadening the aspects of interoperability and cooperation between the Indian and Bangladeshi Armies. (*The Daily Star*, 2017)

2) **Bilateral Trade and Investment**

The first Trade Agreement between India and Bangladesh was signed in 1972. During the visit of Prime Minister Narendra Modi to Bangladesh in June 2015, the trade agreement between the two countries was renewed for a period of five years (2015-2020) with a provision for auto renewal. There are a number of other trade related agreements that have been signed between both countries. Bilateral trade between India and Bangladesh has grown steadily over the last decade. In the past five years, total trade between the two countries has grown by more than 17%. India's exports to Bangladesh in the period July 2016 – March 2017 stood at US$ 4489.30 million and imports from Bangladesh during FY 2016-17 stood at US$ 672.40 million. (MEA, GoI, 2017)

Moreover, India has provided duty free quota free access to Bangladesh on all tariff lines except tobacco and alcohol under South Asian Free Trade Area (SAFTA) since 2011. Four Border Haats, two each in Tripura and Meghalaya, have been established for the benefit of bordering communities. Additional Border Haats on the India-Bangladesh border are under consideration. Total Indian investment proposals in Bangladesh registered with the Bangladesh Investment Development Authority (BIDA) exceed US$ 3billion. Indian Foreign Direct Investment (FDI) in Bangladesh reached US$ 88 million in 2015-16. During PM Sheikh Hasina's visit in April 2017, 13 agreements worth around US$ 10 billion, mainly Indian investment in power and energy sectors in Bangladesh were signed. (MEA, GoI, 2017)

3) Economic Assistance to Bangladesh

India has extended 3 Lines of Credits (LoCs) to Bangladesh in the last 7 years amounting to US$ 8 billion. This makes Bangladesh the largest recipient of LoC funds from India till date. The first LoC of US$ 1 billion was extended to Bangladesh in 2010 for developing infrastructure projects, mostly in the infrastructure and communications sector. The second LoC of US$ 2 billion was announced during the visit of the PM Narendra Modi to Bangladesh in June 2015. And the third LoC was signed during the visit of Bangladesh PM to India in April 2017. The new Indian LoC, worth a staggering $4.5 billion, will be used to fund 17 major projects in Bangladesh, which include electricity, railroads, roads, shipping and ports. (*Business Today*, 2017) This is the biggest-ever credit New Delhi has given to any country.

In addition to LoC funds, Government of India also provides grant assistance to Bangladesh for projects under 'Aid to Bangladesh'. Projects such as construction of school/college buildings, laboratories, dispensaries, deep tube wells, community centers, renovation of historical monuments/ buildings etc, have been financed by Government of India under this programme. At present, three Sustainable Development Projects (SDPs) are being undertaken in the cities of Rajshahi, Khulna and Sylhet. The extended development work of Rabindra Nath Tagore's ancestral house in Shilaidaha is as well as 36 community clinics in selected districts of Bangladeshis also being undertaken. One of the biggest projects under the Indian grant assistance is the Bangladesh section of the Agartala-Akhaura rail-link. (MEA, GoI, 2017)

4) **Power and Energy Cooperation**

Cooperation in power sector has become one of the hallmarks of India Bangladesh relations. India currently exports 660 MW of electricity, on a daily basis, to Bangladesh. Of the total, 250 MW is sold through a bilateral agreement at India's domestic generation tariff. The rest are open market purchases. Of the total supplies, 500 MW is transmitted to Bangladeshi power grid through Bheramara in Mursidabad and the remaining 160 MW through Suryamaninagar in Tripura to meet the local demand of South Comilla district of Bangladesh. The current supplies are over seven per cent of Bangladesh's own generation of 9,000 MW and five per cent of the projected demand of 12,600 MW by the Bangladesh Power Development Board. (*Hindu Business Line*, 2017) Supply of another 500 MW is expected to begin in 2018.

Energy sector cooperation between India and Bangladesh has also seen considerable progress in the last two years. With power and gas leading the $9-billion investment projects India has proposed to make in Bangladesh to help strengthen Dhaka's emerging industrial base. The Reliance and Adani Groups, and power behemoth National Thermal Power Corporation (NTPC) were among the Indian companies that concluded investment proposals on April 10, 2017, to supply electricity, and enhance power generation in the easterly neighbour. (*Economic Times*, 2017) Notably, on May 24, 2017: Reliance Group of India was awarded a deal without any tender for setting up a Liquefied Natural Gas (LNG)-based 750 megawatt power plant at Meghnaghat in Narayanganj. This will allow Indian company to sell per unit of electricity at BTK 5.80 to the state-owned Power Development Board (PDB). The deal would cost cash-starved PDB BTK 80,945.41 crore in 22 years. PDB would buy electricity for 22 years after commissioning of the plant scheduled in 2019. (*New Age*, 2017) Meghnaghat is one of three power plants Reliance Group proposed to set up to produce 3000mw electricity. Two other proposed power plants would be set up in Chittagong and Maheshkhali.

5) **Connectivity**

India-Bangladesh is a good example of connectivity through all modes of transport. The movement of goods by road is operationalised through 36

15

functional Land Customs Stations (LCSs) and two Integrated Check Posts (ICPs) along the border. The Protocol on Inland Water Trade and Transit (PIWTT) which has been operational since 1972, permits movement of goods over barges/vessels from India through the river systems of Bangladesh on eight specific routes. Coastal Shipping Agreement signed during the visit of Prime Minister Narendra Modi to Bangladesh in June 2015 has also enabled direct sea movement of containerized/bulk/dry cargo between the two countries. Out of the erstwhile six rail links that existed, four Broad Gauge inter-country rail links between the two countries are operational now. There are regular bus services between Kolkata-Dhaka, Shillong-Dhaka, Agartala-Kolkata and Dhaka-Khulna-Kolkata. There are presently around 100 flights operating weekly between India and Bangladesh connecting various Indian cities like New Delhi, Kolkata, Mumbai and Chennai to Dhaka and Chittagong. From Bangladesh, US-Bangla Airlines, NOVOAIR, Regent Airways and Biman Bangladesh; and from India, Jet Airways, Spice Jet and Air India are operating flights between India and Bangladesh. (MEA, GoI, 2017)

One more new rail link between Akhaura (Bangladesh) and Agartala (India) is proposed to be built. The Foundation stone of the project was jointly laid by the Hon'ble Railway Ministers of both the countries on July 31, 2016. And on October 16, 2017, the invitation for Tender (International)-Construction of Akhaura-Agartala Dual Gauge Railway Link (Bangladesh Portion) was announced by the Ministry of Railways, Government of the People's Republic of Bangladesh. (Ministry of Railways, GoB, 2017) Separately, as part of the India-Bangladesh cooperation for inland water transport, India on May 24, 2017, announced that India will finance 80 per cent of the estimated 220 crore required for dredging to maintain navigability in the Sirajganj-Daikhawa on the Jamuna Ashugunj-Karimgunj stretch of the Kushiyara river in Bangladesh to improve cargo movement from Kolkata to North-East through Bangladesh. India is already developing the Varanasi-Kolkata stretch, called NW (National Waterway)-1 as a fairway at an estimated 5,369 crores under World Bank assistance. A similar project for developing the NW-2 from Dhubri to Sadiya (MP), with World Bank assistance, is currently under consideration. (*Hindu Business Line*, 2017)

6) **Security and Border Management**

India and Bangladesh share 4096.7 km. of border, which is the longest land boundary that India shares with any of its neighbours. The India-Bangladesh

Land Boundary Agreement (LBA) came into force following the exchange of instruments of ratification in June 2015. On July 31, 2015, the enclaves of India and Bangladesh in each other's countries were exchanged and strip maps were signed. Residents of these erstwhile enclaves, who opted to retain their Indian citizenship made a final movement to India by November 30, 2015. A number of agreements related to security cooperation have been signed between both the countries. The Coordinated Border Management Plan (CBMP) signed in 2011 aims to synergize the efforts of both the Border Guarding Forces for checking cross border illegal activities and crimes as well as for maintenance of peace and tranquility along the India-Bangladesh border. The settlement of the maritime boundary arbitration between India and Bangladesh, as per United Nations Convention on the Law of the Sea (UNCLOS) award of July 7, 2014, has paved the way for the economic development of this part of the Bay of Bengal. (MEA, GoI, 2017)

India and Bangladesh on October 4, 2016, agreed to an effective implementation of a Coordinated Border Management Plan (CBMP) to prevent cross-border criminal activities and other issues. The decision was taken during the 43rd Director General (DG)-level border dialogue between India and Bangladesh. The Border Security Force (BSF) and Border Guards Bangladesh (BGB) agreed to take measures like additional vigilance in areas vulnerable to trans-border crimes like smuggling of drugs, cattle, gold and fake currency as well as human trafficking. (*Business Standard*, 2016) And during the 44th DG-level talks, on February 21, 2017, India and Bangladesh have agreed to conduct joint spot verification and appraisal after any major incident/killing of smugglers on the Indo-Bangla border in order to minimize misunderstandings over such incidents. The two sides also agreed to sensitize the border population on the sanctity of the border. (*Business Standard*, 2017)

7) Sharing of River Waters

India and Bangladesh share 54 common rivers. A bilateral Joint Rivers Commission (JRC) is working since June 1972 to maintain liaison between the two countries to maximize benefits from common river systems. Besides the meetings of the JRC (37 meetings held so far), JRC Technical level meetings are also held regularly. The Ganga Waters Treaty signed in 1996 for sharing of waters of river Ganga during lean season (January 1-May 31) is working satisfactorily. Regular meetings of the Joint Committee on

Sharing of Ganga Waters are held to take stock of the implementation of the provisions of the treaty. (MEA, GoI, 2017)

However, a very emotive issue in Bangladesh is the non-signing of Teesta river water sharing agreement with India. The Teesta deal was set to be signed during the then Prime Minister Manmohan Singh's visit to Bangladesh in September 2011, but was postponed at the last-minute due to objections by West Bengal Chief Minister Mamata Banerjee, who had also dropped out of the Prime Ministerial delegation. Assuring to sign an agreement on Teesta River water sharing at the earliest, on April 08, 2017, Indian Prime Minister Narendra Modi said an "early solution can and will be found" to the Teesta water sharing issue. (*Press Trust of India*, 2017) He said this during making a statement after official talks with visiting Bangladesh Prime Minister Sheikh Hasina in New Delhi.

8) Training and Capacity-Building

A number of training courses are being conducted for interested Bangladesh officials /nationals including personnel of administration, police, judiciary, fire-fighters, narcotic officials, nuclear scientists, teachers etc. Bangladesh is also an important India Technical and Economic Cooperation (ITEC) partner country, and around 800 participants from Bangladesh avail of training courses under the ITEC programme annually. In addition, scholarships are granted by ICCR (Indian Council for Cultural Relations) every year to students from Bangladesh. The scholarships are awarded to meritorious Bangladeshi nationals to pursue various courses in India at the Under Graduate, Post Graduate and PhD level, except in Medicine. Around 3000 ICCR Scholarships have been granted to Bangladeshi nationals by the Government of India till date. (High Commission of India, Dhaka, 2016)

A bilateral MoU on 'Training and Capacity Building of Bangladesh judicial officers in India' was concluded during the state visit of Prime Minister Sheikh Hasina to India in April 2017. Under the framework of MoU, India will extend training and capacity building to 1500 Bangladesh judicial officers at the National Judicial Academy and various State Judicial Academies in India. All expenses on the training, including international and domestic air fares, will be borne by the Government of India. Remarkably, the first batch of 40 Judicial Officers, comprising Senior Judicial Magistrates, Senior Assistant Judges, and Metropolitan Magistrates left for Bhopal, India, to attend the 'Training and Capacity Building Programme for Bangladesh Judicial Officers' on October 9, 2017. The training programme for Bangladesh Judicial Officers was administered under the ITEC plan of the Ministry of External Affairs, Government of India. (High Commission of India, Dhaka, 2017)

9) **Visa**

Large number of people from Bangladesh visit India frequently. They go for a variety of reasons - whether it is for maintaining family ties or for education, for business or for pilgrimage, for tourism or for medical treatment - there is always a reason to travel to India. The Indian High Commission in Dhaka and the two Assistant High Commissions in Chittagong and Rajshahi together issue the highest number of Indian visas compared to any other Indian Mission. The numbers are increasing manifold with the figures touching 9.33 lakhs in 2016. There are 12 Indian Visa Application Centres (IVAC) in Bangladesh managed by the State Bank of India (SBI): 4 in Dhaka (Gulshan, Dhanmondi, Motijheel and Uttara), Chittagong, Sylhet, Rajshahi, Khulna, Mynmensingh, Rangpur, Barisal and Jessore. (MEA, GoI, 2017)

Remarkably, during Sheikh Hasina's New Delhi tour from April 7-10, 2017, India liberalized rules for medical visas for Bangladesh nationals in an effort to further strengthen people-to-people ties between the two countries. (*The Independent*, 2017) In fact, according to a report by the Directorate-General of Commercial Intelligence and Statistics, Kolkata, one in three foreign patients in India are from Bangladesh. The report said of the 460,000 inbound patients to Indian hospitals, more than 165,000 were from Bangladesh in 2015-16 making Bangladesh the largest foreign user of India's health services. Over 58,000 medical visas were issued to Bangladeshi nationals in 2015-16. Since 2016, Bangladesh has unseated the US as the origin of the highest number of foreign tourists, mostly due to medical tourism. (*Business Standard*, 2017) Further, on July 25, 2017, the Indian government removed entry and exit restrictions on visas issued to Bangladesh nationals. Through removal of this restriction, now any Bangladesh national having Indian visa with name of entry or exit point (i.e. by air/ by road) will be able to enter to or exit from India through any of the 24 international airports and two ICPs (Petrapole-Benapole and Agartala-Akhaura). Previously, Bangladeshis could only travel through the ports indicated on their visas. (*Dhaka Tribune*, 2017)

10) Cultural Exchanges

The Indira Gandhi Cultural Centre (IGCC), High Commission of India, is a Cultural Centre of the Indian Council for Cultural Relations (ICCR) of India in Bangladesh. Inaugurated in 2010, IGCC regularly organizes programmes covering a wide-gamut of cultural activities. The IGCC also holds regular training courses in Yoga, Hindi, Hindustani Classical Music, Manipuri Dance, Kathak and Painting. The courses are very popular with the Bangladeshi students. On June 6, 2015, India and Bangladesh signed the Cultural Exchange Programme (CEP) for the years 2015-2017. According to the CEP, among other things, both sides will exchange the visits of scholars and academicians in the field of art, culture and literature and also dance, music, theatre, Jatra groups, art exhibitions, mime shows, performing art groups, exhibitions and other cultural events to meet the local demands for exposure to each other's rich cultural tradition. (Ministry of Foreign Affairs, GoB, 2015)

Conclusion

Indo-Bangladesh relations have gone through many ups and downs in the past. There are many broad areas of contentions which dominate Indo-Bangladesh relations. The state of friendly relations between India and Bangladesh cannot continue if key bilateral issues are not resolved peacefully and equitably. India, as an emerging regional power has the responsibility to understand and respect the sensitivity of a small neighbor such as Bangladesh. And it needs to take initiative to settle the bilateral issues with sensitivity and common sense. Although there is a small group of anti-India elements in Bangladesh, no one can deny that there is also a tremendous goodwill in Bangladesh for people in India. Thus, there is no adequate reason why relations cannot be friendly between the two neighbors. And there is every possibility that the unsettled issues between the two neighbouring nations will be settled scaling the new heights.

References

1. Ahsan, Abdul, 'Foreign Policy in a Changing World – Bangladesh's Foreign Policy: In Search of Security and a New Role', *World Affairs*, Vol. 3, No. 1, 1999, p. 50.

2. Bangladesh gets $4.5 billion line of credit from India; loan to be paid back at 1% interest rate, *Business Today*, October 4, 2017.

3. Bangladeshi, Indian armies complete counter-terrorism exercise, *The Daily Star*, November 17, 2017.

4. Bangladeshi-India Cultural Exchange Program 2015-2017, *Ministry of Foreign Affairs*, Government of the People's Republic of Bangladesh (GoB), May 13, 2015.

5. Foreign Secretary's Keynote Address at the International Conference on "India and her Neighbours: Revisiting relations with Nepal, Bangladesh, Bhutan, Myanmar, Sri Lanka and Maldives", Speeches & Statements, *Ministry of External Affairs (MEA)*, Government of India (GoI), August 17, 2012.

6. Home Minister level bilateral talks between India and Bangladesh held in New Delhi, *Ministry of Home Affairs (MHA)*, GoI, July 28, 2016.

7. ICCR Scholarships 2017-2018, *High Commission of India*, Dhaka, December 15, 2016.

8. India - Bangladesh Joint Statement during the State Visit of Prime Minister of Bangladesh to India, *MEA*, GoI, April 8, 2017.

9. India - Bangladesh Relations, Briefs on India's Bilateral Relations, *MEA*, GoI, December 2016.

10. India eases medical visa rules for Bangladeshis, *The Independent*, April 18, 2017.

11. India removes entry and exit restrictions for Bangladeshis, *Dhaka Tribune*, July 25, 2017.

12. India to fund river dredging in Bangladesh to ease cargo movement to North-East, *Hindu Business Line*, May 24, 2017.

13. India, Bangladesh agree for coordinated border management plan, *Business Standard*, October 4, 2016.

14. India, Bangladesh to strengthen border management, *Business Standard*, February 21, 2017.

15. India-Bangladesh Relations, Briefs on India's Bilateral Relations, *MEA*, GoI, September 2017.

16. Indian companies to invest $9 billion in Bangladesh energy projects, *Economic Times*, April 11, 2017.

17. Indian Finance Minister: Bangladesh-India relations at their all-time best, *Dhaka Tribune*, October 04, 2017.

18. Invitation for Tender (International), *Ministry of Railways*, GoB, October 16, 2017.

19. "Joint Declaration between Bangladesh and India during Visit of Prime Minister of India to Bangladesh-NotunProjonmo - Nayi Disha", *High Commission of India*, Dhaka, June 07, 2015.

20. Nair, P.Sukumaran, *Indo-Bangladesh Relations*, APH Publishing, New Delhi, 2008, p. 84.

21. Neighbours first, Bangladesh foremost: Sushma Swaraj, *The Hindu*, October 24, 2017.

22. One in three foreign patients in India from Bangladesh: Report, *Business Standard*, April 26, 2017.

23. Pattanaik, Smruti S., "Indo-Bangladesh Relations: Need to Evolve a New Paradigm", *World Focus,* Vol. 27, No. 2, February 2006, p. 24.

24. Power exports from India to meet 25% of Bangladesh demand, *Hindu Business Line*, October 20, 2017.

25. Press Statement by External Affairs Minister during her visit to Bangladesh, *MEA*, GoI, October 22, 2017.

26. Reliance Group awarded power plant project without tender, *New Age*, May 25, 2017.

27. Speech by the President of India, Shri Pranab Mukherjee at the Cavalry Memorial Lecture organized by the Cavalry Officers' Association, *President's Secretariat*, GoI, November 19, 2015.

28. Training and Capacity Building Programme for Bangladesh Judicial Officers in India, *High Commission of India*, Dhaka, October 09, 2017.

29. Visit of External Affairs Minister of India to Bangladesh, *MEA*, GoI, October 21, 2017.

30. Visit of Foreign Minister of Bangladesh H. E. Mr. Abul Hassan Mahmood Ali to India, *MEA*, GoI, March 2, 2016.

31. Visit of Foreign Secretary of India Dr. S Jaishankar to Bangladesh, *MEA*, GoI, February 23, 2017.

32. Visit of Foreign Secretary to Bangladesh, *MEA,* GoI, May 12, 2016.

Security Environment of Afghanistan: Implications for India

Dr. N. Koiremba Singh and Ms. Richa Dohgera

Introduction

India and Afghanistan's relationship traces back to the Indus valley civilization and it has strong archeological evident for having prominent trade relationship between two, later on both areas were under the control of the Mauryan Empire. In the wake of 16th century, the Mughals aggressive expansion in the Asia further leads to India and Afghanistan get closer even shared the borders. In the modern days India and Afghanistan has shared long history of struggle against British Empire during anti-colonial movement of both countries. 1979 was also another breakthrough in the India and Afghanistan relations due to the former Soviet invasion on latter. India was the first non-communist country to recognize Afghanistan's new Soviet backed government. As Afghanistan transitioned out of Soviet rule a decade later, India sent aid and supported every succeeding government. However, their relationship hit a roadblock in 1996, when the Afghan government was seized by the Taliban and India refused to recognize the Taliban rule.[1]

With the end of Taliban regime, a hope of reconciliation of the relation came alive between the two countries. Many investment and aid are been concertize by India to restructure Afghanistan economy, infrastructure and even the security. In September 2016, India announced it would provide Afghanistan with $1 billion dollars in economic aid.[2] So far, India has pledged more than $2 billion dollars in aid money, and, according to the government, roughly around four thousand Indian personnel are carrying out aid and security projects.[3] As India-Afghan ties have grown, so has their shared economy. Bilateral trade between the two countries has roughly doubled in the last decade, reaching more than $680 million dollars in 2015. India has also invested in Afghan infrastructure, including power projects, mines, and more than 400 miles of roads, a parliament building and a hydroelectric "India-Afghan friendship dam", the Salma dam.[4]

India is going to be beneficiary for having good relations with Afghanistan for making easy access to central Asian countries by considering Afghanistan as a gateway to the oil and mineral rich central Asian countries. The TAPI pipeline, it's a natural gas pipeline connecting Turkmenistan, Afghanistan, Pakistan, and India. Moreover, US Geological Survey conducted a hyper spectral survey. Jack Medlin, a geologist and program manager of the USGS's Afghanistan project said, "Afghanistan is a country that is very rich in mineral resources and identified the potential for at least 24 world-class mineral deposits."[5]

Hence Afghanistan had immense potential and is home to minerals worth more than $1 trillion dollars, it's not very poor after all.[6] This untapped potential can be used to revive its economy, increase employment and improve the GDP of the country. But the only big challenge would be the "security" issue. If the government of Afghanistan takes care of the security issues, it would be very welcoming to investors from all over the world, including India. This is a modest attempt of this chapter to bring out various aspects of Indo-Afghan relation in general and security in particular. Comprehending with the security dynamics of the chapter, we would like to highlight centrality of instability in Afghanistan and its major effects of security on South Asian region. Moreover, this chapter would like to throw a light on the various obstacle and opportunities of India and Afghanistan relations for their better future especially for the stability with prosperity.

Soviet to US Invasion of Afghanistan

The history of Afghanistan as an independent country is like a roller costar ride. It is one of the country which is directly affected by the war in reselling of the two giants during the cold war. The story of the invasion did not end with former Soviet Union but it was the starting of the various invasions in many forms ranging from Socialism, radical Islamism, and Liberalism which leads to the constant turmoil in the country and became one of the unsafe place in the world.

The Soviet-Afghan war started in December 1979, when the Soviet Union sent in troops to help the then Afghan communist government to suppress an armed uprising that was led by 'Mujahideen', anti-communist Muslim guerillas.[7] The majority of Afghans were not happy with the communist government that came to power by overthrowing the centrist government of president Mohammad Daud Khan in April 1978.[8] The new government which had minority popular support developed close ties with the Soviet Union and began extensive land and social reforms which were resented by the devoutly Muslim and largely anti-communist population. Insurgencies arouse against the government among all groups of Afghans, both rural and urban, they were collectively known as the 'Mujahideen'.

These ongoing protests and revolts prompted the Soviets to invade the country on December 24, 1979. The Mujahideen were backed by the US, Soviet Union's rival, and proliferated to all parts of the country. They received immense support from the US, who sent arms and ammunition via Pakistan, and also other sympathetic Muslims across the globe. They gave a tough fight to the Soviet army. In 1988, the Soviets agreed to withdraw forces and signed an accord with the US, Pakistan, and Afghanistan. In February 1989, the withdrawal of troop was completed and Afghanistan reverted back to its non-aligned status.[9]

In the meantime, there developed many fragmented factions of the Mujahideen, later formed into independent groups, few of them are the al-Qaeda formed in 1988, led by Osama Bin Laden, and the Taliban. One of them took responsibility for the 9/11 attacks, which claimed the lives of around 3000 people, to which the US retaliated by invading Afghanistan.[10] This happened in three phases, first, one aimed at toppling the Taliban, a religious faction that ruled Afghanistan and provided sanctuary to the al-Qaeda, was brief and lasted only for two months.

In the second phase (2002-08), the US targeted at defeating the Taliban military and reconstructing core institutions of the Afghan state.[11] The strategy for the third phase was to temporarily increase the number of the US troops in order to weaken the Taliban and withdraw troops later by giving the responsibility to tackle with the Taliban to Afghan army and police. This strategy miserably failed as the insurgent attacks continued and civilian casualties remained tenaciously high.

Overview of Security Environment in Afghanistan

The story of the Afghanistan is not over yet after the restoration of democracy; however, it creates another avenue of mushrooming asymmetrical warfare within and miles have to go for the end. Conversely instability in Afghanistan is effecting security dynamics of the region in particular and world as a whole. It is very important for us to comprehend the strategic impression of the area i.e. Afghanistan and know something about the primary extremist groups working there. Firstly, we have the Taliban and the Al-Qaeda, both of which are distinct terrorist gatherings of radical Muslims who misinterpret the fundamentals of Islam to promote a brutal plan. While there might be some similarity in these two groups, they are both diverse.

The Taliban that ruled Afghanistan from 1996-2001 is an Islamic gathering established by Mullah Mohammed Omar which takes after a blend of Sharia Law and Pashtun tribal codes.[12] It shares a few ideas of jihad taken after by the Al-Qaeda gathering. Al–Qaida is a fundamentalist Islamist regime that follows the Sharia law and was established in the vicinity of 1988 and 1990 by Osama Bin Laden and Mohammed Atef.[13]

Next, we have the ISIS (Islamic State of Iraq and Syria or the Islamic State of Iraq and al-Sham (ISIS), or basically the Islamic State (IS), Daesh or ISIL (Islamic State of Iraq and the Levant).[14] The ISIS is a vicious jihadist association that has developed from a fear based oppressor association and insurrection to a proto-state in parts of Iraq and Syria. Al-Qaeda and ISIS see America and the West as foes, while the Taliban essentially wishes to be allowed to sit unbothered.

The present connection between Al-Qaeda and the Taliban is exceptionally cold, as the Taliban feel they have been abused by Al-Qaeda. The ISIS sees itself as double-crossed Al-Qaeda and is additionally battling the Taliban in Afghanistan. The Taliban, need to topple the parliament of Afghanistan. Al-Qaeda needs to free the center, East of American impact, and certain different governments. ISIS needs an overall caliphate and will do anything for land and power, paying little heed to the likelihood that infers cutting their allies in the back. By and by, the essential amassing that opposed ISIS and declined dedication to its organization is the Taliban. Up till now, the two gatherings have had clashes in various parts of Afghanistan.

Another very important terrorist organization functioning in Afghanistan is the Haqqani Network. The Haqqani network is one of Afghanistan's most experienced and sophisticated insurgent organizations, which has the backing of elements within the Pakistani security establishment. The Haqqani network was able to provide the network with the ability to execute attacks in the Afghan capital by expanding beyond Loya-Paktia towards Kabul from 2005 to 2006.[15]

Despite recent progress, Haqqani network operations can regenerate if not continually pressured. Therefore, efforts to neutralize the Haqqani network's operation in Afghanistan require continuous and aggressive counterterrorism operations in Afghanistan and Pakistan in addition to sustained counterinsurgency operations in key populations in and around the Southeast. Overall, other insurgent groups continued to have a much smaller impact than the Taliban, the Al-Qaeda or Haqqani Network e.g. Hezb-i-Islami-Gulbuddin and Islamic Movement of Uzbekistan (IMU).[16]

One such late occasion is the Kabul hospital attack on March 8, 2017 where the ISIS aggressors dressed as doctors slaughtered at least 38 people in the assault. The shooters were disguised as specialists who entered the hospital and combated security powers for quite a long time. Every now and then, there have been operations against these organizations and one such operation in the recent time came in the spotlight, as it was the first of its kind. On April 13, 2017 at 7:32 pm local time, the United States dropped Massive Ordnance Air Blast (MOAB), famously known as the "mother of all bombs" - GBU-43 bomb- on an Islamic State cave complex in Nangahar Province, Afghanistan on Thursday, killing at least 35 ISIS militants.[17]

Thus, 2017 is not going to be an easy year for the Afghan government as it will go up against difficulties at various levels. The organization still does not have a method for key changes at the administrative level. Thus, the Afghan government needs to devise a balanced remote system that ensures that greater powers grasp the stakes in the country in 2017 and leads the country to be a better tomorrow.

Impact of Afghanistan's Security Environment on South-Asia

Afghanistan has always played pivotal role in security dynamics of Indian sub-continent as well as South Asia due to its geostrategic location. Moreover, the geo-key area of Afghanistan is its contiguity to the key districts the Persian Gulf, Central Asia, and South Asia sucked in the meddlesome impact of outer forces like the United States, Russia and China as well. Thus, the Instability in Afghanistan and its unpredictable future has become the most serious security problem for the whole of the Central and South Asian region.

The major impact of the regions is the coming up of the jihadi crescent in the Af-Pak which has become the breeding ground of terrorism. The main consequence is that if instability arises in India due to the spread of terrorism through the borders, then the smaller countries of the South Asian subcontinent also gets affected as India is the biggest stakeholder in South Asia and all the other countries are some way or the other related to India and thus will also get affected.

Pakistan

The exit of the Taliban from Afghanistan forces overwhelming misfortunes on Pakistan in every possible field. Afghanistan alongside Kashmir was the vital focus bit of Pakistan's foreign, military and state-supported terrorism strategies for over 10 years.[18] Pakistan today, loses key profundity that it attempted to develop so passionately amid the most recent decade. Its Western outskirts can at no time in the future be seen as secure. With the turbulence produced, it is likely that the Durand Line debate and the calls for 'self-determination' among the Pashtuns may get resurrected.

Politically, in South Asia, Pakistan's picture gets influenced significantly. South Asian states which would be comfortable up with Pakistan otherwise to bring inconvenience to India would now have to reconsider Pakistan's reliability to remain by them. The key misfortunes of Pakistan coming about because of the Afghanistan events affect vigorously on Pakistan's claims to rise as the 'second pole' in the South Asian geopolitics. Pakistan's state-funded terrorism strategies get affected in two courses due to Afghan improvements, to be specific, the loss terrorist foundations and systems and infrastructure and furthermore, the mental impact on Islamic Jihadi psychological oppressors.

Pakistan had burned through millions to make terrorist organization bases and militant training frameworks in Afghanistan. It filled two needs: (1) Provided Pakistan, a deniability leave that Pakistan does not have any terrorist organizations functioning on its soil; and (2) the flotsam from Pakistani madrassas was conveniently diverted from Pak soil to Afghanistan territory for re-processing as Islamic Jihadis for export to India in particular and globally, elsewhere.[19]

Notwithstanding the above, Pakistan is unlikely to be restrained in the field of state-sponsored terrorism. Rather than hosting its own creations, Pakistan is likely to facilitate the transfer of the Islamic Jihadis influx into

Pakistan to Jammu and Kashmir. India may then be willy-nilly forced into cross-border counter-terrorism operations against such an Islamic Jihadi influx if the United States sequential tackling of global terrorism does not coincide time-wise with the threat against India.

Bangladesh

The Islamic Jihadi terrorist network Al Qaeda is gradually finding its roots in the Muslim dominated country of Bangladesh. These roots provided bases for bin Laden's various plans against India. Sheikh Abdul Salam Mohammad, Emir of the Bangladesh Jihad Movement was one of the signatories of Osama bin Laden's original fatwas declaring war against USA, Israel, Russia and India. Bangladeshi Jihadis were present in Afghanistan till recently.[20]

In the aftermath of the Afghan developments, the impact on Bangladesh could be: The Bangladeshi Jihadis will have to secretly go back to Pakistan to find safe sanctuaries and this would also increase the Islamic fundamentalist activities in the state. This may lead to the strengthening of Pakistan's intelligence bases in Bangladesh for operations against India.[21]

Sri Lanka

The progressing ethnic strife in Sri Lanka is inseparably connected to India's local government issues of its southern state of Tamil Nadu. Pakistan could be expected to exacerbate the problem to its own advantage. It may be recalled that Pakistan had in the past supplied arms to the LTTE in exchange for transporting drugs from Pakistan. Hence it may be possible that in future also Pakistan tries to get Sri Lanka on their side just to create irritants for India.

Maldives

Though there is no physical intimacy between the two countries, the Islamic jihadi ideologies spread without any physical connectivity. So, in future, if conditions tighten in Afghanistan, then, can an unstable Maldives that is showing some kind of Islamic Wahabi tendency provide safe haven to the surplus soldiers? Thus, this may cause further turbulence in the geo politics of South Asia.[22]

In summary, the analysis has shown the high degree of security interdependence, which exists in the western theater of South Asia, that is, between India, Pakistan, and Afghanistan. As the security issue is vital for Pakistan, it cannot afford misjudgments of Indian motivations. To change the situation, it is necessary to strengthen Pakistan's sovereignty. Therefore, the border issues between India, Pakistan, and Afghanistan need to be resolved. India, as the strongest and most consolidated of the three states, would have the best chances of making unilateral concessions, for example, regarding the Siachen Glacier. The extension of the principle of non-reciprocity to Pakistan would be domestically costly for any Indian politician. But according to the logic of signaling, it is these costs that make a signal credible.

Given this, it appears doubtful that India aspires to a leading role in South Asia. What would be the benefits? The most convincing answer to this question refers to two preferences in India's grand strategy: India wants to (1) exclude external powers from its immediate neighbourhood and (2) be recognized as a global major power. *If* these assertions are correct, India will not be able to avoid taking on responsibility for security in its sphere of influence. *Whether* they are correct and how they relate to one another should be the subject of further investigation.

Impact of Afghanistan's Security Environment on India

Afghanistan has filled in as the springboard for al-Qaeda and the Taliban as well as for Kashmir-centered terrorist gatherings. The re-development of al-Qaeda's camp and the Kashmiri activist gatherings in Afghanistan could be adverse to Indian local security and economic premiums. Another part of India's enthusiasm for Afghanistan identifies with its need to diminish Pakistani impact in the area. India ought to contain and adjust Pakistan's impact, which may in some way or the other hamper Indian interests.

The impact of Afghanistan security environment in India does not end with the traditional strategic issue, alarming status of non-traditional Security including terrorism, illegal emigrants, illicit drug trafficking are also in forefront in this region. It is an urgent call for the in-depth analysis of probable security threats which may lead to collateral damage to entire region and hampering the prosperity and stability of both countries in near future. Being one of the rising countries in Asia after China, India needs extensive amount of stability as also sustainable amount of the recourses to fulfil the growing demands of energy which are enormously affected by Afghanistan in multifarious ways in the forms traditional and non-traditional security threats.

Throughout history, India did not want to see Afghanistan under the control of outside powers. Today too, it is not in India's interest to have a long-term presence of NATO forces so close to its borders. NATO may be benign towards India today, but not necessarily tomorrow. If the Afghanistan region remains unstable, then it can attract western players to come in like the US already came in the past and in future other countries like China may come up as well. The economic footprints first come in and then they become strategic footprints just like in the case of India, how the East India Company came to India to trade and gradually ended up becoming the colonizers. The regional character of the area gets adversely affected. On the other hand Afghanistan has always been a vital geographical neighbour for India's security. Both India and Afghanistan shared inimical relations with Pakistan. As long as the relations between India and Pakistan aren't getting better, it is in India's best interests that Afghanistan does not come under the influence of Pakistan. India's presence in Afghanistan can increase Pakistan's fears. Having Afghanistan on our side, India can keep a check on Pakistan's actions by projecting 2 front dilemmas that is India and Afghanistan.

The new dimension of transnational Security is also one of the alarming endeavours in Asiatic region where the Afghanistan and neighbouring countries plays a vital role in propelling instability in entire region. For instance, Af-Pak was a neologism used within US foreign policy circles to designate Afghanistan and Pakistan as a single theatre of operations. It has become the epicenter of terrorism in the world with the jihadi crescent coming up. Conversely this kind of activities leads to great challenge of India specially the terrorism and militant issue in northern border of India. India, with its rising capability and by using its newfound military, economic and political assertiveness, India is looking forward to playing a role in global geo-politics. The biggest worry for India today is terrorism abetted by Pakistan and the possible spillover of the ISIS and/or the Taliban and Afghanistan/ Syrian based jihadi and extremist groups. This jihadi crescent can move towards the Bangladesh and have further implications for India.

Every day, thousands of Afghans and Pakistanis cross the Durand Line - the 2,430-kilometer (1,510 miles) long boundary established by the British during their colonial rule. Neither the Pashtuns who live on either side of the border who share the same historical, cultural and family ties and nor does the afghan government recognize the Durand line as the official boundary of the country.[23]

A decade of instability along this border has led to the spread of terrorism through these porous borders which in turn can become a major issue for India as terrorism from Pakistan can easily spread to India through these borders in a no. of ways and soon may become a threat to the country. Thus, we cannot afford to have an unstable Afghanistan and further an unstable Pakistan.

We cannot have an unstable, dependent Afghanistan as India is not economically ready to provide shelter to immigrants from Afghanistan in the case of any war in Afghanistan that may take place in the future. This will thus challenge the basic characteristic of our country and would further lead to a shift in the demography.

Last but not least energy is also another quest of India where Afghanistan is alone of greater prospect of new growing economy. 2008 Agreement for the TAPI gas pipeline is an important development with far-reaching geo-strategic implications. At a cost of approximately $ 10 billion, the proposed 1,700-km-long pipeline will transport 33 billion cubic meters of natural gas annually.[24] The pipeline commences from Daulatabag gas field in Turkmenistan, through Herat in northwest Afghanistan to Kandahar, further to Quetta and Multan in Pakistan and, finally, terminating at Fazilka in India. It would mitigate India's energy resource crunch and provide an assured supply at competitive rates. A strong and stable government in Afghanistan is essential to Indian security, trade, commercial and strategic interests as Afghanistan's unique geo- strategic location positions it as a viable land bridge to Central Asia, Iran and Afghanistan's energy resources which will cater overarching demand of energy in India.[25]

India's role in Peace Keeping and Capacity Building in Afghanistan

India and Afghanistan have been cooperating for the last 10 years. India has provided nearly $ 1.5 billion worth of assistance and trained a large number of Afghans in India including the Afghan police.[26] Afghanistan has sought close ties with India. In October 2011, Afghanistan and India signed a "Strategic Partnership Agreement." A large number of specific areas of cooperation have been mentioned under this agreement, including trade, investment, science & technology, agriculture, mining, health, regional trading arrangements, quality assurance and standardization, transportation, energy, regional infrastructural projects, annual scholarship programs, sports and student exchanges.[27]

For the first time, India played a formal role in Afghan security by providing for India to train ANDSF personnel, of whom thousands have been trained since 2011. As noted above, India has donated three Cheetah military helicopters to the Afghan Air Force.[28]

At the NATO summit in Brussels in October 2016, India pledged an additional $1 billion for Afghanistan's development needs. Indian officials assert that their projects are focused on civilian, not military, development and are in line with the development priorities set by the Afghan government.

Prime Minister Modi visited Afghanistan in December 2015 and June 2016 to inaugurate India-sponsored projects (a new parliament complex in Kabul and the Afghan-India Friendship Dam in Herat province, respectively). In addition, India

- Along with the Asian Development Bank, financed a $300 million project to bring electricity from Central Asia to Afghanistan.

- Renovated the well-known Habibia High School in Kabul.

- Signed, in May 2016, with Iran and Afghanistan, the "Chabahar Agreement" under which India will invest $500 million to develop Iran's Chabahar port on the Arabian Sea. That port will facilitate increased trade between India and Afghanistan, bypassing Pakistan.

- In December 2011, the Indian firm Steel Authority of India, Ltd. (SAIL) won a bid for three of four blocks of the Hajigak iron ore project in Bamyan Province.

- Helped Afghanistan's Independent Directorate of Local Governance (IDLG) with its efforts to build local governance organizations, and it provides 1,000 scholarships per year for Afghans to undergo higher education in India. Some Afghans want to enlist even more Indian assistance in training Afghan bureaucrats in accounting, forensic accounting, oversight, and other disciplines that will promote transparency in Afghan governance.[29]

Conclusion

Afghanistan has always plays pivotal role in security dynamics of Indian sub-continent as well as South Asia due to its geo-strategic location. The number of invasions, ranging from Socialist, radical Islamism and Liberal leads to the constant turmoil in the country and became one of unsafe place in the world. Even after the democratization of Afghanistan another avenue of asymmetrical warfare coming in the center stage intertwine with global terrorism and safe haven of transnational crime-terror nexus.

In the meantime, Afghanistan has filled in as the springboard for al-Qaeda and the Taliban as well as for Kashmir-centered terrorist gatherings. The re-development of al-Qaeda's camp and the Kashmiri activist gatherings in Afghanistan could be adverse to Indian local security and economic premiums. On the other hand, India quest for the energy for ever growing economic atmosphere is in setback due to the instability in Afghanistan considering Afghanistan is a gateway to the oil and mineral rich central Asian countries.

Being one of the rising countries in Asia after China India needs extensive amount of stability and sustainable amount of the recourses to fulfill the growing demands of energy. It is well evident that impact of Afghanistan security environment In India does not end with the traditional strategic issue, alarming status of non-traditional Security including terrorism, illegal emigrants, illicit drug trafficking are also in forefront in this region. This is the prime time of India to intervene where post-war engagement will prove to be a more crucial battleground than the war itself. India cannot be a spectator as chaos ensues in Afghanistan because of the spillover effect of the crisis in terms of security and economic aspects and may leads to collateral damage.

Unlike the other stake holder in Afghanistan, India is the country which believes in mutual benefits and respects of sovereign status of the concern nation neither fall in the category of neo-imperialism or aggressive economic expansionism. This initiation may be the starting and premature but this is an expedition of imperfect towards perfection with the motto of prosperity and stability. The healthy relation of the two countries may even give a ray of hope to south Asian country for peaceful coexistence and even helping in the revival of the SAARC.

Endnotes

1   Katzman, K., & Thomas, C. (2017, 12 13). *Afghanistan: Post-Taliban Governance, Security, and U.S. Policy*. Retrieved 01 16, 2018, from https://fas.org/sgp/crs/row/RL30588.pdf

2   Nair, K. K. (2015). India's Role in Afghanistan Post 2014. *Manekshaw Paper* , 13-14.

3   Nair, K. K. (2015). India's Role in Afghanistan Post 2014. *Manekshaw Paper* , 13-14.

4   Nair, K. K. (2015). India's Role in Afghanistan Post 2014. *Manekshaw Paper* , 13-14.

5   Choi, C. Q. (2014, September 4). *$1 Trillion Trove of Rare Minerals Revealed Under   Afghanistan*. Retrieved from Live Science: https://www.livescience.com/47682-rare-earth-minerals-found-under-afghanistan.html

6   Choi, C. Q. (2014, September 4). *$1 Trillion Trove of Rare Minerals Revealed Under   Afghanistan*. Retrieved from Live Science: https://www.livescience.com/47682-rare-earth-minerals-found-under-afghanistan.html

7   The Editors of Encyclopædia Britannica. (2009, January 15). *Soviet invasion of Afghanistan*. Retrieved from Encyclopædia Britannica: https://www.britannica.com/event/Soviet-invasion-of-Afghanistan

8   The Editors of Encyclopædia Britannica. (2017, 10 16). *Taliban* . Retrieved 12 01, 2017, fom Encyclopædia Britannica: https://www.britannica.com/topic/Taliban

9   The Editors of Encyclopædia Britannica. (2009, January 15). *Soviet invasion of Afghanistan*. Retrieved from Encyclopædia Britannica: https://www.britannica.com/event/Soviet-invasion-of-Afghanistan

10 Bergen, P. L. (2011, August 23). *September 11 attacks*. Retrieved from Encyclopædia Britannica: https://www.britannica.com/event/September-11-attacks

11 Witte, G. (2017, May 2). *Afghanistan War*. Retrieved from Encyclopædia Britannica: https://www.britannica.com/event/Afghanistan-War

12 Laub, Z. (2014, july 4). *Council on Foreign Relations*. Retrieved may 5, 2017, from The Taliban in Afghanistan: https://www.cfr.org/backgrounder/taliban-afghanistan

13 Bennett, B. P. (2007). *Understanding, Assessing, and Responding to Terrorism: Protecting Critical Infrastructure and Personnel*. Wiley-Interscience.

14 The Editors of Encyclopædia Britannica. (2017, JUNE 16). *Islamic State in Iraq and the Levant*. (Encyclopædia Britannica, inc.) Retrieved august 24, 2017, from Encyclopædia Britannica: https://www.britannica.com/topic/Islamic-State-in-Iraq-and-the-Levant

15 Dressler, J. A. (2010, 10). *The Haqqani Network*. Retrieved may 03, 2017, from Institute for the Study of War: http://www.understandingwar.org/report/haqqani-network

16 Dressler, J. A. (2010, 10). *The Haqqani Network*. Retrieved may 03, 2017, from Institute for the Study of War: http://www.understandingwar.org/report/haqqani-network

17 Safi, M. (2017, march 8). *The Guardian*. Retrieved may 4, 2017, from Isis militants disguised as doctors kill 38 in Kabul hospital attack: https://www.theguardian.com/world/2017/mar/08/gunmen-dressed-as-doctors-attack-military-hospital-in-kabul

18 Kapila, D. S. (2001, 12 4). *South Asia And The Impact Of Afghanistan Events: An Analysis | South Asia Analysis Group*. Retrieved may 4, 2017, from South Asia And The Impact Of Afghanistan Events: An Analysis: http://www.southasiaanalysis.org/paper369

19 Kapila, D. S. (2001, 12 4). *South Asia And The Impact Of Afghanistan Events: An Analysis | South Asia Analysis Group*. Retrieved may 4, 2017, from South Asia And The Impact Of Afghanistan Events: An Analysis: http://www.southasiaanalysis.org/paper369

20 Kapila, D. S. (2001, 12 4). *South Asia And The Impact Of Afghanistan Events: An Analysis | South Asia Analysis Group*. Retrieved may 4, 2017, from South Asia And The Impact Of Afghanistan Events: An Analysis: Http://Www.Southasiaanalysis.Org/Paper369

21 Kapila, D. S. (2001, 12 4). *South Asia And The Impact Of Afghanistan Events: An Analysis | South Asia Analysis Group*. Retrieved may 4, 2017, from South Asia And

The Impact Of Afghanistan Events: An Analysis: http://www.southasiaanalysis.org/paper369

22 Ningthoujam, A. S. (2015, april 2). *RSS*. Retrieved may 4, 2017, from Maldives is No Longer a 'Paradise': https://www.ict.org.il/Article/1372/Maldives-is-No-Longer-a-Paradise#gsc.tab=0

23 Shamil, S. (2017, 03 26). *Pakistan to build fence along disputed Afghan border*. Retrieved 05 04, 2017, from DW.COM: http://www.dw.com/en/pakistan-to-build-fence-along-disputed-afghan-border/a-38125527

24 Nair, K. K. (2015). India's Role in Afghanistan Post 2014. *Manekshaw Paper* , 13-14.

25 Nair, K. K. (2015). India's Role in Afghanistan Post 2014. *Manekshaw Paper* , 13-14.

26 Narain, A. (2016, 05 26). *Afghanistan's Growing Unrest: Implications for India's Security*. Retrieved 05 03, 2017, from The Diplomat: https://thediplomat.com/2016/05/afghanistans-growing-unrest-implications-for-indias-security/

27 *Ministry of External Affairs*. (2011, 10 4). Retrieved from Ministry of External Affairs: Afghanistan: Post-Taliban Governance, Security, and U.S. Policy

28 Nair, K. K. (2015). India's Role in Afghanistan Post 2014. *Manekshaw Paper* , 13-14.

29 Katzman, K. (2015). Retrieved 01 16, 2018

India–ASEAN Maritime Cooperation

Ms. Joshy M. Paul

Introduction

India's engagement with Southeast Asia is a recent one. The opening up of the Indian economy beginning in 1991, ushered in a more outward-looking policy orientation. India's growing engagement with ASEAN, which later became subsumed under the umbrella term of its Look East policy, was primarily driven by prospects of economic collaboration. The *Look East* policy has now gone beyond just increasing trade and institutional linkage with ASEAN and its members, with what has been called 'act east' policy.[1] In fact, India's engagement with Southeast Asia in the post-Cold War period has been gradual and non-threatening, emphasizing the importance of economic linkages and exchange. This economically driven partnership contributes to confidence building and inculcates a political environment that is devoid of "securitization"[2] of India by Southeast Asian states. Southeast Asian countries do not now consider India in any form of security threat, instead started embracing New Delhi as a balancer against Beijing's highhandedness. This approach helped India joining various security related, multilateral mechanisms beginning from being an ASEAN Dialogue Partner status in 1995. India then became a member of the ASEAN Regional Forum (ARF) in 1996 and the East Asian Summit in 2005, and signed on to the Treaty of Amity of Cooperation in 2003, and lately became of member of ASEAN Defence Ministers Meeting (ADMM Plus) in 2009, of which India is an original member of EAS and ADMM Plus. Besides, India engages with some of the Southeast Asian countries in the Indian Ocean multilateral mechanism which includes Indian Ocean Rim-Association for Regional Cooperation (IOR-ARC) and the Indian Ocean Naval Symposium (IONS). The tsunami disaster relief operations of 2004, launched by the Indian Navy initially on its own, and later joined the navies of the U.S., Japan and Australia in Southeast Asia has convincingly changed the perception about India and since then Southeast countries have become more accommodative towards India. Typical of India's emerging maritime power projection in these eastern reaches of the Indian Ocean was the dispatch of a powerful naval group, consisting of *INS Viraat*, accompanied by the guided missile destroyers *INS Rajput* and *INS Ranjit*, the indigenously built missile corvette *INS Khukri* and the replenishment tanker *INS Shakti*.[3] These were deployed to Singapore, Port Kelang in Malaysia and Jakarta in Indonesia during July and August 2005. India's agreement, in October 2008, to start training East Timorese naval personnel is another sign of India's growing maritime influence in the region.

In fact, security cooperation between India and Southeast Asia has become more robust in recent years. India's share maritime borders with Indonesia and Thailand, and long land border with Myanmar, means that India and ASEAN share joint concerns and interests in anti-piracy, counter-terrorism, narcotics, and sea lane protection. In the sea, the shared security interest in protecting the Strait of Malacca, which connects the South China Sea to the Indian Ocean and is one of the world's busiest sea routes, carrying goods vital to the economic viability and energy security of India and ASEAN. Insulating the sea lanes from piracy and crime is thus a key concern for both sides. Although the incidences of piracy have fallen significantly over the last few years, the Malacca Strait still remain a security concern due to various types of terrorist activities.[4]

India's Maritime Security Approach and Southeast Asia

India's own security and prosperity is intimately tied to the security and prosperity of the extended Indian Ocean Region, which also includes the Asia-Pacific region. A significant percentage of India's global mercantile trade – almost 90% by volume and 77% by value – is carried by sea. India has a coastline of over 7,500 kilometers: the chain of the Lakshadweep and Minicoy Islands to the west and the Andaman and Nicobar Islands on the east cover more than 600 islands, the northernmost tip being just 10 nautical miles from Myanmar and the southernmost tip 90 nautical miles from Indonesia. India's exclusive economic zone is more than 2.5 million square km and the mining areas allotted to us under UNCLOS are about 2,000 km from our southernmost tip. As in other parts of the world, the seas around India are now believed to have substantial hydrocarbon potential. As India seeks to satisfy the growing demand for mineral resources, in order to meet the growth and development aspirations, so India has expanded its interest into the maritime domain. Given India's geographical location, extensive maritime interest, dependence on the seas for trade and the evolving asymmetric threats in the form of maritime terrorism, piracy and drug trafficking, maritime security issues have become a strategic priority for India. There are two different aspects to this imperative: the first is the concern for safeguarding India's territories and the adjacent waters against seaborne threats; and, second is the desire to ensure that the traditional freedoms at sea ensure access for all.

In the initial period of the post, Cold-War Southeast Asia viewed India with suspicion India begins upgrading its naval capabilities in the eastern Indian Ocean region, especially in the Andaman Nicobar Islands. Some countries of the Southeast Asian region such as Indonesia and Malaysia expressed their concerns and registered protests as they found themselves in a strategically fragile state. For them, India's rising defence expenditures and its induction of an additional aircraft carrier and a leased Soviet nuclear-propelled submarine were indicators of its desire to become a regional hegemon having an offensive combat force with influence beyond the Indian Ocean and Malacca Straits.[5] They feared that the region would face the consequences of any rivalry between the bigger Asian powers such as China, India and Japan in the event of a withdrawal by the United States.[6] For instance, In February 1990, Singapore's vice Prime Minister, Goh Chok Tong, in a speech anticipated that the dismantling of American bases in the Philippines would lead to competition between India, China and Japan to occupy the void left in Southeast Asia.[7] Indian overcame this puzzle through the look east policy that New Delhi unleashed in the early 1990s. This policy priority has kept as one of the underlying principle in all subsequent effort by India towards the Southeast Asian region in the next two decades. What started as an attempt to dispel the perceived threats led to greater appreciation of Indian maritime threats by the Southeast Asian countries, which in effect created a new era of engagement in India's relations with the region. Highlighting the importance of the Look East Policy, Prime Minister Manmohan Singh said in 2005 that, "In 1992, our government launched India's 'Look East Policy'. This was not merely an external economic policy; it was also a strategic shift in India's vision of the world and India's place in the evolving global economy. Most of all, it was about reaching out to our civilisational neighbours in Southeast Asia and East Asia".[8] A number of confidence-building measures (CBMs) that India undertook, and greater appreciation of Indian maritime threats by the Southeast Asian countries, created a new era of cooperation which began to transcend the naval contours. Perhaps the most important were the joint naval exercises India started holding periodically with Indonesia, Malaysia and Singapore from 1991 near the Andaman and Nicobar Islands.[9] Concretely Southeast Asian countries gradually embraced India as a 'trusted' partner in both economic and security arenas.

A major component of India maritime security policy is that the sea-lanes passing through the Indian Ocean and the western Pacific should not be controlled by anybody. The India's security establishment has stressed repeatedly that it is in favor of "freedom of navigation" and an open and inclusive architecture of global maritime security[10]. In his address at the 2012 Shangri-La Dialogue in Singapore, former Indian Defense Minister A.K. Antony noted that open sea lanes in the South China Sea were critical for global commerce and that "maritime freedoms could not be the exclusive prerogative of a few."[11] Indian officials reiterated this theme during U.S. Defense Secretary Leon Panetta's visit to New Delhi in early June 2012. Maritime freedoms have become so salient in the Asian security discourse today. It is not just the concern of the littoral countries only but the entire maritime fraternity is a stakeholder in it. It should not be changed to suite the interest of new or emerging power which seeks to control maritime trade to consolidate its power position.

India gradually converted its economic strength for military power projection capabilities. Since India is heavily depended on maritime domain for its economic growth threats in the trade routes would cripple Indian economy. Importantly, if that threats take place in the near-vicinity area it would affect India's security also. In this regard India has expanded its security periphery from the Indian Ocean to the near- by area such as Gulf of Aden in the west to the South China Sea in the east and the protection of India's economic interest connected to these parts of the world has become one of the main objective of India's maritime security. In April 2004 India unveiled its first ever public official document on India's maritime security by the India navy known as *Indian Maritime Doctrine*, which describes India's maritime areas extended from "the arc of the Persian Gulf to the Straits of Malacca Straits".[12] Naturally, Malacca Strait is part of Indian Navy's "primary area of interest". The maritime doctrines further revised four times and in the 2007 edition named as "*Freedom to Use the Seas: India's Maritime Military*

Strategy", divided the maritime interest into two areas primary and secondary. The primary areas focus on the Indian Ocean region which include: the Arabian Sea and the Bay of Bengal, which largely encompass our EEZ, island territories and their littoral reaches; The choke points leading to and from the Indian Ocean – principally the Strait of Malacca, the Strait of Hormuz, the Strait of Bab-el-Mandeb and the Cape of Good Hope; while the secondary areas covers the adjacent waterbody which include : The Southern Indian Ocean Region, The Red Sea, The South China Sea, and the west Pacific Region.[13]

India Navy plays an important role in enhancing India's diplomatic relations in its neighborhood. It plays a significant role in India's relationship with Southeast Asian countries. The Indian Navy has thus far played a crucial role in deepening India's security partnerships with ASEAN states, through joint patrols, bilateral exercises, humanitarian assistance and disaster relief; and multilateral engagement, including the biennial MILAN exercises at Port Blair since 1995.[14] India strengthening the tri service command set up in the Andaman and Nicobar Islands in 2001 with better and bigger runways at naval air stations in North Andaman's Shibpur and at Campbell bay in Great Nicobar.[15] These will be extended from the current 3,000 feet to 10,000 feet to accommodate fighter jets and bigger planes such as the navy's Boeing P-8I long-range maritime reconnaissance and anti-submarine aircraft. These airstrips will be kitted out with ammunition dumps too. The airfields are currently used for Dornier aircraft and Mi-17 helicopters. The expansion will allow the Lockheed C-130 Hercules transport aircraft to land on and take-off from these airstrips.

In the maritime doctrine, Indian Navy identified four key roles in supporting New Delhi's foreign and defence policies. First, the military function emphasized the development of the capability to project force and the building of trust and inter-operability with foreign navies. Second, the navy's diplomatic function was to enhance India's relations with its neighbors and with countries of strategic importance in the Indian Ocean region, including Southeast Asian states such as Singapore, Malaysia, Indonesia, Thailand and Myanmar. Third, the navy's constabulary function was to cooperate with the coast guard to maintain stability in the Indian Ocean region with the aim of reducing disruption of maritime commerce and energy supplies between the Middle East and East Asia. Finally, the doctrine emphasized the navy's humanitarian role, which included search and rescue missions and assistance during calamities such as floods, tsunamis and earthquakes. Indeed, Indian Navy was the first foreign navy that visited the coast of Southeast Asia when tsunami struck the western coast of Southeast Asian regional and did a commendable job in rescue and relief operations.

Naval cooperation

With the evolution of India as a major economic and military power in the last decade, New Delhi became increasingly pro-active in Southeast Asia by strengthening its bilateral defence ties with the regional countries. India had, in fact, signed defence cooperation MoUs with Southeast Asian countries in the 1990s as part of the look east policy, but it got strengthened only during the middle of the last decade. In other words, it can be said that, when China began to flex its muscles in Southeast Asia, the regional countries considered India as the best which responded positively. Former PM Vajpayee was instrumental in selling India's hard power diplomacy to the Asia-Pacific region as he sought defence cooperation with the regional countries. In 2001, Vajpayee visited Vietnam, Indonesia, Malaysia and Japan that emboldened India's politico-strategic position in the Asia-pacific region as it was the first visit by Indian Prime Minster after the nuclear test of 1998 after which India's major western trade partners had imposed economic sanctions, but India recovered from that crisis without giving any commitment to their demands such as signing NPT. This gave lot of credence to India's political profile in the region.

India- Singapore

With Singapore, Malaysia and Indonesia, India has had deep bilateral defence engagements which include joint exercises, training for personnel and regular interaction of top level defence officials. India and Singapore started bilateral naval exercise in 1999 called SIMBEX (Singapore-India Maritime Bilateral Exercise) and for the first time it held in South China Sea in 2005, and also the edition held in the SCS in May 2017. In the week long SIMBEX exercise Singapore Navy deployed two frigates (RSS Formidable, equipped with an S-70B naval helicopter, and RSS Supreme) and a missile corvette (RSS Victory), while the Indian Navy participated with two frigates (INS Sahyadri and INS Shivalik), a corvette (INS Kamorta), an oiler (INS Jyoti) and a P8-I maritime patrol aircraft.[16] It is the 24th iteration of the annual bilateral exercise held since 1994. Over the years, SIMBEX has grown in scope and complexity, expanding beyond its traditional emphasis on anti-submarine warfare to incorporate elements of maritime security, anti-air and anti-surface warfare. Singapore participated in the Malabar naval exercise in 2007 as part of the quadrilateral but both countries wanted to continue the bilateral mechanism strongly.

When Singaporean Defence Minister Ng Eng Hen visited India in November 2017 for the second defence Ministers level dialogue both countries signed 'India-Singapore Bilateral Agreement for Navy Cooperation'. Under this agreement Indian navy will be able to use Singapore's Changi naval base located near the disputed South China Sea for logistical support, including refueling purpose.[17] Singapore even proposed a multilateral naval drill in the areas between the Andaman Sea and Malacca Strait with the participation of more South Asian nations.[18] The naval logistics agreement is the first for India with a country located east of Malacca, which will enhance Indian navy's operational reach, keeping in mind that the navy from June this year began its Malacca patrol to protect the SLOCs. India and Singapore on Wednesday favoured having a naval exercise in an area - a move that may upset China."Both countries want to see more participation and more activity in the Malacca strait and Andaman sea. We left it to the officials to flesh it out," Singapore Defence Minister Ng Eng Hen said here after bilateral talks and signing of a naval cooperation agreement.

India-Indonesia

India-Indonesia maritime cooperation growing strongly in addressing the non-traditional security challenges facing the region such as terrorism and maritime piracy. To enhance their cooperation in an institutionalized manner India and Indonesia signed a defence cooperation agreement in 2001. In 2002 India and Indonesia launched coordinated naval patrols - codenamed *Ind-Indo Corpat – twice a year* of their shared maritime boundary with the aim of keeping this vital part of the Indian Ocean Region safe and secure for commercial shipping, International trade and legitimate marine activities.[19]. The CORPAT has strengthened understanding and interoperability between the two navies and promoted net maritime security in the region. During the visit of the Indonesian President, Susilo Bambang Yudhoyono in November 2005, the two countries agreed to hold an annual senior officer level strategic dialogue, and the first meeting held in 2006. While Indonesia has traditionally been opposed to foreign involvement in the Malacca Strait, it formally requested India for assistance in securing the Strait in March 2009. The coordinate patrol in the littoral has significant importance as both countries want to avoid both China's and US presence in the region. The first ever India-Indonesia Bilateral Maritime Exercise held in October 2015.

When Indonesian President Jokowi Widodo visited India in December 2016, both sides committed to strengthening their cooperation in maritime security in the regular sessions of their defense ministers dialogue. The joint statement issued after his meeting with Indian Prime Minister Narendra Modi highlights the "importance of freedom of navigation and overflight on the high seas, unimpeded lawful commerce, as well as resolving maritime disputes by peaceful means, in accordance with universally recognised principles of international law including the UNCLOS".[20] Both leaders identified thrust areas which include maritime security, maritime industry, maritime safety and navigation in their cooperation.

Vietnam and India

They signed a defence cooperation agreement in 1994 but there was little follow-up until recently. Vietnam needed Indian assistance, both in training and hardware procurement, but New Delhi's response was tepid. While Vietnam's eagerness to engage India in a security role continued throughout the 1990s, the major upswing in defence relations between the two states came in 2000 when the Indian defence minister George Fernandes signed a new defence protocol which was more comprehensive and included an institutionalised framework for regular discussions between the two defence ministers, naval exercises between the two navies and coast guards, and training of Vietnamese air force pilots by the Indians. Since March 2000, a high-level security dialogue has been in place to discuss among other issues, piracy on the high seas. In May 2000, Vietnam and India signed a joint declaration on the Framework of Comprehensive Cooperation, which signaled another milestone in the relationship.

When Vietnamese Prime Minister Nguyen Tan Dung visited New Delhi in July 2007, the security cooperation was taken to the advanced level by signing Joint Declaration on Strategic Partnership which includes establishing a Strategic Dialogue and a Joint Working Group (JWG) on counter-terrorism and enhancing cooperation in security and Defence Matters. The Declaration has also "pledged to strengthen cooperation in defence supplies, joint projects, training cooperation and intelligence exchanges". Hanoi is eagerly looking for India's greater role in Vietnam's as well as regional security framework, but New Delhi is not able to elevate its position as they expect including the demand for sale of India made missiles and weaponries. During the visit of Vietnamese President Truong Tan Sang to India on Oct. 12-15, 2011, both countries signed a memorandum of understanding for joint oil exploration activities in the South China Sea, besides initiating a strategic dialogue. China had raised its objection against Indian exploration projects, claiming they are in its "indisputable" area. Admittedly, on Oct. 12, China Energy News, published by Communist Party mouthpiece, the People's Daily, said that cooperation between India and Vietnam in these seas was a bad idea, and warned that "India's energy strategy is slipping into an extremely dangerous whirlpool." By accepting the Vietnamese invitation to explore oil and gas in Blocks 127 and 128, India's state-owned oil company ONGC Videsh Ltd (OVL), not only expressed New Delhi's desire to deepen its friendship with Vietnam, but ignored China's warning to stay away. This display of backbone helped India strengthen its relationship with Vietnam.[21]

In recent time India and Vietnam have strengthened their defence cooperation. When Narendra Modi visited Vietnam in September 2016, both countries elevated the current Strategic Partnership into a Comprehensive Strategic Partnership with increased purpose and content. PM Modi announced a new Defence Line of Credit for Vietnam of USD 500 million for facilitating deeper defence cooperation.[22] Vietnam has evinced interest to buy India's BrahMos missile to boost its defence preparedness to protect its maritime claim in the Spratly island region. Though India has not taken any official stand on the South China Sea dispute, but can help strengthen the defence preparedness of individual countries.

Multilateralism

India is part of most of the multilateral organization which discuss political and security issues in the region. ASEAN countries consider India's presence in the forums is a counterbalance to China's dominance. For example, Indonesia and Singapore's proposal to bring Australia, India and New Zealand into the East Asian Summit was widely perceived as a way to dilute 'Chinese dominance' in regional architecture.[23] Though India's presence in various security forums would not be to contain Beijing, but will help jointly manage China's rising profile in the region in a peaceful and constructive way.

The sub - regional initiative the Bay of Bengal Initiative for Multi – Sectoral Technical and Economic Cooperation (BIMSTEC), which covers India, Thailand, Myanmar, Bhutan, Bangladesh, Nepal and Sri Lanka, was truly a maritime mechanism between India and ASEAN established in 1997. However, it has not produced any significant contribution in the maritime domain for, for that matter, politico-economic aspects. In the biennial 17-nation Milan joint naval exercise, which takes place in the eastern part of Bay of Bengal, Indonesia, Malaysia, Myanmar, Brunei, Singapore, Thailand, Philippines and Vietnam take part in it.[24] 'MILAN', with its emphasis on building friendship and understanding between personnel at the tactical level, also presents ample opportunities for the sailors to build personal bonds and friendships. The Western Pacific Naval Symposium (WPNS) is another platform where navies from India and Southeast Asian countriesinteract, and in 2015 a multilateral exercise was conducted under WPNS name in the Singapore waters.[25] And if the Quad come into materialize Southeast Asia will be an integral part of it, though none of the regional countries is a member of it.

India launched Project Maussan as a foreign policy initiative aims to revive India's ancient maritime routes, cultural and trade linkages with a diverse group of states and regions that are connected to the Indian Ocean.[26] The project commenced in April 2015 with a total cost of the project as Rs. 150 crone ending March 2017 under the Ministry of Culture to promote research on themes related to the study of Maritime Routes through international scientific seminars and meetings and by adopting a multidisciplinary approach.[27] Though, it was touted as India's response to China's OBOR, but has not been supplemented by any policy or specific agenda to make it a real counterbalance to China's Maritime Silk Route. Recently New Delhi signed an MOU with Myanmar to strengthen maritime security cooperation including developing infrastructure which is measured as counter to China's increased influence in Myanmar.[28]

South China Sea

The South China Sea is vital for India not only as a gateway for shipping in East Asia but also as a strategic maritime link between the Pacific and the Indian Oceans. It profoundly affects India's strategic vision as a growing power, in terms of its expanding economic and security role in the broader "Indo-Pacific," where the Indian navy is best positioned to play a crucial role.

While India does not have an official position on the maritime territorial disputes in the South China Sea, it has a huge economic stake in the region, with state-owned Oil and Natural Gas Corporation's foreign arm, ONGC Videsh, involved in major oil-exploration activity off the coast of Vietnam. [29]

The Indian navy has ramped up efforts at forging closer ties with other navies in Southeast and East Asia. India's partners have their own interests in seeing the South China Sea remain an international waterway, and each is concerned about Chinese assertiveness in the region. India interacts with the regional countries through bilateral and multilateral way, and supports the regional general view on the dispute. But India's naval planners are aware that longer forays into the western Pacific will impose costs and constraints, and these impediments, if not dealt with firmly, could seriously inhibit progress. If India wants to realize its desire to become a dominant maritime power in Asia, it will need to work with like-minded stakeholders in a singular and clear-minded pursuit of common objectives.

Conclusion

India's maritime cooperation with Southeast Asia is increasing important for security peace and stability in the region. India's approach towards the ASEAN region has been directed by restraint by not to provoke any regional countries or for that matter China. However, the Southeast Asian region expects more pro-active role by India in the security mechanism. In the recently concluded biannual naval commanders' conference held in New Delhi in the last week of October held the view that Indian Navy must ramp up its new "mission-based deployments" in the Indian Ocean Region (IOR) stretching from the Persian Gulf to the Malacca Strait.[30] Similarly, The conference upheld the need of 12 to 15 destroyers, frigates, corvettes and large patrol vessels on long-range deployments in the IOR at any given time now, which are backed by naval satellite Rukmini (GSAT-7) and daily sorties by Poseidon-8I maritime patrol aircraft to keep tabs over the vast oceanic expanse. Like the recent three-month deployment of INS *Satpura* and INS *Kadmatt* to East and Southeast Asia as part of the commemoration of 25 years of India-ASEAN partnership which further by attended an International Fleet Review hosted by the ASEAN in Thailand, India needs to send its warship on a permanent basis into the Southeast Asian waters. A quad maritime exercise can also be held in the territorial waters of either of the ASEAN countries. More India's presence in the Southeast Asian region would counter China's presence in the Indian Ocean region.

Endnotes

1   Ministry of External Affairs, "Act East: India's ASEAN Journey", November 10, 2014. http://www.mea.gov.in/in-focus-article.htm?24216/Act+East+Indias+ASEAN+Journey

2   Securitization theory highlights the process through which security threats are constructed. Under securitization a specific act or an object is casting as an issue of "existential threat" which calls for extraordinary measures beyond the routines and norms of everyday politics, for details see Williams MC (2003) Words, Images, Enemies: Securitization and International Politics. International Studies Quarterly47 (4), 511–531.

3   David Scott, "India's "Extended Neighborhood" Concept: Power Projection for a Rising Power", India Review, 8 (2), 107-143.

4   Neil Chatterjee. "Security Raised in Malacca Strait after Terror Warning", Reuters, 4 March 2010. https://www.reuters.com/article/us-malacca-threat/security-raised-in-malacca-strait-after-terror-warning-idUKTRE62335120100304

5   Rahul Mishra, "India's Maritime Diplomacy in Southeast Asia: An Assessment of the INS Sudarshini Expedition", Strategic Analysis, 37(5), 526-533

6   Chandra Jeshurun (ed.), China-India-Japan and the Security of South-East Asia, ISEAS, Singapore, 1993, p. 136.

7   The Strait Times, 26 February 1990 (cited in KripaSridharan, The ASEAN Region in India's Foreign Policy, Dartmouth Pub. Co., Aldershot, UK, 1996, p. 174).

8   Prime Minister Manmohan Singh, 'Make the 21st Century Truly an Asian Century', keynote address at special leaders' dialogue of the ASEAN business advisory council, 12 December 2005.

9   Gurpreet S. Khurana, 'Cooperation among Maritime Security Forces: Imperatives for India and Southeast Asia', Strategic Analysis, 29(2), 2005, 295-315.

10 Abhijit Singh, "India's 'Look East' Policy Takes on Maritime Edge" The World Politics Review, 09 Jul 2012. https://www.worldpoliticsreview.com/articles/12139/indias-look-east-policy-takes-on-maritime-edge

11 "Protecting Maritime Freedoms: A K Antony", *Shangri-La Dialogue 2012 Second Plenary Session A K Antony, Minister of Defence, India,* 02 June 2012. http://www.iiss.org/en/events/shangri-la-dialogue/archive/sld12-43d9/second-plenary-session-25b4/a-k-antony-a296

12 See ReshmiKazi, "India's Naval Aspirations", Article No. 1472, Institute of Peace and Conflict Studies, August 23, 2004.

13 Indian Navy (Integrated Headquarters), Freedom to Use the Seas: India's Maritime Military Strategy,28 May 2007, New Delhi, p. 59-60

14 David Brewster, "India's Defence Strategy and the India-ASEAN Relationship," in *India-ASEAN Defence Relations,* ed. Ajaya Kumar Das (Singapore: S. Rajaratnam School of International Studies, 2013), 124-145.

15 More muscle for India's Andaman and Nicobar defence posts to counter hawkish China, *The Hindustan Times*, Aug 26, 2017.

16 *The Indian Express*, "India-Singapore joint naval exercise SIMBEX 2017 concludes", May 25, 2017. http://indianexpress.com/article/india/india-singapore-joint-naval-exercise-simbex-2017-concludes-4673123/

17 The Times of India, "Navy gets access to Singapore's Changi naval base", November 30, 2017.

18 Deccan Herlad, India, "Singapore favour multilateral naval drill with ASEAN", Nov 29 2017.http://www.deccanherald.com/content/645399/india-singapore-favour-multilateral-naval.html

19 Indian Navy, "Coordinated Patrol and India-Indonesia Bilateral Maritime Exercise commence at Belawan, Indonesia". https://www.indiannavy.nic.in/content/coordinated-patrol-and-india-indonesia-bilateral-maritime-exercise-commence-belawan

20 Ministry of External Affairs, joint statement on "India-Indonesia Joint Statement during the State visit of President of Indonesia to India", December 12, 2016. http://mea.gov.in/bilateral-documents.htm?dtl/27805/IndiaIndonesia_Joint_Statement_during_the_State_visit_of_President_of_Indonesia_to_India

21   Harsh V. Pant, "The India-Vietnam Relationship: Beyond the BrahMos Connection", *The Diplomat*, August 22, 2017. https://thediplomat.com/2017/08/the-india-vietnam-relationship-beyond-the-brahmos-connection/

22   "PM Modi Announces $500 Million Credit Line For Vietnam" NDTV, September 03, 2016. https://www.ndtv.com/india-news/defence-security-high-on-agenda-as-pm-modi-visits-vietnam-10-points-1453980

23   Dick K. Nanto. "CRS Report for Congress: East Asian Regional Architecture: New Economic and Security Arrangements and U.S. Policy." 4 January 2008.

24   "17 Nations 15 Ships Demonstrate a Momentous 'Milap': Milan 2014 an Unequivocal Success", Press Information Bureau, Government of India, 9 February 2014. http://pib.nic.in/newsite/PrintRelease.aspx?relid=103278

25   "WPNS Multilateral Joint Maritime Exercise kicks off in Singapore", Ministry of Defence, Singapore, May 21, 2015.**http://eng.mod.gov.cn/TopNews/2015-05/21/content_4586180.htm**

26   Thomas Daniel, "Project Mausam: A Preliminary Assessment of India's Grand Maritime Strategy from a Southeast Asian Perspective" National Maritime Foundation, 21 July 2015.http://www.maritimeindia.org/View%20Profile/635730250805439349.pdf

27   "Project Mausam of M/O Culture", Press Informati0n Bureau, 25 April 2016. http://pib.nic.in/newsite/PrintRelease.aspx?relid=141133

28   *Nikkei Asian Review*, "India inks maritime partnership deals with Myanmar", September 7, 2017. https://asia.nikkei.com/Politics-Economy/International-Relations/India-inks-maritime-partnership-deals-with-Myanmar

29   Abhijit Singh, "India's 'Look East' Policy Takes on Maritime Edge", *World Politics Review*, 9 July 2012.   https://www.worldpoliticsreview.com/articles/12139/indias-look-east-policy-takes-on-maritime-edge

30   The Times of India, "Eye on China, India expands naval footprint in Indian Ocean", Oct 25, 2017.

The Major Irritants in Sino-Indian Relations: The Way Forward

Dr. Madhumati Deshpande and Ms. Apoorvi Mishra

The Doklam standoff between India and China in 2017 brought to focus the border skirmishes that the two countries have been having since 1947. Dokalm issue was not specific to Indian border with China but it showed that China has issues with the currently demarcated border with not just India but many other countries as well. It was seen as Chinese flexing their muscles and trying to see how far they can go in intimidating neighbouring countries in accepting their supremacy in the region. But India's reaction also showed that India has been trying to resolve the issues and are now exasperated by the brazen action of the Chinese troops. Ever since Communist revolution in China, the Chinese government has de-recognized all the treaties and agreements that the earlier Chinese governments had signed. This meant that the border agreements signed before 1949 were not recognized by the Chinese government.[1] China currently has territorial disputes with many of its neighbours. This is one of the major issues that hinders relations between the two countries. The other major issue in the recent past has been the Brahmaputra river that flows both in India and China. Without a formal water sharing agreement the problem may escalate to bring both the countries once more in a face off. Despite the increasing trade and commerce between the two countries, the unresolved issues in the recent past have led to a deteriorating relationship.

Sino-Indian relations have a long history. Scholars have traced several contacts between the two oldest civilizations in the ancient and medieval times. The history of modern times also shows a relationship that was of mutual respect and cordial relations. It is only in the 20th century that we see the two countries coming in to conflict.

The Four Periods of Sino-Indian Relationship

Since India's independence and the founding of the People's Republic of China, development of Sino-Indian relations may roughly be divided into four periods: peace and friendship for the most part in the 1950s; war and hostility in the 1960s and the first half of the 1970s; and détente and negotiations in the 1980s; and, the beginning in the early 1990s, joint efforts to re-establish Sino-Indian friendship during the post-Cold-War era.

In 1950s, particularly from the signing of the 1954 agreement on trade and intercourse between the Tibet region of China and India to the 1959 Tibetan Revolt, Sino-Indian relations were characterized by the cordiality and brotherhood of "Hindi-Chini Bhai Bhai!" based on the five principles of peaceful coexistence. The Panchsheel agreement between China and India was a political rather than a trade pact in which the Indian government recognized China's sovereignty over Tibet and gave up all its extra-territorial rights in Tibet, inherited from the British in 1947. During this period, global and regional security concerns of both sides overweighed their bilateral differences, including the border dispute. Facing hostile Pakistan allied with the west, Indian policy makers saw friendship with China as the best guarantee for security on India's northern frontier. In terms of interests of the Chinese Strategic Security, India played a mediating role during the Korean War, advocated China's representation in the United Nations and supported china on the question of integration of Taiwan with the mainland. While this made the period of friendly relations between these both nations, irritants started from the issue of Tibet.

The Chinese have a fundamental national interest in having control over Tibet, because Tibet is the Chinese anchor in the Himalayas. If that were open, or if Xinjiang were to ever become independent, the vast buffers between China and the rest of Eurasia could possibly break down. The Chinese can't predict the evolution of Indian, Islamic or Russian power in such a circumstance, and they certainly don't intend to find out. They will hold both of these provinces, particularly Tibet. The Chinese note that the Dalai Lama has been in India ever since China invaded Tibet. The Chinese regard him as an Indian puppet. They see the latest unrest in Tibet as instigated by the Indian government, which uses the Dalai Lama to try to destabilize the Chinese hold on Tibet and open the door to Indian expansion. To put it differently, their view is that the Indians could shut the Dalai Lama down if they wanted to, and that they don't signal Indian complicity.

With the growing tensions between India-Sino relations, the situation of Tibet worsened subsequently and reached its worst in 1959. Some rebellious separatist groups broke out in eastern and central Tibet. The rebels, however, spread the rumour that the PLA would detain Dalai Lama and staged the arm rebellion. Dalai Lama and his followers fled to India with the assistance of the Central Intelligence Agency (CIA) of the United States and the Tibetan rebels. Dalai Lama and his followers were given political asylum in Mussoorie where he first made his headquarters.

While the rebellion took place, the Chinese government requested the Indian government to halt the subversive activities against China and pointed out that these separatist elements were taking advantage of the current (then) border issue between India and China and were using the Indian border town Kalimpong as a base. The Indian government however, denied these charges and stated that there was no evidence of any of the charged activities.

The denial of the Indian government made the Chinese believe that the Indian government was indulging and supporting subversive activities in Tibet. The Chinese suspicion of the Indian government's role in Tibetan rebellion was intensified by the fact that the Tibetan local government invited Nehru to visit Lhasa without the consent of the Chinese central government in 1958, when rebellious activities were spreading in central and eastern Tibet. In the Chinese eyes, political asylum given to Dalai Lama and the Tibetan rebels and the warm welcome Nehru himself had extended to the Dalai Lama at that moment were at least an unfitting reception, if not a proactive act to give rebels against a friendly neighbouring state.

From 1959 to the mid-1970s, Sino-Indian relations experienced the coldest period, the Sino-Indian cold war was interwoven with the American-Soviet-Chinese triangular relations within the context of the global cold war. The Chinese all-out counterattack along the entire Sino-Indian border from October 20 to November 21, 1962, has usually been defined as the Sino-Indian war. In the Karakoram borderlands between India and China lies the high plateau of the Aksai Chin, an extension of the Tibetan plateau reaching into Kashmir. In September 1958, an Indian reconnaissance party, which had been sent to the area to identify where the Chinese Xinjiang-Tibet highway ran, was detained and then deported by the Chinese frontier guards. This border incident was the beginning of the subsequent Sino-Indian border dispute. India's border policy of "non-recognition and non-negotiation", its forward policy, and the Chinese tit-for-tat countermeasures pushed the inevitability of war. In the Indian version, the war was a Chinese invasion of the Indian Territory, while the Chinese term it as a war of self-defence counterattack. They justified their respective war behaviours on the basis of the disputed areas being their own territories. The Chinese asserted that they had taught India a good lesson, and India accused China of an ungrateful betrayal. This war has made the relationship worse for decades.

The third phase is made of economic ties between the two nations which eased out by the end of 1970s, and China took the lead in easing strained relations. Mr. Moraji Desai welcomed this gesture, but he was faced with harsh criticism. When receiving a delegation from the Indian council of Social Science Research in 1982, Deng Xiaoping stated: "We cannot afford to not understand each other and promote the friendship between us. The problem between China and India is not a serious one. Neither country poses a threat to the other. The problem we have is simply about the border. If we want to change the international economic order, we must, above all, settle the question between South and North, but at the same time we have to find new ways to increase South-South cooperation".[2] (Liu, 1994). India and China despite having symbolic and strategic sensitivity held eight rounds of border negotiations between December 1981 and November 1987.

Arunachal Pradesh was announced as a state of the Indian union by the Indian Parliament in December 1986. This demarche enraged the Chinese government. Deng warned India not to take possession of the disputed terrain. Troops mobilized on both sides of the border and media reports are mentioned new armed skirmishes in the months following December 1986. Rajiv Gandhi paid a historical visit to China in 1988, despite the opposition from the media and several congress party members. Deng clearly identified China's internal quandaries with those of India: "The world is changing, so peoples mind have to change with it. Because of mistakes made in the past, especially during the Cultural Revolution, we have wasted about twenty years when we could have been building our country. After the downfall of the Gang of Four, everything has been changing here in China too. For example, we have changed from taking class struggle as the central task to concentrating on modernization, we have changed from stagnation and closed- door policy to reform and a policy of opening to the outside world, and we are carrying all sorts of reforms. I think your country will also encounter this problem of change. Development means change; without change, there can be no development".[3] (Liu, 1994)

A group was formed to deal with the boundary question additionally. Between December 1988 and June 1993, six rounds of talks of the Joint Working Group on the India-China Boundary Question were held, which led to concrete confidence building measures which included mutual troop reductions, regular meetings of military commanders and advanced notification of military exercises. Three agreements were signed on important issues like economic cooperation and established a Joint Ministerial Committee on economic and scientific cooperation and approved direct air links. The shift to appeasement was to a large extent the consequence of the economization of foreign politics during the 1980's.

During the 1990s, which is fourth phase, the further economization of diplomacy was most obvious in several institutional reforms in the civil service. A New Economic Coordination Unit and Investment Promotion Unit were created when The Ministry of External Affairs revamped its Economic Relations Division. The increasing importance of commercial interests in China's external affairs also resulted in profound organizational reconfiguration. Between 1990 and 1999, bilateral trade volume multiplied ten times.

In 1992, consulates reopened in Mumbai and Shanghai. In June 1993, the two sides agreed to open an additional border trading post. Under Rao's government, the two sides prepared memorandums of understanding pertaining to the avoidance of double taxation, banking relations and coal. In 1995, trade between china and India exceeded US $1 billion for the first time.

Commercial and Economic Relations Trade and economic relationship has seen rapid progress in the last few years. India-China bilateral trade which was as low as US$ 2.92 billion in 2000 reached US$ 41.85 billion in 2008, making China India's largest trading partner in goods. By 2015, as per DGC&IS provisional data India-China bilateral trade stood at US$ 70.4 billion. India's exports to China touched US$ 8.86 billion whereas China's exports were US$ 61.54 billion. However, India still faces a growing trade deficit vis-a-vis China. In 2015 trade deficit stood at US$ 52.67 billion. Apart from trade, India is also one of the largest markets for project exports from

China. Currently, projects under execution are estimated at over US$ 63 billion. As per Chinese figures, cumulative Chinese investments into India till December 2014 stood at US$ 2.763 billion while Indian investments into China were US$ 0.564 billion.[4] Chinese provinces have been courting several Indian states for investments specially West Bengal and Gujarat.

India-China Border Issues

The Sino-Indian boundary has never been formally delimited or demarcated; and no boundary treaty has been mutually accepted by both governments. The Sino-Indian border is generally divided into the eastern, middle and western sectors. The western sector involves dispute over the Aksai Chin area which India claims as a part of Ladakh and China claims as a part of Xinjiang. The middle sector involves dispute over various points between the Tibet-Kashmir-Himachal Pradesh border junction and the Nepal-Tiber-Uttarakhand border junction. The eastern sector involves the disputed area which lies within the territory claimed by India as a part of Arunachal Pradesh—formerly the North-East Frontier Agency (NEFA) of Assam and claimed by China as a part of Tibet. The McMahon line in the eastern sector and the Aksai Chin in the western sector have been central to the Sino-Indian border dispute.

The Chinese side called for major mutual territorial adjustments by advocating "mutual understanding and mutual accommodation", while the Indian side insisted on minor territorial adjustments on the eastern sector and China's unilateral concession in the western sector by advocating "mutual understanding and mutual adjustments". These differences over the words represent a fundamental difference over the basic principles of defining the border. Both sides share the view that the border dispute should be settled through peaceful negotiation and friendly consultation. They have agreed that stability and tranquillity along the entire Sino-Indian border should be maintained pending a final solution.

In December 1988, bringing an end to a prolonged hostility post 1962 war, Indian Prime Minister Rajiv Gandhi paid an official visit to China and was warmly welcomed by the Chinese government. During his talk with Mr. Gandhi, Deng Xiaoping, the paramount Chinese leader, proposed the principle of "forget the past, look forward to the future" in re-establishing

Sino-Indian friendship. Rajiv Gandhi responded favourably, but Indian officials later took a more cautious stance.

In September 1993, During Mr. P.V. Narsimha Rao's visit to Beijing, a "landmark" agreement was signed on recognizing the current line of actual control (or LAC) separating their troops since the 1962 border war. This pact is by far the most important, conducive to promote mutual interest and establishing stable relations by laying down the framework for maintaining peace and tranquillity along the LAC. India and China agreed to respect and observe the LAC and where there are differences on alignment, to let experts check and determine the line. The two countries also agreed to undertake a series of series of confidence- building measures (CBMs), including the reduction of military forces along the border keeping their levels in conformity with the principle of "mutual and equal security".

The Looming Water Crisis in South and South East Asian Region

Brahmaputra River originates in Tibet where it is locally known as the Yarlung Tsangpo, meanders across the LAC and into the Indian state of Arunachal Pradesh. Brahmaputra ranks low in terms of institutionalized management, among the world's international rivers. Countries along the Nile, for instance have formed the Nile Basin Initiative to encourage peace and security. States in the lower Mekong region have formed the Mekong River Commission (of which china is an observer, but not a full member). However, Brahmaputra doesn't have any such management system.

Considering from a security point of view, there are three major challenges for China and India. The first is the challenge of flood control and prevention. In June 2000, a natural dam on the Chinese- controlled side of the Brahmaputra broke free, leading to a massive flood in Arunachal Pradesh. Thirty Indian nationals were killed, and fifty thousand displaced from their homes. Indian authorities charged that China had withheld vital information that could have improved flood forecasts.[5] This led to a 2002 agreement by which China supplies river flow data to India during flood season which is roughly half the year. Flooding still remains a concern, and might worsen in the long term due to the melting of Tibetan Glaciers as a result of Global Warming.

Second, there are concerns that China might build dams capable of diverting the Yarlung Tsangpo away from India. These concerns have circulated in India for years. The Chinese academics have considered a variety of river diversion plans focused on alleviating domestic water shortages, including one by a former PLA officer titled Tibet's Waters Can Save China that received much domestic and international attention. The Chinese officials have frequently reiterated that China is building only "run-of-the-river" dams on the Yarlung, with no ability to impound or divert water.

Third, Chinese observers are concerned about the ramifications of planned Indian hydropower and other infrastructure development along the Brahmaputra in Arunachal Pradesh.[6] The Chinese however fear that this development will strengthen India's "actual control" over the region by facilitating large influx of Indian migrants into the contested territory. This would further complicate border negotiations and make it harder for China to ever regain southern Tibet. China has even taken steps to try to complicate Indian development in Arunachal by seeking to deny international financing for these types of projects. Interviews with Chinese experts suggest that Beijing does not have much hope of being able to forever forestall India's progress in this arena, though the projects themselves will probably continue to be an irritant in broader Sino-Indian political relations.

China and India could work closely to address the risks of flooding. For instance, the two militaries might organize combined exercises based on a flooding scenario. Chinese and Indian civilian ministries might also join forces to discuss how flood control measures in the region might be strengthened, and exchange information on other topics of mutual concern, such as river safety and pollution mitigation. Although this type of cooperation will not resolve underlying tensions related to the border dispute, it could build trust at a low level and strengthen both sides' capacity to respond to emergencies.

Another step would involve greater information sharing regarding dam building and other infrastructure development on both sides of the LAC. China, for instance, might consider allowing Indian officials to conduct site visits to the Zangmu dam, which became fully operational in October 2015. China might also provide more details on planned additional dams, to respond to Indian concerns about ulterior motives.

India should levy taxes on goods imported China so that they can work at power with other goods. (India-China Relations, 2016)

Conclusion

The growing economic and commercial relations between the two countries make it imperative for them to solve their political dispute beginning with the border issues. The past year has shown that mistrust in one field leads to misunderstandings in others. Chinese support to Pakistan and opposition to Indian entry in to NSG is the case in point. In a globally dependent world the two most populous nations of the world cannot afford to be at logger heads with each other. Both countries will have to come up with workable solutions to the existing disputes which will then make the environment conducive for a better and more trust worthy cooperation on the global stage. Putting the border dispute on the back burner as has been done since Rajiv Gandhi's period will not suffice anymore. Lesson of Doklam should be that both countries need calm the irritants before it breaks out in to a bigger conflict that will affect the trade, investment and cooperation.

References

1. India China Relations (2016) Retrieved from Ministry of External Affairs ath-ttps://www.mea.gov.in/Portal/ForeignRelation/China_Jan_2016.pdf

2. Wuthnow, J. (2016, April 16), *Water War: This River could Sink China-India Relations.* Retrieved from The National Interest, http://nationalinterest.org/feature/water-war-river-could-sink-china-india-relations-15829?page=2

Endnotes

1   Bandopadyaya J. (1973), The making of India's Foreign Policy, 2nd ed. New Delhi, Allied Publishers Limited. (p.300)

2   Liu, X. (1994).The Sino-Indian Border Dispute and Sino-Indian Relations.1st ed. (p.44). New York: University Press of America.

3   Liu, X. (1994).The Sino-Indian Border Dispute and Sino-Indian Relations.1st ed. (p.45). New York, University Press of America.

4   *India-China Relations.* (2016, January). Retrieved from Ministry of External Affairs: https://www.mea.gov.in/Portal/ForeignRelation/China_Jan_2016.pdf

5   Wuthnow, J. (2016, April 16). *Water War: This River could Sink China-India Relations.* Retrieved from The National Interest: http://nationalinterest.org/feature/water-war-river-could-sink-china-india-relations-15829?page=2

6   Wuthnow, J. (2016, April 16). *Water War: This River could Sink China-India Relations.* Retrieved from The National Interest: http://nationalinterest.org/feature/water-war-river-could-sink-china-india-relations-15829?page=2

India and China: Eying New Foreign Ports in Sri Lanka

Mr. Ramprasad P

History has witnessed how controlling the seas are, crucial in projecting power, trade, resources etc. This was well substantiated by Alfred Thayer Mahan in his book, 'The Influence of Sea Power upon History'. Indian Ocean is the world's third largest body of water and has become a growing area of competition among the major economies. Indian Ocean Region (IOR) strategically provides intersection of critical sea routes which connects the West Asia, Africa and South Asia, with the broader Asian continent and the Pacific belt. Thus, this region has become an inevitable area of competition for Asian giants – India and China. During the Cold War, commercial transport in this region was not as full of activity as it was in the Pacific and in the Atlantic. But with economies like India, China etc. growing at a rapid rate than ever before, and the resource crisis across the world, has raised the importance of this region. With that context, if we try to understand then Indian Ocean has access to 70% of the world's petroleum - which is in the Persian Gulf, and offshores around Indonesia, Australian Northwest Shelf. Above all Indian Ocean itself contains 65% of global strategic raw materials which include metal reserves like 85% of world manganese, 60% vanadium, 86% of chromium, 50% of uranium etc.[1] Growing dependence on natural resource flow, rising prosperity around the region, globalized supply chains and distribution networks have made the Indian Ocean strategically more significant to the global security.

Owing to the voluminous trade through IOR, it has become important to make the Sea Lanes of Communications secure. States not only have the responsibility to protect them from sea aggression, but also have to protect economic interests, and further, small countries feel insecure because of the force projection of bigger countries.

So, in order to keep themselves safe and secure, they, in turn, take sides of a bigger country or just encourage all countries to invest in their country in order to gain economic leverage. Nevertheless, these nations are not ready to give up their sovereignty because of some economic aid. The emergence of nationalism and local pressure in littoral countries tend to complicate the situation.[2]

This paper concentrates on one such small littoral state which has ancient ties with India – *Sri Lanka*.

India's main concern in 1980s was that it did not want any foreign players to have their bases in Sri Lanka. So before even the US or UK could take that opportunity to get advantage of the region, India stepped in. It offered to negotiate between Tamil fighters and Sri Lankan Government. After the backlash which India received, and with the assassination of Indian Prime Minister Rajiv Gandhi, the sensitivity heightened. The Indian government started supporting the Sinhalese by providing lot of war techniques and radar surveillance covertly to Sri Lankan government in defeating LTTE (Liberation Tigers of Tamil Eelam). With India being reluctant in openly providing military assistance or financial aid to the Sinhalese government, because of the increasing pressure from the Tamil population of India, China and Pakistan were supplying them with armored personnel carriers, air surveillance radars and rocket propelled grenades.[3] In return, Lankan side allowed China to build a port in Hambantota which was earlier offered to India. China's need for maritime access is the main motivation for China in helping Sri Lanka with economic aid, weapons and making security partnership. This was the beginning of India-China competition, as China entered into India's traditional area of influence.

Chinese New Ports in Sri Lanka

Hambantota, which is in the middle of the Strait of Malacca and the Persian Gulf, seemed a critical link in the Chinese pursuit to construct a "string of pearls" in the Indian Ocean. Many Indian strategists crib that it was India's lack of decisiveness and fear that Hambantota port would give tough competition to its own ports in South India that kept India from taking the opportunity.[4] Though US ignored Sri Lanka as a small island nation, China understood its geographical importance in the Asian rim land. While Americans were busy with Western and Central Asia, China utilized the opportunity to partner with Sri Lanka, economically and diplomatically. China drew a budget of $1 billion - to build this port. On the first phase, of the fifteen-year project, China provided loan of $361 million.[5] Again as a second phase, it invested $810 million for the construction and also 200 million separately for the airport in Hambantota.[6] There are interestingly a few advantages for India as well. As 70 per cent of shipping to and from Indian ports is handled by Colombo, the Hambantota port complex can ease pressures on Colombo. India also depends on the adjoining maritime territory for its energy needs. The sea lanes a few miles south of Hambantota are used for about 50 per cent of India's energy supplies. China too gains 80 per cent of its oil supplies through this route.[7] The economic significance of the Hambantota project has ripples across the globe in other states as well, especially in South East Asia. Perception that developing Hambantota port would bring exponential increase in Sri Lanka's revenue is actually blurred. Because, there are high chances that Sri Lanka may not be able to pay back the loans which it had borrowed from China. For Hambantota port project, Sri Lanka has borrowed from China -with an interest rate of 6.3%, while the interest rates on soft loans at World Bank and Asian Development Bank are just 0.25-3%. Interest rate which India provides to neighboring countries is just around 1%.[8] In the future, using this debt as leverage, China might seek Sri Lankan government's permission for China's military use if necessary.

Another port on which China laid its hands is, the Colombo Port City project. It was inaugurated by Chinese President Xi Jinping in September 2014, with a budget of $1.4 billion; it is financed by China's state-controlled China Communication Construction Company (CCCC) Ltd., a subsidiary of the China Harbor Engineering Company. The Colombo port city project aims to play a key role in the Maritime Silk Road (MSR) project of China.[9]

With the change of government in Sri Lanka, the projects of previous government are under scrutiny for its high interest rates deals, corruption, environment issues etc. China's intensifying investments in Sri Lanka have not gone unquestioned within the civic society of that country. Many opposition parties have criticized former president Mahinda Rajapaksa for mounting an over-reliance on China for infrastructure financing, and for accumulating debt. Between 2009 and 2014, Sri Lanka's total government debt has been tripled and external debt has been doubled. Yet, Chinese economic aids are too luring; the Indian government and private players cannot compete with the size of Chinese investment capacity. The current president Maithripala Sirisena has found himself continuing to seek Chinese investment to finance his grand infrastructure projects.

Possible New Ports in Sri Lanka and Indian Investment

Now that Sri Lanka wants to balance the relationship which it maintains with China and India, which is again a clever way, to gain maximum out of the regional power rivalries, it has allowed India to jointly build a sea port in the Norther Eastern part of Sri Lanka. The memorandum of agreement is all set to be signed by the top leadership when Prime Minister Modi visits Sri Lanka in May 2018. Even though jointly developing the Trincomalee port does not offset the Chinese pull over Sri Lanka, it can develop countervailing influence. In 2013 the Indian Oil Company announced it would invest USD 40 million to renovate about 30 oil tanks at this port city. Coast Guard maritime exercises were also carried out between India, Sri Lanka and Maldives in Trincomalee recently.[10] But there is an implication beyond strategic concerns in this port city, given its nature as an energy hub.

As Shiv Shankar Menon had stated, "given the need for energy security, it is natural that Indian companies would operate oil tank farms in Trincomalee, in Sri Lanka. There is immense potential in this region for India to protect its interests.[11] But the problem is the financial ability and political willingness of India to invest in this port. Currently, India itself needs more funds to develop its own naval ports like Tuticorin port trust and Madras Port in Tamil Nadu. One of the reasons why it will show hesitation to invest in Trincomalee is that it doesn't want it to give competition to the ports in its own backward.

Though the investment by Chinese in Sri Lanka is continuing, India has not stopped its investments. It has signed the agreement for rehabilitation of Kankesanthurai Harbour in 2011, which was supposed to have been competed in six stages. It planned to build a new port as the existing one was inoperative after being attacked by LTTE during the civil war. India had completed the first four phases by 2013, with the removal of six sunken vessels, at a grant of $19.5 million. The first three phases were a preliminary hydrographic survey, dredging and geotechnical investigation and preparation of a detailed project report by RITES.[12] It is clear that India is only interested in economic prospects, and accordingly, as part of its line of credit USD

382.37 million has been given to lay the track on the railway line which connect Kankesanthurai with Pallai, another coastal town. Besides, India has no strategic reason or need to dock its naval vessels at the renovated harbor, as the subcontinent state already possess the expertise and logistics required.[13]

Conflict of Interests between India and China

After globalization, the Asian economies have been growing at a rapid rate and thereby their energy consumptions are also increasing. As most of their energy imports travel through IOR, securitization has also increased by both the states. Even though experts predict that the chances of military conflict between India and China remains low, the competition between two countries are getting intensified day by day making it difficult to predict immediate future. By slowly expanding its naval presence in the India Ocean, China is trying to create a new status-quo. Both the nations are involving themselves in developing ports, bases and military exercises. India realized the strategic importance and growing influence of China in the Indian Ocean only after 1980s. Until 1980, India allocated only 10% of its defense budget to Navy. It always considered IOR as its own backyard and gave less importance to it and its naval development. In the 1990s, India became enthused about regional maritime cooperation and considerably increased its spending on developing its Navy. Thanks to the increasing number of regional trading blocs across the world, that played a positive factor for India to integrate itself with various regional groupings.

On the other hand, China has been rapidly developing its blue water capabilities. Although not officially confirmed, China has military bases in the Indian Ocean. The Chinese Navy possess the Liaoning aircraft carrier which is already in service, about 60 submarines (including nuclear and conventional submarines), over 50 frigates, nearly 30 destroyers, along with 80 amphibious and other ships that enable it to introduce a 'far sea defense' strategy.[14] The projects invested by China in Hambantota (Sri Lanka), Chittagong (Myanmar), Gwadar (Pakistan) and in Seychelles are said to be base for China to enter the Indian Ocean. With the rising the economic strength of China, the littoral states in the Indian Ocean are getting closer to China. The sudden appearance of Chinese submarines in Colombo created dissatisfaction with Delhi because over 70 percent of the transshipment business at the Colombo port is India-related.

Later that month, Indian Prime Minister Narendra Modi personally reminded the then Sri Lanka Prime Minister Rajapaksa that Sri Lanka was obliged to inform its neighbors about such port calls under a maritime pact. Yet the same submarine resurfaced in Colombo again without prior notice to Delhi.[15] Two years later Sri Lankan President Sirisena has stated that "India is a good neighbor and China is a good ally.[16] This statement by the Sri Lankan President shows that they are more inclined and thankful to China than India. China's economic hegemony and their investments in smaller countries make the smaller countries bend down to China politically. If not for now, there are high chances that it may happen in future. Currently, this is one of the prime concerns of India in this region and the expansion of Chinese presence in the Indian Ocean has heightened India's concerns, even though Beijing is assuring that its activities are commercially motivated and intended to protect its interests and people.

Challenges for Sri Lanka

There are two main challenges which Sri Lanka is facing currently. The first one is to try and lessen its dependence on China. The official estimate of what Sri Lanka currently owes its financiers is $64.9 billion — $8 billions of which is owned by China. The country's debt-to-GDP currently stands around 75% and 95.4% of all government revenue is currently going towards debt repayment. By 2015, China had become the largest provider of Official Development Assistance (OPA) to Sri Lanka standing at $12 billion, with a long lead over India's $1.9 billion, and Japan's $175 million.[17] This statistic shows how much Sri Lanka is dependent on China for its economic development. In 2016, Sri Lanka took a bailout of $1.5 billion dollar from IMF (International Monetary Fund) to avert its balance of payment crisis.[18] Recently Sri Lanka has allowed Chinese companies to have control of 80% of Hambantota port because of its incapability to pay back loans or interest within the stipulated time. Also, it is not able to convince the civic population that these projects are useful to the public. There is a feeling among the Tamil population that the Sri Lankan government is not concentrating much in the war tone regions of Jaffana. The current situation is that it is not even able to generate employment in the infrastructure projects. The Chinese firms bring laborers and raw materials from China. Lack of confidence among the local people of Sri Lanka has stirred up a lot of protests in the recent years. However, the biggest problem is that the Sri Lankan government has no road plan of how to pay back the loans which it has been acquiring for some time now. There are high chances that Sri Lanka might fall into the debt trap of China.

The second challenge for Sri Lanka is balancing the relationship with India and China. Despite China contributing 12 times more than India for its development projects, it still doesn't want to completely align with China. There are lot of Indian public private partnership projects going on like construction of damaged railway lines, schools, hospitals and houses on the north-eastern part of Sri Lanka. The Sri Lankan government has to give confidence to the Indian counterparts that the port in Hambantota will remain as a commercial venture in order to maintain the balance.

The Future Ahead for Both Players in Sri Lanka

"Bases is going to be the name of the game in the Indian Ocean, and that game is going to be pretty attractive in the coming years.",

–C. Raja Mohan, Director, Carnegie India

China is taking a big risk by providing loans to all the South Asian countries. It is giving loans which are beyond the financial strength of the littoral countries to pay back. There are chances that they may default the loans in future. If they are not able to persuade the littoral states to support them politically, all their investments in those countries do not make much sense.

There was always an uncertainty of whether China can have access to the ports its building in Sri Lanka for military purposes. As it was also the case with United States, every time it builds ports and bases aboard with lot of enthusiasm, but due to unforeseen political circumstances, it could not use them for its military purposes.[19] This may repeat with China too, in Sri Lanka. Even though Chinese company owns 80% of the Hambantota port, it still cannot access it for its military purpose as of now. So, China is in every possible way, trying to pull those small countries towards their side. It is also important for China to take cautious steps. China should make sure that it doesn't precipitate any conflict, by increasing its presence of naval ships, or make India uneasy in the Indian Ocean region. If it does, India would also start to involve actively in the South China Sea conflict. That would create pressure for the Chinese navy on both sides. But some feel that China's involvement in Indian Ocean is detriment for its long-term interest. But with the strained ongoing bilateral relations between these two nations, neither

China nor India can trust each other. As an aspiring super power, China may think of trying to cut down their vulnerability to protect itself, from India –United States collaboration.

In such scenario, India needs to have strong ties with close friends in Indian Ocean region. As of now, many littoral countries are politically staying neutral in order to get investments from both the big countries. Countries like Sri Lanka are in a serious debt-trap created by the Chinese which shows the other side of the Chinese investments. That is where the role of India as a big regional power comes into play. Even though India can't bail out Sri Lanka from its debts because of its own financially reasons, it can still help them get a major bailout from World Bank and other International organizations. India can be a mediator to lobby for Sri Lanka in the West.

India being geographically dominant in IOR, it must act as a regional leader. In order to be so, it must expand its naval strength and ports both within its sovereign land and outside. Without reacting to the investments of China, India has to tactically invest, to counter the strategy of China. Developing Vizhinjam Port in Kerala to counter Hambantota is one such step. If in IOR geo-political game is being played then India can expand the game to South China Sea too. India can build a port in Cam Ranh Bay in Vietnam in South China sea as a counter measure for Chinese activities in IOR in future. This may not sound practical, but, it is a sensible strategy for a long-term goal. The Quadrilateral partnership which comprises of Australia, Japan, the US and India to deter China is also a step in the right direction.

If there are issues where both the Asian giants stand against each other, there are also diverse nontraditional security challenges like piracy, natural calamities, etc in the Indian Ocean Region (IOR) where both states can cooperate. Both countries should collaborate and work together to reduce tensions and build confidence. Both the countries should create an understanding, that they will not get involved in each other's ocean that would be a good start. But this is dependent upon the willingness of the political leadership of the two countries. Incase if they decide on working together, India can even consider the possibility of inviting China as an observer of the IONS. However, this seems to be a difficult proposition at the moment. India, in order to retain its position as net security provider, must draft a long-term strategy, even if that means, it has to take some strong decisions against other emerging powers in the region.

References

1. Monsoon- the Indian Ocean and the Future of American Power. (Robert Kaplan)

2. Geopolitics, Security and Bilateral Relations: Perspectives from India and South Korea. (B K Sharma)

3. Maritime Safety and Security in the Indian Ocean. (BhagyaSenaratne)

4. Indian Ocean Challenges: A quest for cooperative solutions. (Sureesh Mehta)

5. Evolving dynamics of the Indian Ocean. (Vijay Sakhuja and Raghaventra Mishra)

6. Indian Ocean Region: Emerging Strategic Cooperation, Competition and conflict Scenarios. (BK Sharma, Dr. Adil Rasheed)

7. Michael Vurens van Es, (2014 Jul). Sri Lanka: Export Powerhouse?.The Diplomat. Retrieved from http://thediplomat.com/2014/07/sri-lanka-export-powerhouse/

8. Goh Sui Noi, "China Not Planning Sri Lanka Naval base," *Strait Times*, June 24, 2009.

9. Nihal Rodrigo, 2012: "Emerging China: Prospects for Partnership in Asia- A Perspective from Sri Lanka" in Sudhir T.Devarr, Swaran Singh, Reena Marwah (Ed.) *Emerging China: Prospects for Partnership in Asia*. Routledge, India. Pp.241-255.

10. Nilanthi Samaranayake, 2014: "China's Relations with the Smaller Countries of South Asia" in Donovan C. Chau, Thomas M. Kane (Ed.) *China and International Security: History, Strategy and 21st Century Policy*. Praeger, U.S.A. PP. 217- 238

11. S.I Keethaponcalan, 2011: " The Indian Factor in the Peace Process and Conflict Resolution in Sri Lanka" in Jonathan Goodhard, Jonathan Spencer, BenediktKorf (Ed.) *Conflict and Peacebuilding in Sri Lanka- Caught in the Peace Trap?*. Routledge, Oxon. Pp 39- 53.

12. Shine Jacob, (2013 Apr) IOC's Lanka plans on the table despite Colombo's takeover threat. Business Standard. Retrieved fromhttp://www.business-standard.com/article/economy-policy/ioc-s-lanka-plans-on-the-table-despite-colombo-s-takeover-threat-113041000104_1.html

Endnotes

1   Cuiping, Z. (n.d.). Turbulence and Strategic competition in Indian Ocean. In *Evolving Dynamics of The Indian Ocean* (p. 38).Shipra publications.

2   Mohan, C. R. (2013). "*SamudraManthan: Sino-Indian rivalry in the Indo-Pacific.*" (p.135) New Delhi: Oxford University Press.

3   Peter Popham, "How Beijing Won Sri Lanka's Civil War," Independent, May 23, 2009, www.independent.co.uk/news/world/asia/how-beijing-won-sri-lankas-civil-war-1980492.html

4   Mohan, C. R. (2013). "SamudraManthan*: Sino-Indian rivalry in the Indo-Pacific.*" (p.149) New Delhi: Oxford University Press.

5   Smith, J. M. (2016, November 20). China and Sri Lanka: Between a Dream and a Nightmare. Retrieved May 13, 2017, from http://thediplomat.com/2016/11/china-and-sri-lanka-between-a-dream-and-a-nightmare/

6   ibid

7   India - Sri Lanka - China Relations: Building Bridges via Infrastructure. (n.d.). Retrieved May 13, 2017, from http://www.mmbiztoday.com/articles/india-sri-lanka-china-relations-building-bridges-infrastructure

8   Chaudhury, D. R. (2017, May 02). China may put South Asia on road to debt trap. Retrieved May 13, 2017, from http://economictimes.indiatimes.com/news/politics-and-nation/china-may-put-south-asia-on-road-to-debt-trap/articleshow/58467309.cms

9   Geopolitics of Chinese Investments in Sri Lanka.(n.d.). Retrieved May 13, 2017, from http://www.ipcs.org/article/india/the-geopolitics-of-chinese-investments-in-sri-lanka-4862.html

10 C3s » India- Sri Lanka- China Relations: Building Bridges via Infrastructure ByAsma Masood. (n.d.). Retrieved May 18, 2017, from http://www.c3sindia.org/uncategorized/4809

11 India - Sri Lanka - China Relations: Building Bridges via Infrastructure. (n.d.). Retrieved May 13, 2017, from http://www.mmbiztoday.com/articles/india-sri-lanka-china-relations-building-bridges-infrastructure

12 N. (n.d.).India Refloats Plan for Lanka Port. Retrieved May 18, 2017, from http://www.newindianexpress.com/thesundaystandard/2015/sep/27/India-Refloats-Plan-for-Lanka-Port-821094.html

13 C3s » India- Sri Lanka- China Relations: Building Bridges via Infrastructure ByAsma Masood. (n.d.). Retrieved May 18, 2017, from http://www.c3sindia.org/uncategorized/4809

14 Rasheed, A. (n.d.). Indian Ocean Region - Emergic Strategic Cooperation, Competition and Conflict Scenarios (B. Sharma, Ed.).Pg 42 New Delhi: Vij Books.

15 Smith, J. M. (2016, November 20). China and Sri Lanka: Between a Dream and a Nightmare. Retrieved May 13, 2017, from http://thediplomat.com/2016/11/china-and-sri-lanka-between-a-dream-and-a-nightmare/

16 Storm in a port. (2015, March 19). Retrieved May 18, 2017, from http://www.economist.com/news/asia/21646757-islands-largest-infrastructure-project-governments-first-big-test-storm-port

17 Shepard, W. (2016, October 03). Sri Lanka's Debt Crisis Is So Bad the Government Doesn't Even Know How Much Money It Owes. Retrieved May 18, 2017, from https://www.forbes.com/sites/wadeshepard/2016/09/30/sri-lankas-debt-crisis-is-so-bad-the-government-doesnt-even-know-how-much-money-it-owes/#25a205304608

18 C. (2016, April 30). Sri Lanka, IMF agree on $1.5B bailout to avert balance of payments crisis. Retrieved May 18, 2017, from http://www.cnbc.com/2016/04/30/sri-lanka-imf-agree-on-15b-bailout-to-avert-balance-of-payments-crisis.html

19 Mohan, C. R, (2013). "SamudraManthan: Sino-Indian rivalry in the Indo-Pacific.", (p.149) New Delhi: Oxford University Press

Strategic Importance of Myanmar for India

Ms. Shivangi Shrivastava

Introduction

India as an emerging economy needs to maintain a good strategic relationship with its neighbours for its future endeavours and national security. It aims to become a global power and for that it needs to show concern and interest in Asian countries. Myanmar is one of the most enriched countries in terms of natural resources in Asia, and provides a gateway for South East Asian countries for India.

With the rise of China's influence amongst India's neighbours, and the introduction of CPEC, under its famous One Belt One Road project, it is important that India builds a strong strategic relationship with other neighbouring countries to counter China.

Myanmar plays a very important role in India's take on its 'Act East Policy', because of its geopolitical location. Myanmar is a gateway for India to South East Asia, both in terms of geography as well as economic connectivity, thus a good relationship with Myanmar will help in the development of India's economy as well as benefit India's Northeast region. This is due to the fact that, Myanmar not only shares border with India but a lot of Northeastern states share same ethnicity, as a result there is a sense of commonality.

A good strategic development with Myanmar will be the key factor in the success of the government's look east policy (Act East Policy)[1].

India shared a historical relation with Myanmar, even after independence India maintained a good relationship with Myanmar, but due to different political governance structures, the progress became stagnant. Further the

Chinese inroads in Myanmar isolated Myanmar and it was a cause of concern for India too as it made India vulnerable to China.

China has carried out a lot of projects/trade in Myanmar and both the nations do consider each other very important in terms of building a strategic partnership. If China has a strong control over Myanmar both strategically and economically then this will affect India's Act East Policy. China will also be encircling India from all sides as China's influence in Pakistan is already growing and China is also trying to build its relationship with other neighbouring nations of India. China might not consider Indo-Myanmar relation as a threat, but it is so for India. The nation thus needs to enhance its various ongoing projects and create better strategies to maintain a good relationship with Myanmar. Myanmar, at present, is being targeted by lot of countries, including USA, but due to Myanmar's rich natural and energy resources and geostrategic location, India needs to focus on its development and trade relations.

Issue of Border Management

India and Myanmar relations are also of utmost importance for India's internal security. Due to partition[2] there are ethnic and community differences/similarities, because of which there always have been cultural divisions, which has resulted in cases of insurgency and militancy in the north-eastern region, where Myanmar had played a very significant role. The other issue is- India shares a porous border with Myanmar. Poor border management has resulted in drug problems, human and weapon trafficking, etc. Narco trade is a serious concern for both the states.

If both the states want to maintain good economic and strategic relations, then the issue of porous borders and poor border management needs to be addressed. Especially, for the India side, because there are cases where Chinese goods have been dumped into the Indian Border States, as a result this has created a parallel economy and the local goods manufactured by the locals suffer. Apart from this there also have been the issue of illegal immigration coming into the country, causing an upsurge in terrorist activities. Recent is the issue of Rohingya Muslims, who are following the route from Bangladesh and trying to enter the country.

The Indo-Myanmar border needs to be demarcated. It will be difficult to follow a traditional method of border security; therefore, new scientific method such as smart borders can be used to deal with border management issues.

Along with that proper development, the building of roads, better security check, implementation of smart borders, less corruption by security forces and a collective support from the Northeastern states are required.

India and Myanmar a Historical Perspective

India shares the same history with Myanmar, as they both were part of British colony, till 1935, Myanmar and India use to come under the same territory for the British Empire, culturally and religiously also both were connected. India is a birth place of Buddhism which is the most followed religion in Myanmar; Bodh Gaya always had been a pilgrimage for Myanmar people[3]. Myanmar also has lot of people of Indian origin. With respect to Northeast region, Myanmar shares common ethnicity with four states mainly, Arunachal Pradesh, Nagaland, Mizoram, and Manipur. Manipur shares the closest ties with Myanmar, because of Asiatic kingdoms[4]. There was and is still a strong social - the cultural interaction between Manipur and Myanmar.

Even our leaders has always showed soft corner towards Myanmar, starting from the first prime minister Jawaharlal Nehru, when he gifted the Kabaw valley in 1952 to Myanmar as part of the peace treaty[5,] which was signed in 1951. However, the relations became sour when the military junta took control in Myanmar, and India was not in favour of such political regime, as it had always supported pro-democracy institutions. It always supported the NLD intentions, but India never allowed it to become a hub, for their political activities. India was always critical of the military junta.

The visit of erstwhile Prime Minister Rajiv Gandhi in 1987 laid the foundations for a stronger relationship between India and Myanmar, keeping aside the political turmoil in Myanmar. India's relation with the state since then, has improved and various bilateral trade agreements have been signed, which include exchange of high-profile bilateral visits to initiate dialogue. India even carried out disaster relief projects for Myanmar. At present, India is working on improving its relationship with Myanmar in terms of infrastructure development, economical trade, and strategic development. Myanmar has become more politically stable now as it has come out of its international isolation.

Geo-Strategic Importance of Myanmar

Myanmar shares common border with five countries Bangladesh, China, India, Laos, and India. India dominates Myanmar's westerns borders; it provides convenient external land and sea communication to India's landlocked north- eastern states[6]. Myanmar is a gateway between India and ASEAN. Myanmar became a member of ASEAN in 1997. Myanmar is the key factor in the success of India's Act East Policy, as it provides linkages to the South East Asian countries for India. It occupies the most strategically important location, connecting the South Asian countries to South East Asian countries and provides littoral to the Bay of Bengal[7] Myanmar is very rich in natural resources; especially it has abundance of energy resource. Having a good strategic and economical relation with Myanmar, will help India primarily in two ways, firstly it can help in controlling insurgency, and secondly the connectivity can aid in the development of Northeastern states of India. Myanmar can serve as a buffer zone between India and China. It is also the key country for the strategic trilateral highway, which passes through India, Myanmar, and reaches to Thailand.

India maintains a good relationship with most of its neighbours, if it develops a strong bond with Myanmar, it will help in building a positive international network in the neighbourhood.

India's Present Position

Infrastructure

Slowly India is trying to mark its footprints in Myanmar, Indian army border roads organization had built the Tamu-Kalewakalemyo highway[8], now the famous Kaladan multi-modal transit transport project, which aims to connect Eastern seaport of India with that of Myanmar, is being built. After the coming of Prime Minister Narendra Modi, the bus service will be started soon which follows the Tamu-Kalewa-Mandalay highway route famously quoted as the road to Myanmar. Cooperation with Myanmar in various multilateral forums such as ASEAN and BIMSTEC[9] can strengthen the relationship. However, like the Chinese, India needs to build soft power in Myanmar.

Politics and Defence

There have been conferences and exchange of dialogues at political level but nothing very significant has come out of it, therefore, India can engage such dialogues. Till now, China holds the maximum investment in Myanmar's defence[10], however things can change in future, and India can start by conducting joint military exercise with Myanmar and help the country by giving military weapons and aid.

Act East Policy

Act East Policy is the changed/new name given to India's Look East Policy, which was initiated in the early 90s. It took its wings under the leadership of erstwhile Prime Minister Narasimha Rao and was later renamed as Act East Policy after Narendra Modi became the Prime Minister. The policy aims to create better economic and strategic ties with the South East Asian countries and also aims to develop India's Northeastern states. It is a proactive initiation on the part of India to respond to the changing geopolitics of South East Asian countries at a global and a regional level. Hence it becomes imperative that India develops good relationship with Myanmar so that its Act East Asia policy becomes successful.

Implémentation

A good border management between India and Myanmar is essential and on economic level BIMST-EC (Bangladesh, India and Myanmar, Sri Lanka, Thailand- Economic Cooperation) and Mekong Ganga project have gained prominence.

China's Influence

A Historical Perspective

China and Myanmar's historical connect is older than that of India and Myanmar. They have seen dynasties together, though there were struggles and disputes too, between the two states; however, friendly relations were restored in the 1950s. China seized the opportunity when it saw that Myanmar was being isolated internationally, she supported Myanmar politically, economically and through the development of infrastructures. In terms of politics it always took a neutral stand as far as military junta was concerned but covertly it supported the military, however, it concentrated on economics and tried to build peace with the state, which increased its value in their eyes. Military junta even claims to have called China as its elder brother, On the other hand, Myanmar was the first non- communist country which recognized China after its foundation[11], All this show that both the countries were close allies. Though the period from 1950-1970 was tumults, but things improved later and China has invested a lot in Myanmar's defence and this helped China to carry out its military projection at Myanmar's base[12].

China's influence in Myanmar is the maximum in the economic sector as China is the largest investor in Myanmar. China considers Myanmar as an economic corridor. First China tried to support Myanmar politically and by providing defence equipment, now it is trying to help economically. Though there has been a democratic revolution in the country, China's closeness with political leaders is still maintained.

Curent Situation

China's good relationship with Myanmar will have a strategic impact on India. It can provide China a pathway to access Northeastern regions of India. Already some of the Indian territories has been claimed by China, thus this can affect the sovereignty of India. Chinese companies have built 190 miles of highway in Myanmar with a special emphasis on roads leading up to Arunachal Pradesh, which China persist in claiming as its rightful territory of southern Tibet[13].

China has already invested a lot in Myanmar, China has pumped approximately 5 billion US$ in the hydropower sector of Myanmar[14], Chinese companies like 'Human Machinery & Equipment Import and Export Company Limited' has been involved in 25 projects in past one decade[15]. Not just economically, but even military it is supplying equipment and giving training facilities, thus it will be difficult to counter Chinese influence in Myanmar. China is also extracting Myanmar's natural resources and China's economic assistance is very crucial to Myanmar.

In terms of geography, China already enjoys more stable connectivity to Myanmar than India, Yunnan province of China which shares a border with Myanmar is more developed than that of our Northeastern states[16], therefore, it is very important for India to increase its investments in Myanmar, and to engage with the political leadership of Myanmar. A friendly and good strategic support from India will help Myanmar to overcome China's influence, and may prevent forced opium cultivation, trafficking and environmental degradation, all these factors had led to animosity among Burmese people[17]. This can thus provide a better opportunity for India to enhance trade and have good relations with Myanmar.

Political Stability

A good strategic relation will result in tackling of political issues. There has been political instability between the Northeastern regions of India and Myanmar, Northeast India had faced strategic insecurity and at that time Myanmar did become a haven for insurgent groups- like the Nationalist Socialist Council of Nagaland and the United Liberation Front of Assam[18]. Though, efforts from both states were taken to counter insurgency, through initiatives like the "operation golden bird[19]". However, the issue of Rohingya Muslim refugees is a serious concern for both the countries. Islamic radicalization is another area of concern for India; a lot of terrorist groups have been traced back to Bangladesh and Myanmar.

Need for Border Management

If India wants to maintain a good strategic relation with Myanmar, it needs to work on the loopholes, and one of the major loopholes is the issue of the porous border. The opening of border trade between India and Myanmar has indirectly helped in exposing the porous nature of border[20]. A good border management is the need of the hour. Because of the same ethnicity and very high terrain, the border is porous in many areas; and many tribes are allowed free trade on either side because of ethnic similarity.

Poor border management has led to the issues of drug trafficking and smuggling, which is creating a parallel economy and affecting the health of the youth. 'Heroine and synthetic drugs come from Myanmar to India while chemicals like acetic anhydride and ephedrine, essential for converting raw opium into heroin, are transported from India (linter 1994:29)[21]. It is also the source for illegal migrants. With such conditions, it is essential that both countries monitor the border through the creation of smart borders.

Endnotes

1   Sahi.S.K (2017), 'China Strides in Bhutan, Nepal and Myanmar Options for India'. Delhi: G.B Books Publishers & Distributors, p. 161.

2   Ibid., p.150.

3   Available at https://www.mea.gov.in/Portal/ForeignRelation/myanmar-july-2012.pdfpg1 accessed on 11 May 2017 available at https://www.mea.gov.in/Portal/ForeignRelation/myanmar-july-2012.pdfpg1 accessed on 11 May 2017.

4   Singh.L.k (2009) Look East Policy & India's North East- Polemics and Perspective. Delhi: Centre for Alternative Discourse,Manipur: Concept Publishing Company, "Indo-Myanmar Relations in the Greater Perspective of India's Look East Policy: Implication on Manipur", p 168.

5   Available at https://www.mea.gov.in/Portal/ForeignRelation/myanmar-july-2012.pdfpg1,2 accessed on 11 May 2017.

6   Sahi.S.K (2017), "China Strides in Bhutan, Nepal and Myanmar Options for India". Delhi: G.B Books Publishers & Distributors, p 123.

7   Ibid., p. 123.

8   Ibid., p. 154.

9   Ibid., p. 162.

10   Sahi.S.K (2017), "China strides in Bhutan, Nepal and Myanmar Options for India". Delhi: G.B Books Publishers & Distributers, pp 141-142

11   Sahi.S.K(2017) ,China Strides in Bhutan, Nepal and Myanmar Options for India', Delhi: G.B Books Publishers & Distributors, pp 126

12   Ibid., p. 126-127.

13   Ibid., p. 138.

14   Ibid., p. 137-138.

15   Ibid., p. 137-138.

16   Ibid.,p 122

17   Ibid., p. 147.

18 Ibid., p. 150-151.

19 Singh. L. K (2009) 'Look East Policy & India's North East- Polemics and Perspective Delhi: Centre for Alternative Discourse,Manipur: Concept Publishing Company', "Indo-Myanmar Relations in the Greater Perspective of India's Look East Policy: Implication on Manipur", p. 165

20 Ibid., p. 168-169.

21 Ibid., p 166

The Changing Trajectory of the Indo–US Relations

Mr. Gaurav Kumar

US President Donald Trump on December 18, 2017 released the US National Security Strategy (NSS) 2017, documenting its strategy, for the global security, that promotes and safeguards American interests, under the fast changing, unpredictable world order. The paper discusses ways in which it can uphold US supremacy, while confronting new challenges posed by the resurgent Russia, China, North Korea, and global terrorism. Amidst all this, the document welcomes "India's emergence as a leading global power, and being a stronger US strategic and defence partner." Emphasising India's role in the region the paper further states, "We will expand our defense and security cooperation with India, a Major Defense Partner of the United States, and support India's growing relationships throughout the region."

The reference to India has been particularly in the context of Indo-Pacific region, and in countering Chinese Influence in South Asia, as stated, "We will encourage India to increase its economic assistance in the region."

The reference to India as a global power has been well received in the country, and much of the discourse on the US NSS has been on India's newly gained stature of a leading global power; this is in contrast to the past reference of "regional provider of security" in 2015. The NSS reflects the US's growing confidence in India. Indo-US relation has never witnessed such an improved cooperation between two countries as it has witnessed in the last few years. The current state of the relation is a sharp contrast to the age-old policy of "one-step-forward, two-step-backward" approach, born out of lack of confidence / indifference. However, once the two countries gained confidence and aligned their interests, the relationship witnessed unprecedented upsurge. The most striking feature of the relationship is that all the new developments have taken place within a short period of time.

Brief History- Baggage of Communism and Pakistan Factor

The Indo-US relations have the most distinctive quality of being world's most inconsistent relationship in the last seventy years. The nature and the content of the relationship have varied with the kind of strategical and ideological preferences the governments of the two countries have shown over the period of time. The other factors that have strained the relations have been the geographical location, cultural differences, political perspectives, and attitude. The celebration of the most distinguished and most cherished characteristic of being world's largest and oldest democracy came into play much later with the change of the US national interest towards India.

The US hostility or at times indifference to India was largely shaped by its strategy of berating Communism that dominated from 50s to early 20th century. In order to choose an ally against communism in South Asia, US, choose Pakistan over India. The underlining reason has been aptly stated by the then secretary of state, John Foster Dulles an interview with the New York Times, when he stated, "The strong spiritual faith and martial spirit of the people make them a dependable bulwark against communism[1]." He saw in India, "Soviet Communism exercising a strong influence through the interim Hindu government" led by Jawaharlal Nehru[2]. The doctrine of John F Dulles had huge impact on the future of US policy in South Asia.

The former US diplomat Dennis Kux has called India and the US as "estranged Democracy." According to Kux the two factors of friction that has dominated Indo-US relation are the U.S. arms to Pakistan, and India's close ties with the Soviet Union[3]. Other strategical and political factors were either offshoot or subset of these two critical factors. In contrast, today, the two countries boost of more than 50 bilateral dialogue mechanisms between them, clearly highlighting the kind of engagement the two countries currently have.

If the communism and the Pakistan factor dominated Indo-US relation in 20th century; the relationship in the initial decades of 21st century was primarily shaped by the shared concern over the rise of transnational problems such as terrorism, along with other issues likes defence and security, environment, trades and commerce etc.

Terrorism as a Common Threat

Terrorism as an expanding threat to the sovereignty of the United States and to international order has important implications for the Indo-US relations. Both India and the US have faced horrific impact of state sponsored terrorism by Pakistan. Pakistan, which has history of providing logistical support, money, weapons, training, and safe havens and passage to terrorists, has consistently used terrorism as a foreign policy tool, to uphold its strategic grip over the Kashmir issue, as also in Afghanistan. India has long witnessed Pakistan's sponsorship of terrorism on its soil; however, the US is slowly waking up to this reality in Afghanistan, where its troops are battling the resurgent Islamist groups backed and patronised by Pakistan.

Similarly, India has faced the menace of terrorism right since independence, and has continuously appealed to international community to take note of Pakistan sponsored terrorism. However, due to difference in the interests of the United States and India, the US was never been able to fully acknowledge India's grievances in the region. Over the years in the last two decades, the US governments have shown understanding of Indian problem; however, it had remained limited to diplomatic circles, and never reached operational level of cooperation. The new government in the US under Trump administration has shown some signs of revising its policy in the region, when it announced its new South Asia policy in August. It appears that the Trump government understands that India is the key player in the region and therefore it wants to make India the core of his Asia strategy. While unveiling its South Asia Policy in August 2017 Trump had underlined the importance of India, when he said that a critical part of the South Asia strategy for America is to further develop its strategic partnership with India, and he wants India to help the US more with Afghanistan, especially in the area of economic assistance and development. [4] This was a departure from the past policies of the previous governments in the US. As professor, Harsh Pant has suggested that the Trump's policy is a remarkable turnaround for Washington, which had wanted to keep India out of its "Af-Pak" policy for long, for fear of offending Rawalpindi. India was viewed as part of the problem and now Trump is arguing that India should be viewed as part of a solution to the Afghan imbroglio.[5] The turnaround has significant implication for the regional security structure and it is up to India now how it utilizes the growing convergence of its interest with the US.

The renewed Indo-US strategic partnership is not limited to South Asia alone. The US is giving new impetus to its nearly dormant Indo-Pacific policy. In doing so, it has shown the willingness to engage India along with Japan and Australia. Trump's frequent use of the term "Indo-Pacific" instead of commonly used word "Asia-Pacific" reveals the kind of importance the US places on India. The nomenclature has more than semantic importance and recognises the region a natural extension of the India centric maritime space. According to Alyssa Ayres, senior South Asia fellow at the Council on Foreign Relations, the label underscores "India's geographic connection to the Asia-Pacific as a cornerstone of the Trump administration's strategic thinking." [6] To many analysts the term Indo-Pacific now seems to be a means of including India in the military calculations of U.S. strategy in the Pacific. [7]

Growing Defence and Security Partnership

There has been an alignment of interests, leading to building a strategic partnership, as also an increase in the military and defense relationship. India's growing stature as global power requires it to develop its military power. It is equally important for India to modernize its defence capacity and capabilities, amid growing threats from two of its neighbours- China and Pakistan. India had historically, close defence ties with Russia. India had an extensive military cooperation (both in volume and quality) with the Russians, and is exclusively dependent on Russian for its military purchases. In the last couple of decades, India has however, diversified its military cooperation, building strong ties with the US, France and Israel. The US has been the most significant beneficiary of India's new diversification of defence policy. Even the US understands that a militarily strong India in the region, is in the interest of the US.

Under the Obama Administration, India was designated as a major defence partner of the US. The Trump administration equally values India's role as a global player, and it has continued the policy of the Obama government of seeing India as the net security provider of the region. Similar sentiments were expressed by the US defense Secretary James Mattis during his visit to India in September 2017, when the US agreed to boost their defence ties, with the US willing to share some of its most advanced technologies with India. Mattis had said that India as a major defence partner reflected the recognition of India as a "pillar of regional stability and security."[8] The Trump has gone a step further and has shown keenness to accommodate India's demand for state-of-the-art technology. It has been widely reported that the Trump government has informed the Congress that it "strongly supports" transfers of F-18 and F-16 fighter proposals put forth by Boeing and Lockheed Martin respectively. These proposals have the tremendous potential to take Indo-US defence ties to the next level. [9]

The most important dimension of these strong military ties is the US renewed approach towards the Indo-Pacific region. To counter the Chinese growing presence, and to maintain the freedom of navigation in the region, US needs more participation from militarily strong regional players like Japan and India. According to Alice Wells, acting Assistant Secretary of State for the South and Central Asian Affairs, the reason why defence cooperation with India is so vital to US interests is because we (the US) need India to be a net security provider in the Indo–Pacific, a region that serves as the fulcrum of global trade and commerce, with nearly half of the world's 90,000 commercial vessels—many sailing under the US flag—and two-thirds of traded oil travelling through the region." [10] The formulation aptly sums up the US interest in a militarily strong India.

India, on the other hand has its own interest in having strong strategic and security ties with the US, particularly after the rise of resurgent and aggressive China. India's own interest coincides with the American interest in the region. For example, the South China Sea is India's gateway to the pacific region. With changing nature of its trade and commerce in the last two decades, with volume of trade and commerce shifting towards East away from West, it is imperative for India to maintain and safeguards the freedom of navigation and the security of sea lanes in the Indo-Pacific region. Around 55 per cent of India's trade in the Indo-Pacific transits through the SCS region, secondly some of its energy requirements are met by the supplies through the SCS. Therefore, India's increasing involvement in the SCS region illustrates the relationship between its strategy and the need for resources, and for the routes and logistical systems necessary for their transportation.[11]

India's Emerging Economy and the Indo-US Cooperation

India's desire to be seen as a global player cannot be fulfilled unless and until its economy grows in leaps and bounds. Economic development is the key to overall development of its strategical and military goals. The US has played significant role in helping India build its economy. India's financial crisis of

1990s and subsequent economic liberalisation had direct and immediate impact upon US–India relations. The changes in India's domestic economic structure began in the early 1990s. It played an important role in changing the texture of their relationship. In his historic visit to India in 2010, US Treasury Secretary, Timothy Geithner launched the U.S.-India Economic and Financial Partnership, with Indian Finance Minister Mr. Pranab Mukherjee. The ministerial-level meeting was first of its kind to institutionalize deeper bilateral relations on economic and financial sector issues.[12] Today, India-US bilateral trade in goods and services increased from $104 billion in 2014 to $114 billion in 2016. Two-way merchandise trade stood at $66.7 billion. Of this, India's exports of goods to the US were valued at $46 billion and India's imports of goods from US were valued at $21.7 billion. India-US trade in services stood at $47.2 billion.[13] The journey of India right from the time when India was facing economic sanctions and embargo after its nuclear tests to the current intense economic partnership is the key indicator of growing ties between the two countries. Off late the US has evolved as an inevitable partner for India and vice versa, and requires another decade or so for India to fully gain the benefits from the strong multifaceted cooperation.

Way Ahead

The end of the US–Soviet Cold War and the subsequent downfall of communism had significant impact on Indo-US relations. The soured relation slowly and subtly started to develop into friendship. The growing economic, defence and security cooperation were corollaries of those epochal geopolitical transformations, the world has witnessed after the disintegration of the Soviet Union. However, the renewed vigour in the relationship is also an outcome of another transformation shaping the global order, the decline of the US domination in the Indo-Pacific, and the rise of revisionist powers like China and Russia. India with its healthy economy and vibrant democracy is seen by many global actors to be the new face of the emerging global order. India too appears willing to play the role of global power in the region and finds US a competent partner, in this new game. As far as US views are considered it considers India a "central strategic partner" of the US in pursuing common interests in the region, and is willing to step up cooperation to complement the common strategic interest in the region.[14] In Indo-Pacific region both the US and India's interests now are focused on enhancing connectivity towards the east, while trying to balance the aggressive rise of China. At the same time, both countries would be wary of military confrontation and would like to negotiate its interests in peaceful terms. Indo-US cooperation is more likely to witness upswing in the region as compared to South Asia.

Cooperation on terrorism is another area that is more likely to witness enhanced cooperation in the coming years, as hinted by the new Trump administration. South Asia, which is the hub of terror networks, and the key to the stability of the world, has become important for the US policy makers. With Pakistan's duplicity exposed by the Trump government, India stands as the only reliable partner with some hold over the region. The US government might not be willing to completely break its ties with Pakistan, but recent signals from the US suggest that the government is looking at an alternative model in South Asia. They desire more participation of India at the regional level, which is a clear shift from the past policies, where India's participation was merely symbolic in nature. During his recent visit to India, Secretary of States Rex Tillerson had made a veiled attack at Pakistan, while extending the US support for India's growing role in the region. He said, "In the fight against terrorism, the United States will continue to stand shoulder to shoulder with India. Terrorist safe havens will not be tolerated." [15] Similar sentiments were expressed for India in the US South Asia policy and National Security policy, which talks about 'deepening strategic ties with India.' Therefore, it appears that a new policy is shaping up at Washington D.C at the strategic level in South Asia, involving India as compared to Pakistan.

However, the new policy has its own short comings and lacunae as far as the evaluation of the role of India in Afghanistan is concerned, and the cooperation that India and the US can have in Afghanistan. The role India is playing in Afghanistan may not be up to the expectation of the current US government. India has been actively involved in infrastructural development initiatives in Afghanistan, showcasing its soft power along with economic incentives. After US President Trump's speech in August, calling for India's greater involvement in the region, there were speculations that India might be asked to send troops to Afghanistan. However, during a joint press conference with US secretary of defense James Mattis, Indian Defence Minister categorically denied sending Indian military to Afghanistan. India has avoided this, even though it has been involved in providing all kind of security assistance including training and some non-lethal military equipment to Afghan forces. In future, the US would like India to step up its involvement in the region, whereas, India would be cautious and watchful of the Pakistan-US relation, and as long as Pakistan remains in the game, India would avoid any direct military role.

Apart from the defence and security cooperation, the two countries are likely to enhance trade and economic ties, as India remains one of the most lucrative markets, as well as one of the key investor for the US. The bilateral trade has grown from $19 billion in 2000 to over $100 billion in 2014, and the current governments believe that increasing the annual trade between the US and India to $500 billion is feasible under the opportunities that New Delhi offers to American companies, particularly in aviation and defence sectors.

In a relatively short time, Indo-US relation has witnessed unprecedented cooperation and the future appears to be more vibrant and positive than the past. More importantly, the two countries have successfully diversified cooperation which is the hallmark of the growing confidence, between the two nations.

References

1. Wetering, Carina. Changing US Foreign Policy toward India: US-India Relations since the Cold War. New York: Palgrave Macmillan US, 2016. E-Book.

2. Pant, Harsh V. Contemporary debates in Indian foreign and security policy: India negotiates its rise in the international system. New York: Palgrave Macmillan, 2008. Print.

3. Sikri, Rajiv. Challenge and strategy: rethinking India's foreign policy. New Delhi, India Thousand Oaks, Calif: SAGE Publications India Sage, 2009. Print.

4. Mohan, C. Crossing the Rubicon: the shaping of India's new foreign policy. New Delhi New York: Penguin Books, 2005. Print.

Endnotes

1   Haqqani, H. (2013). Magnificent Delusions: Pakistan, the United States, and an Epic History of Misunderstanding (2013 ed., Vol. 1, SBN 978-1-61039-318-8)

2   Chabbra, A. K. (2011, November 22). Breakthrough or Breakdown?U.S.-Pakistan Military Alliance of 1954.Foreign Policy Journal. Retrieved January 29, 2018, from https://www.foreignpolicyjournal.com/2011/11/22/breakthrough-or-breakdown-u-s-pakistan-military-alliance-of-1954/view-all/

3   Zagoria, D. (1994, May & June). India and the United States: Estranged Democracies. Foreign Affairs. Retrieved December 07, 2017, from https://www.foreignaffairs.com/reviews/capsule-review/1994-05-01/india-and-united-states-estranged-democracies.

4   Full texts of Donald Trump's speech on South Asia policy. (2017, August 22). The Hindu. Retrieved January 30, 2018, from http://www.thehindu.com/news/international/full-texts-of-donald-trumps-speech-on-south-asia-policy/article19538424.ece.

5   Pant, H. (2017, August 29). A new chapter in the US's South Asia policy? Live Mint. Retrieved January 30, 2018, from http://www.livemint.com/Opinion/i4OLNTeyseyHJYkqiFl14O/A-new-chapter-in-the-USs-South-Asia-policy.html.

6   Chandran, N. (2017, November 14). Trump wants to make India the core of his Asia strategy — but he needs to know a few things first. CNBC. Retrieved February 01, 2018, from https://www.cnbc.com/2017/11/14/trump-asia-strategy-india-will-be-at-the-center-of-white-house-policy.html

7   Joshi, M. (2017, November 13). Why India Should Be Wary of the Quad. The Wire. Retrieved February 01, 2018, from https://thewire.in/196540/india-us-japan-australia-quadrilateral-alliance/

8   Roche, E. (2017, September 26). James Mattis in India: US commits to transfer advanced defence technology for Make in India. Live Mint. Retrieved February 02, 2018, from http://www.livemint.com/Politics/07dee1V8WtcWlYPFcFeslM/US-commits-to-transfer-advanced-defence-technology-for-Make.html

9   Defence cooperation with India important for Indo-US ties. (2017, September 07). Indian Express. Retrieved February 02, 2018, from http://indianexpress.

com/article/india/defence-cooperation-with-india-important-for-indo-us-ties-4832464/

10   Defence cooperation with India is vital for Indo-US ties: Top US diplomat. (2018, January 10). The Hindu Business Line. Retrieved January 03, 2018, from http://www.thehindubusinessline.com/news/world/defence-cooperation-with-india-is-vital-for-indous-ties-top-us-diplomat/article9848890.ece

11   Chaturvedy, R. R. (2014, February 22). India's maritime gateway to the Pacific. The Hindu. Retrieved February 03, 2018, from http://www.thehindu.com/opinion/op-ed/indias-maritime-gateway-to-the-pacific/article5714122.ece

12   Timeline: U.S.-India Relations 1947 – 2015, Council on Foreign Relations. Retrieved February 03, 2018, from https://www.cfr.org/timeline/us-india-relations

13   Ministry Of External Affairs, GOI. (2017, June 06). Brief on India-U.S. Relations [Press release]. Retrieved February 04, 2018, from http://mea.gov.in/Portal/ForeignRelation/India_US_brief.pdf

14   Will deepen ties to fight Sino sea challenges: US Air Chief. (2018, February 05). The Tribune . Retrieved February 6, 2018, from http://www.tribuneindia.com/news/nation/will-deepen-ties-to-fight-sino-sea-challenges-us-air-chief/538831.html

15   Pasricha, A. (2017, October 25). Tillerson's Visit to India Highlights Strong Emerging Alliance.Voice of America. Retrieved February 05, 2018, from https://www.voanews.com/a/tillerson-india-/4085312.html

India and Japan: Confluence of Strategic Interests

Cdr Subhasish Sarangi

The restoration of India-Japan ties, post the nuclear explosions by India in 1998, occurred, with Japanese Prime Minister Yoshiro Mori's visit to India in 2000, when both the countries reached an agreement to establish a "Japan-India Global Partnership in the 21st Century"[1]. The next major watershed in the bilateral relationship occurred with the visit of Japanese Prime Minister Junichiro Koizumi's visit to India in April 2005 and both the countries announcing an "India-Japan Partnership in a New Asia Era"[2]. Till 2005, India-Japan relations were driven by economic factors. However, the joint statement now stated that "The global partnership between India and Japan reflects a broad convergence of their long-term political, economic and strategic interests, aspirations, objectives and concerns. India and Japan view each other as partners that have responsibility for, and are capable of, responding to global and regional challenges in keeping with their global partnership. A strong, prosperous and dynamic India is, therefore, in the interest of Japan and vice-versa". The two countries agreed on an eight-point initiative that included high level strategic dialogue, comprehensive economic engagement, enhanced security cooperation, science and technology initiative, strengthening people-to-people contacts, cooperation in ushering a new Asian era, cooperation in United Nations and other international organizations, and cooperation in responding to global challenges and opportunities. It was agreed that summit-level (Prime Minister-level) talks will be held annually alternating between New Delhi and Tokyo. This commitment has been adhered to till date except in 2012, when Japan held unscheduled parliamentary elections.

In December 2006, Prime Ministers Manmohan Singh and Prime Minister Shinzo Abe elevated the relationship to a "strategic and global partnership"[3]. The 2006 Joint statement stated that "the two leaders share the view on the usefulness of having dialogue among India, Japan and other like-minded nations in the Asia-Pacific region on themes of mutual interest".

The reciprocal visit of Japanese Prime Minister Shinzo Abe to India happened in August 2007. In his speech on 'The Confluence of the Two Seas' delivered to a joint session of the Indian Parliament, Prime Minister Shinzo Abe spoke of the "dynamic coupling" between the Pacific and the Indian Oceans as seas of freedom and of prosperity and the idea of a "broader Asia"[4]. He spoke of the need for the two countries, to "ensure that it broadens yet further and to nurture and enrich these seas to become seas of clearest transparence". He mentioned about incorporation of USA and Australia in this endeavour "spanning the entirety of the Pacific Ocean". He urged the "two democracies, Japan and India, to carry out the pursuit of freedom and prosperity in the region". For the security of sea lanes, that are the most critical for the world economy, he mentioned the need to "together bear this weighty responsibility" "by joining forces with the like-minded countries". The roadmap to realize the "strategic and global partnership" was also unveiled during this visit.

During Prime Minister Manmohan Singh's visit to Japan in October 2008, a "Joint Declaration on Security Cooperation between Japan and India" was signed[5]. Japan had earlier signed such a security declaration with only the US (in 1996) and Australia (in 2007). In December 2009, Japanese Prime Minister Yukio Hatoyama visited India. The visit resulted in the "Action Plan to Advance Security Cooperation" and the establishment of a regular two-plus-two dialogue (that is dialogue between the foreign and defence secretaries)[6].

Emperor Akihito visited India in December 2013 and Prime Minister Shinzo Abe was the chief guest for India's Republic Day celebrations in 2014.

During Prime Minister Narendra Modi's visit to Japan in September 2014, the relationship was elevated to a "special strategic and global partnership"[7]. Both sides also agreed to establish the 'India-Japan Investment Promotion Partnership'. As part of this "special strategic and global partnership", during Prime Minister Shinzo Abe's visit to India in December 2015, the Vision 2025 for the Indo-Pacific region was unveiled[8]. Among the 16 Agreements/

MoUs signed during the visit included the agreement concerning transfer of defence technology and equipment that enabled joint research, development and production of military equipment[9].

Resonant Factors

Since 2005, the India-Japan partnership has enjoyed bipartisan political support in both countries irrespective of the parties in power. The biggest advantage in the relationship is that there is no negative historical legacy between the two nations and no direct conflict of strategic interests. The bilateral relationship has moved in tandem with the India-US relationship and it is not a coincidence that it has flourished with the increased US interest in India as a stabilising factor in Asia.

Greater International Engagement

One of the primary factors in the trajectory of India-Japan relations has been the increasing international engagements by both nations in recent decades.

The post-war Japan saw two constants – the security guarantee of the USA and consensus on a pacifist foreign policy. A turning point came in 2001 when Japan provided troops for logistics support during the US campaign in Afghanistan. Since then, Japanese troops have participated in UN Peacekeeping Missions and humanitarian missions like in the aftermath of tsunami of 2004 and Typhoon Haiyan in the Philippines in 2013. Prime Minister Shinzo Abe has endeavored to further alter the post-war status quo with a more robust policy with internal reforms and greater engagement with the world. Under his leadership, Japan created a National Security Council (NSC) in 2013. Two strategic documents were adopted on 17 December 2013 – National Security Strategy (NSS) and National Defence Program Guidelines (NDPG). In September 2015, he managed to push through legislation that allowed for Japanese military forces to be deployed abroad under certain circumstances. He has also announced his intentions to the amendment of Article 9 of the Constitution that forbids military action by Japan. In April 2014, he amended policy, by declaring the 'Three Principles on Transfer of Defense Equipment and Technology', to enable Japan to export military hardware and technology[10]. Military cooperation with ASEAN countries has been enhanced through the Vientiane Vision of 2016[11]. In 2015, the ODA charter was replaced with the Development Cooperation

Charter that seeks to provide ODA on a strategic rationale[12]. The Partnership for Quality Infrastructure (PQI) initiative was launched in May 2015 with a commitment of $110 billion funding by the Japanese government and Asian Development Bank for international infrastructure development over the next five years[13].

Prime Minister Abe has consistently sought to set the agenda with concepts such as the "arc of freedom and prosperity" proposed by his foreign minister in 2006[14]. In 2012, he mooted the idea of a "Democratic Security Diamond" to "safeguard the maritime commons stretching from the Indian Ocean region to the Western Pacific"[15]. On 30 May 2014, in his address at the Shangri-La Dialogue, he unveiled his vision by stating that "Japan intends to play an even greater and more proactive role than it has until now in making peace in Asia and the world something more certain"[16]. Even before he became Prime Minister, in a book authored by him, he had identified India as a pivotal partner and described how Japan could advance its national interests by strengthening ties with India[17]. The NSS identifies India and China as the primary drivers of change in balance of power. The NDPG reiterates that Japan will strengthen its relationship with India "in a broad range of fields, including maritime security"[18].

With economic development, India's radius of strategic interest has also been expanding. In recognition of the global economic center of gravity shifting to Asia, India unveiled its 'Look East' policy in 1992. India became a dialogue partner of ASEAN in 1994 and joined the ASEAN regional Forum (ARF) in 1996. Prime Minister Narendra Modi has sought to invigorate it with the 'Act East' policy unveiled during the India-ASEAN Summit in Myanmar in September 2014. This was epitomized with the unprecedented event of ten heads of state/government of ASEAN attending the 2018 Republic day celebrations in New Delhi.

The greater engagement between India and Japan has also become imperative due to the concurrent phenomenon of the rise of China and the relative decline of the US power in Asia.

Security Environment

The security environment has significantly degraded for Japan in the last one year. Overlapping Air Defence Identification Zones (ADIZs) with China and disputed maritime territories have resulted in repeated Chinese incursions in the maritime and air domain. Nuclear brinkmanship by North Korea, in the form of missile tests and detonations, has added to the vitiated atmosphere. With the gradual withdrawal of the USA and its stated desire for allies to shoulder more responsibilities, Japan has concluded that it will have to contend with securing its security interests on its own. The tension with China in recent years commenced, with the collision between a Chinese fishing vessel and Japanese coast guard patrol boats in 2010 near the disputed Diaoyu/Senkaku Islands. The Japanese government nationalized the islands in September 2012 and in December 2013, China declared an ADIZ that included these islands.

India has disputed land borders with China. The China-Pakistan nexus has ensured that India remains pre-occupied in its region due to security threats emanating from Pakistan. China has also been increasing its forays into the Indian Ocean region. With greater presence and investments, it is constricting India's strategic options in the region.

Hence, the security relationship between India and Japan has been driven by shared concerns about rise of China. During the stand-off between India and China at the Doklam region near the India-China-Bhutan tri-junction, Japan's ambassador to India supported the Indian action. Both countries need to hedge against the possibility of China becoming the predominant power in Asia.

Maritime Security

The maritime security cooperation is driven by economic and strategic factors. With its energy sources located in West Asia and dependence on sea-borne trade, the security of the Sea Lanes of Communication (SLOCs) is of utmost importance to Japan. However, the assertive behavior of China in the South China Sea, non-traditional security threats and the extended lines of its sea lanes has created anxiety in Japan. India's east-bound sea trade has been increasing over the years and hence, India too is concerned about its sea lanes to the Pacific.

The catalyst for maritime cooperation was provided by the rescue from hijackers of the Japanese freight ship MV Alondra Rainbow by the Indian Navy and Coast Guard in 1999. The Coast guards of the two nations concluded an agreement for cooperation in 2000 and have conducted bilateral exercises since then. Both countries are also involved in the Regional Cooperation

Agreement on Combating Piracy and Armed Robbery against Ships in Asia (ReCAAP), which was started in 2006 based of Prime Minister Koizumi's 2001 anti-piracy proposal. It is in the context of India-Japan maritime cooperation that the term 'Indo-Pacific' was first used in India.

In 2007, Prime Minister Shinzo Abe suggested the formation of a "quadrilateral forum" between USA, Japan, India and Australia. The suggestion died down due to the protests of China and subsequent backing down by Australia. The buzz over this configuration erupted again in 2017 when officials of the four nations met on the margins of the ASEAN-led meetings in Manila.

The first trilateral naval exercises between USA, Japan and India were held in April 2007 in the western Pacific Ocean. The India-US naval exercise 'Malabar' is conducted annually and Japan was included in it - in 2007, 2009 and 2014. In 2015, it was decided that Malabar would henceforth be a trilateral naval exercise between USA, Japan and India. The bilateral Japan-India Maritime Exercise (JIMEX) has been conducted annually since 2012. Bilateral and trilateral maritime security dialogues are also conducted between USA, Japan and India.

This bonhomie has however not translated in transfer of any defence technology or equipment till date. Stalemate continues over India's procurement of Japanese US-2 amphibious aircraft and diesel engine submarines.

Value Oriented Diplomacy

China has laid claim on almost the entire South China Sea. It has created artificial islands by reclaiming from the sea. Airstrips have been constructed and military equipment has been stationed on these artificial islands, raising concerns on freedom of navigation in the South China Sea. China has not accepted the 12 July 2016 ruling of the Permanent Court of Arbitration regarding the legality of its maritime features in the South China Sea under UNCLOS. It has maritime boundary disputes with the other littoral states and has clashed with Vietnam and Philippines over ownership of maritime features. China has also objected to the award of oil exploration license given by Vietnam to ONGC Videsh Ltd. (OVL) in the South China Sea.

Japan and India have sought to counter this assertive behavior of China by mobilising opinion on values such as "peaceful, open, equitable, stable, rule-based order", "open global trade regime", "freedom of navigation and over-flight", compliance to international norms and laws and peaceful settlement of disputes. Prime Minister Abe presented the three principles of the rule of law at sea for resolution of disputes at the 13th Shangri-La Dialogue in 2014[16] and his government announced the "Free and Open Indo-Pacific Strategy" in April 2017[19]. The India-Japan Vision 2025 for the Indo-Pacific region unveiled in 2015 also presents these values.

Connectivity

The unbridled ambition of the Chinese Belt and Road Initiative (BRI) has necessitated a response to provide an alternative to the nations of the region. The Asia-Africa Growth Corridor (AAGC) is one such alternative announced jointly by India and Japan in May 2017[20]. Both countries have also affirmed their commitment to infrastructure and connectivity projects with a special emphasis on the development of India's northeast region and increased connectivity between India and Southeast Asia. The Japan International Cooperation Agency (JICA) is supporting construction of highways in North East India[21]. The India-Japan Act East Forum was launched on 05 Dec 2017 to provide a platform for India-Japan collaboration under the rubric of India's "Act East Policy" and Japan's "Free and Open Indo-Pacific Strategy"[22]. The Forum will identify specific projects for economic modernization of India's North-East region including those pertaining to connectivity, developmental infrastructure, industrial linkages as well as people-to-people contacts through tourism, culture and sports-related activities.

Infrastructure

Japanese ODA has financed numerous major infrastructure projects in India that include the Bombay High Deep-Sea Drilling Project, Visakhapatnam harbor, Cochin Shipyard and New Delhi Metro.

The visit of Prime Minister Abe in September 2017 saw the unveiling of the high-speed rail project, incorporating *Shinkansen* technology, between Mumbai and Ahmedabad being undertaken with Japanese assistance. Japan is providing a loan of $12 billion to cover the project cost of $15 billion.

The Mumbai-Delhi Dedicated Freight Corridor (totaling 1,490 km) that envisages a double line electric track with average speed to be 100 km per hour is being progressed with Japanese assistance. The Delhi-Mumbai Industrial Corridor (DMIC) envisages setting up of industrial zones and cities along the Dedicated Freight Corridor. Part of the estimated $90 billion cost of the project is being financed through Japanese funding. The other major infrastructure projects being undertaken with Japanese assistance include the Chennai-Bengaluru Industrial Corridor and development of Andaman and Nicobar Islands.

Trade and Investment

Intuitively, India and Japan seem complementary to each other for trade and investment. India is a developing country that requires capital infusion and technological know-how for infrastructure development, prosperity and growth. With its large and young population, it provides a ready availability of labour and market for consumption. Japan is a developed country that is capital surplus and possesses cutting edge technological know-how. Its ageing and declining population means that it requires new markets to sustain its economy. However, trade and investment has not matched this potential, although Japan is the fourth largest foreign investor in India.

A Comprehensive Economic Partnership Agreement (CEPA) was signed on 16 February 2011 and came into effect from 01 August that year. It covers trade in goods and services, investments, intellectual property rights and other trade related issues. Although it seeks to reduce tariffs and provide Most Favoured nation (MFN) status to each other, numerous barriers still remain.

In May 2012, both countries agreed to jointly extract rare earth minerals in India[23]. Rare earth minerals are essential for manufacturing electronics products and Japan is heavily dependent on China for it. During the diplomatic row of 2010, China had restricted the supply and hence, Japan desires to diversify its sourcing. In 2014, Japan committed to earmark $33.55 billion, through loans and investments, for India for the next five years under the bilateral Investment Promotion Partnership. India is the biggest recipient of Japan's ODA. 2,590 crores of loan were committed in financial year 2016-17[24]. Bilateral trade rose from $13.4 billion in 2010-11 to $18.51 billion in 2012-13 but has since then come down to $14.51 billion in 2015-16[25]. There have also been concerns about the growing trade deficit in favour of Japan.

Nuclear

The India-Japan Civil Nuclear cooperation agreement was signed in November 2016 and came into force in July 2017. This will enable foreign nuclear reactor manufacturers to enter the Indian nuclear energy market. All the major manufactures are either owned by Japanese companies or source technology from them.

Multilateral Forums

India and Japan have mobilized global opinion for reforms in the United Nations. The G4 (Germany, Japan, India and Brazil) had sought permanent membership of the UN Security Council to provide better global representation. They also share space in multilateral platforms like ASEAN, APEC, ARF, EAS, RCEP and IORA. Japan's support has enabled India to actively participate in the West Asia/Pacific based forums.

USA-Japan and India have institutionalized trilateral strategic dialogues since 2011. Similarly, the India- Australia-Japan trilateral dialogue commenced in 2015.

Conclusion

The India-Japan relationship has flourished due to the convergence of strategic interests. However, it should not be seen merely through the prism of competing with China. The fact that Sino-Indian and Sino-Japanese trade is much larger than Indo-Japanese trade should be a sobering thought. India, in particular, has been careful to dispel any notion of containment or counterbalancing. The two countries continue to pursue their independent policies vis a vis China. India is a founder member of AIIB but declined to attend China's Belt and Road Forum (BRF) meeting held in May 2017 at Beijing. Japan has done the opposite in both cases.

India and Japan are important players in the evolving security architecture of the region. Their bilateral relationship is a significant factor in building the Asian power equilibrium.

Endnotes

1   Ministry of External Affairs, Government of India .(2013, January), India-Japan Relations. Retrieved February 02, 2018, fromhttps://www.mea.gov.in/Portal/ForeignRelation/Japan_Relations_-_Jan_2013.pdf accessed on 02 Feb 18.

2   Ministry of External Affairs, Government of India. (2005, April 29). Joint Statement, India-Japan Partnership in a New Asian Era: Strategic Orientation of India-Japan Global Partnership [Press release].Retrieved February 02, 2018,fromhttp://www.mea.gov.in/bilateral-documents.htm?dtl/2498/Joint+Sta tement+IndiaJapan+Partnership+in+a+New+Asian+Era+Strategic+Orientation +of+IndiaJapan+Global+Partnership accessed on 02 Feb 18.

3   Ministry of External Affairs, Government of India. (2006, December 15), Joint Statement Towards India-Japan Strategic and Global Partnership, Retrieved February 02, 2018, fromhttp://mea.gov.in/bilateral-documents.htm?dtl/6368/ Joint+Statement+Towards+IndiaJapan+Strategic+and+Global+Partnership accessed on 02 Feb 18.

4   Abe, S. (2007, August 22). Confluence of the Two Seas. Address presented in Parliament of the Republic of India, New Delhi. Retrieved February 02, 2018, from http://www.mofa.go.jp/region/asia-paci/pmv0708/speech-2.html accessed on 02 Feb 18.

5   Ministry of External Affairs, Government of India. (2008, October 22). Joint Declaration on Security Cooperation between India and Japan. Retrieved February 02, 2018, from http://mea.gov.in/bilateral-documents.htm?dtl/5408/ Joint+Declaration+on+Security+Cooperation+between+India+and+Japan accessed on 02 Feb 18.

6   Ministry of External Affairs, Government of India. (2009, December 29). Action Plan to advance Security Cooperation based on the Joint Declaration on Security Cooperation between Japan and India.Retrieved February 02, 2018, from http://mea.gov.in/bilateral-documents.htm?dtl/5089/Action+Plan+to+ad vance+Security+Cooperation+based+on+the+Joint+Declaration+on+Security+ Cooperation+between+Japan+and+India accessed on 02 Feb 18.

7   Ministry of External Affairs, Government of India. (2014, September 01). Tokyo Declaration for India - Japan Special Strategic and Global Partnership [Press release]. Retrieved February 02, 2018 fromhttp://www.mea.gov.in/bilateral-

documents.htm?dtl/23965/Tokyo+Declaration+for+India++Japan+Special+Stra
tegic+and+Global+Partnership accessed on 02 Feb 18.

8   Ministry of External Affairs, Government of India. (2015, December 12). Joint Statement on India and Japan Vision 2025: Special Strategic and Global Partnership Working Together for Peace and Prosperity of the Indo-Pacific Region and the World [Press release]. Retrieved February 02, 2018, fromhttp:// www.mea.gov.in/bilateral-documents.htm?dtl/26176/Joint_Statement_on_ India_and_Japan_Vision_2025_Special_Strategic_and_Global_Partnership_ Working_Together_for_Peace_and_Prosperity_of_the_IndoPacific_R accessed on 02 Feb 18.

9   India and Japan sign 16 agreements. (2015, December 12). Business Standard. Retrieved February 02, 2018, fromhttp://www.business-standard.com/article/ news-ians/india-and-japan-sign-16-agreements-115121200435_1.html accessed on 05 Feb 18.

10   Ministry of Foreign Affairs of Japan. (2014, April 01). The Three Principles on Transfer of Defense Equipment and Technology [Press release]. Retrieved fromhttp://www.mofa.go.jp/press/release/press22e_000010.html accessed on 05 Feb 18.

11   Ministry of Defense of Japan. (2016, November 16). Vientiane Vision: Japan's Defense Cooperation Initiative with ASEAN [Press release]. Retrieved February 02, 2018, fromhttp://www.mod.go.jp/e/d_act/exc/vientianevision/index.html accessed on 05 Feb 18.

12   Ministry of foreign Affairs of Japan. (2015, February 10). Development Cooperation Charter [Press release]. Retrieved February 02, 2018, fromhttp:// www.mofa.go.jp/policy/oda/page_000138.html accessed on 05 Feb 18.

13   Ministry of foreign Affairs of Japan. (2015, May 21). Announcement of "Partnership for Quality Infrastructure : Investment for Asia's Future" [Press release]. Retrieved February 02, 2018, fromhttp://www.mofa.go.jp/policy/oda/ page18_000076.html accessed on 05 Feb 18.

14   Aso, T. (2006, November 30). Arc of Freedom and Prosperity: Japan's Expanding Diplomatic Horizons. Lecture presented in Japan Institute of International Affairs, Tokyo. Accessed on February 02,http://www.mofa.go.jp/announce/fm/ aso/speech0611.html accessed on 05 Feb 18.

15 Abe, S. (2012, December 27). Asia's Democratic Security Diamond. Project Syndicate. Retrieved February 02, 2018, from   https://www.project-syndicate.org/commentary/a-strategic-alliance-for-japan-and-india-by-shinzo-abe accessed on 05 Feb 18.

16 Abe, S. (2014, May 30). Peace and prosperity in Asia, forevermore". Speech presented at 13th IISS Asian Security Summit - Shangri-La Dialogue in Republic of Singapore. Retrieved February 02, 2018, fromhttp://www.mofa.go.jp/fp/nsp/page18e_000087.html accessed on 05 Feb 18.

17 Shamshad Ahmad Khan, Changing Dynamics of India-Japan Relations, Pentagon Press (2017), pp.64.

18 Shamshad Ahmad Khan, ibid, pp. 78-80.

19 Celine Pajon, "Japan's Security Policy in Africa: The dawn of a strategic approach", Asie. Visions, No. 93, IFRI (May 2017), pp. 13.

20 Asia Africa Growth Corridor – A Vision Document, http://www.eria.org/Asia-Africa-Growth-Corridor-Document.pdf accessed on 05 Feb 18.

21 "Cooperation with India not in disputed area: Japan to China", Mint, 18 Nov 2014 and "Japan funds to improve NE roads", The Telegraph, 18 Apr 2016. Press Information Bureau release dated 03 Mar 2016, http://pib.nic.in/newsite/PrintRelease.aspx?relid=137251 accessed on 05 Feb 18.

22 Ministry of External Affairs, Government of India. (2017, December 05). Launch of India-Japan Act East Forum [Press release]. Retrieved February 02, 2018, fromhttp://www.mea.gov.in/press-releases.htm?dtl/29154/Launch_of_IndiaJapan_Act_East_Forum accessed on 05 Feb 18.

23 Ritu Sharma, "India Japan ink pact on rare earth exports", The New Indian Express, 17 Nov 12.

24 Press Information Bureau release dated 31 Mar 2017, http://pib.nic.in/newsite/PrintRelease.aspx?relid=160362 accessed on 05 Feb 18.

25 Shamshad Ahmad Khan, ibid, pp. 111.

India's Nuclear Doctrine: It's Features and Challenges with Respect to China and Pakistan

Mr. R.L. Abishek

Introduction

It is widely believed that the 21st century belongs to Asia and that the two giants of Asia, namely, China and India are going to dominate the world in the coming decades. It is also implicitly accepted that the nuclear weapons are going to be present, at least for the foreseeable future. It is therefore very important to analyse nuclear weapons and its implications on the emerging epicentre of global affairs i.e. Asia.

The Cold War mind set of viewing nuclear weapons is little different than the way it is viewed by the nations of Asia today. It is due to the nature of disputes and the security environment present in Asia and which will continue in the foreseeable future. The geopolitical and geo-strategic uncertainties in South Asia, where China is on the threshold of becoming a major power due to its emergence as an economically strong nation, and its efforts on modernisation, with an objective of having a greater global presence, as also Pakistan's cloak-and-dagger nuclear capability which is constantly increasing its nuclear stockpile is creating stability-instability paradoxes in Asia. India which is also emerging as a powerful state has no choice but to increase its nuclear stockpile to restore balance in the region and in doing so, enhance its options.

Having gone nuclear, and going in for nuclear weapons the next step had been to develop its triad. A strategic shift has begun in Asia, and the researcher tries to analyse India's nuclear doctrine, it's features, and challenges with respect to China and Pakistan.

Motivation for India to go Nuclear

It is important to assess the invariables that have influenced India's nuclear posture and the roles these variables might play in shaping the nation's future choices. In this context, it is important to analyze what India's strategic posture has been for most of the post-independence period. Summarizing the complex evolution of Indian attitudes and capabilities will require the simplification of certain historical details. The objective is to point out India's policy shift which from the background condition of "nuclear ambiguity" ended with the resumption of nuclear testing in May 1998.

Indian nuclear program predates the country's independence in 1947. India's indigenous efforts in nuclear science and technology was established by Dr. Homi Jehangir Bhabha in March 1944. This led to the creation of the Tata Institute of Fundamental Research (TIFR) on 19 December 1945. The new government of India passed the Atomic Energy Act, on 15 April 1948, leading to the establishment of the Indian Atomic Energy Commission (IAEC) one year after independence. At that time, Prime Minister Jawaharlal Nehru declared[1]:

> "We must develop this atomic energy quite apart from war - indeed I think we must develop it for the purpose of using it for peaceful purposes. ... Of course, if we are compelled as a nation to use it for other purposes, possibly no pious sentiments of any of us will stop the nation from using it that way."

"Apsara" India's reactor began functioning on 4 August 1957, thus, becoming the first operating reactor in Asia. India, having recently emerged from the colonial era, desired, at the global stage to carry out a moralistic brand of politics, hence adopted a policy which emphasized comprehensive economic development and, the objective was to use the nuclear energy for peaceful purposes. This uncompromising opposition to nuclear weapons and to nuclear weaponry per se as Instruments of "high politics", changed after the 1960s, when India – having become conscious, both of the Chinese threat and of the Chinese nuclear prowess, following Sino-Indian border dispute of 1962 and the Chinese Nuclear test subsequently. India began to consider the possibility of extending civilian nuclear technology to defence applications, through its Subterranean Nuclear Explosion Project (SNEP)[2].

The reasons to develop nuclear weapons and declare India as a Nuclear Weapon State were: -

- China had already developed its nuclear capability in 1964.

- During the 1971 war U.S.A had sent the 7th fleet, which led to a need to develop deterrence capabilities.

- China-Pakistan Nuclear Collaboration - In July 1984 the *New York Times* reported that US intelligence had learned that in the previous year China had supplied Pakistan with the design of nuclear device. Gary Milhollin, a leading expert on nuclear disarmament, stated that "China, a staunch ally of Pakistan's, provided blueprints for the bomb, as well as highly enriched uranium, tritium, scientists, and key components for a nuclear weapons production complex, among other crucial tools". Without China's help, Pakistan could not have developed the bomb, further China helped in missile development programme also, as a result in March 1997 Pakistan tested Ghauri missile having a range of 1500 km (900 miles) and a payload of 700 kg. All these pushed India to develop nuclear capabilities for deterrence purposes[3].

Evolution of India's Nuclear Doctrine

Initially there was ambiguity as far as India's nuclear programme was concerned. Though, throughout the 1990s India had started developing its missile programme. India had to show restraint due to international pressure, as going nuclear might have impeded economic development of the nation.

India had not signed the Non-Proliferation Treaty (NPT) despite being one of its original supporters, because it believed that it was discriminatory in nature. India has not signed the CTBT, but follows its major tenants of not undergoing any further nuclear testing. However, India remains committed to support the Fissile Material Cutoff Treaty (FMCT). India is now also the member of MTCR, Wassenaar Agreement and the Australian Group[4].

India's Nuclear Doctrine

The U S department of defence defines a doctrine as: "Fundamental principles by which the military forces or elements there can guide their actions in support of national objectives. It is authoritative but requires judgment in application.[5]"

A doctrine consists of a policy which can be stated as a set of ideas as to what to do in a particular situation, that has been officially agreed. A strategy refers to achieving a particular goal therefore, a doctrine basically states the objectives of a nation and general principles as to how it would develop and implement its resources to achieve its objectives. India's nuclear doctrine is as follows: -

Nuclear Draft Report

India's Nuclear Doctrine was first laid out in the Draft Report of 1999, prepared under the chairmanship of nuclear strategist K Subrahmanyam. Based on this draft report, the Cabinet Committee on Security presented India's official Nuclear Doctrine in 2003. This draft contained the preamble, Objectives, nuclear force structure, Credibility and Survivability, Command and Control, Security and safety, Disarmament and Arms Control and Research and Development aspects[6]. Since the official doctrine is based on the draft report I would point out to the differences between the draft and the official report while analyzing the official doctrine as they are similar in many ways.

Cabinet Committee on Security (CCS)

In 2003, the Cabinet Committee on Security presented the Nuclear Doctrine. It is based on the draft doctrine with certain changes such as addition of the clause - In case of first strike the retaliation would be massive, and an attack by nuclear forces would be taken if biological or chemical weapons are used against India or its soldiers[7].

Key Features of India's Nuclear Doctrine

India's nuclear doctrine can be summarized as follows:

1. Building and maintaining a credible minimum deterrent: -which means that the minimum number of weapons needed to deter an attack would be built and maintained.

2. A posture of "No First Use": - nuclear weapons will only be used in retaliation against a nuclear attack on Indian Territory or on Indian forces anywhere. This policy has led to a lot of debate but the posture of no first use is said to be the most salient feature of the doctrine

as it shows that India is a responsible nation which possesses nuclear weapons as a means for self-defence.

3. Nuclear retaliation to a first strike will be massive and designed to inflict unacceptable damage: -This clause states that India would respond to a nuclear attack by causing massive and unacceptable damage which shows the intent to deter any adversary as it would lead to massive losses.

4. Nuclear retaliatory attacks can only be authorized by the civilian political leadership through the Nuclear Command Authority: -This again shows that India has a well-defined structure to prevent unauthorized use of nuclear weapons.

5. Non-use of nuclear weapons against non-nuclear weapon states. This again depicts the responsible posture India has chosen.

6. However, in the event of a major attack against India, or Indian forces anywhere, by biological or chemical weapons, India will retain the option of retaliating with nuclear weapons: -This clause again tries to deter the use of banned biological or chemical weapons.

7. A continuance of strict controls on export of nuclear and missile related materials and technologies, participation in the Fissile Material Cutoff Treaty negotiations, and continued observance of the moratorium on nuclear tests.

8. Continued commitment to the goal of a nuclear weapon free world, through global, verifiable and non-discriminatory nuclear disarmament. Though India is a nuclear power it is willing to cut down nuclear arms but only if all other nation states do so.

Characteristics of Pakistan and China's Nuclear Doctrine and Challenges to India

China's Nuclear Strategy

Chinas nuclear thought process was influenced by the book entitled 'Guidelines for the development of Nuclear Weapons'. In July 2000 at the Central Military Commissions Conference, President Jiang Zemin gave his "Five Musts on Nuclear Weapons", expounding Chinas need to have five key basics, namely "a definitive quality and quantity of nuclear weapons to ensure national security, to ensure safety of strategic nuclear bases, to keep nuclear weapons in high degree of war preparedness, to be able to launch nuclear counter attacks and finally adjust its strategic nuclear weapon development strategy in a timely manner"[8].

Key Elements of China's Nuclear Doctrine

A Conditional 'No-First Use'

China's declared policy is that they will not use or threaten to use nuclear weapons, against any Non-Nuclear Weapon States or those within any Nuclear Weapon Free Zones. However, the major concern for India, is that China might for safeguarding those territories which are perceived by China as theirs, may apply conditional NFU, which will always give an option to China to use these weapons, against India, as there are quite a few contentious territories between India and China. This implies that China can use or threaten to use nuclear weapons against India if they find that their core interests are threatened[9].

Counter strike

Counter strike (zhongdianFanji) is one of the pillars of Chinas policy of 'Active Defence.' It is the offensive after strike that would damage massive military and civilian targets, especially the Command and Control systems, thus reducing the enemy's war making potential so that the adversary ends the nuclear exchange[10].

Though the policy of active defence seems to be a defensive strategy it is actually very offensive as China has stated it will also target the Counter-value assets like cities and civilian population of an adversary, thus forcing the adversary to stop the exchange of nuclear weapons.

A Credible Minimum Deterrence

China has developed a limited, reliable, precise and effective nuclear force capable of surviving the first strike and executing a massive counter strike through its nuclear triad. In recent publications, the PLA has also been using the term 'Effective Nuclear Deterrence' (you xiao he weishe) and this has been interpreted as being a 'reliable, survivable delivery system, capable of penetrating an adversary's missile defenses.[11]'

China has built a large tunnel system which is referred to as Underground Great Wall of China which is about 3000 miles long, and a report written by a Georgetown University team led by Phillip Karber, stated that the Chinese nuclear arsenal is understood to be nearly 3,000 nuclear warheads which may be stored in the underground tunnel network which cannot be destroyed using conventional or low yield nuclear devices[12]. This shows that China is expected to have more nuclear weapons than estimated and the credible minimum deterrence is only on paper which is evident even with its growing missile force capable of carrying nuclear weapons.

Second-Strike Retaliatory Capability

China focuses on the quality rather than the quantity of its nuclear force. The accuracy and the penetrating ability of her nuclear arsenal are important aspects, because a missile that can hit deep and accurately, can only do colossal damage.

They have been revising their missile technology and increasing its precision and range like the DF-31A which is estimated to possess a range of about 11200 km. They have increased the survivability of her nuclear force by replacing older liquid-fueled missiles with solid-fueled, road mobile ballistic missiles and constructing deep underground tunnels that can act as missile bases[13].

Survivability of China's Nuclear Force

China wants to have a strategic missile early warning system, and seeks to launch nuclear missiles immediately if an incoming first strike from an enemy is detected. This practice is called launch-on-warning. And the question is: Will China move to a launch-on-warning posture? Launch-on-warning means China can increase the survivability of its nuclear weapons by launching them before they are hit. This, in turn will increase the credibility of China' nuclear deterrent[14].

Pakistan's Nuclear Strategy

Pakistan believes in theory of "bleeding India through thousand cuts" as their use of overt aggression has failed and they have resorted to the use of covert means like terrorism. Pakistan has always known that India has much more economic and military strength and to attain a kind of parity with India due to their insecurity they started to develop Nuclear weapons. Nuclear weapons are an intrinsic part of Pakistan's military strategy. Their main objective of developing nuclear weapons is to prevent or deter India from using its large conventional force, thus it has also developed the policy of first use.

Pakistan does not have an officially declared nuclear doctrine and Pakistan believe in ambiguity as it gives them more leverage. But various policy makers and military Generals have outlined the basic nuclear policies, based on which, the Pakistani nuclear policy can be described as follows-

First Use

Pakistan has often stated that it will not hesitate to use nuclear weapons, even in the initial stages of a war. This is due to the fact that India has superiority in conventional arms and man power which can only be offset by nuclear weapons. Hence, Pakistan bases its doctrine on first strike and that is, it will use nuclear weapons if attacked by India even if the attack is with conventional weapons.

Professor Stephen P. Cohen feels that Pakistan would use what he calls an 'option-enhancing policy' for a possible use of nuclear weapons. This would entail a stage-by stage approach in which the nuclear threat is increased at each step to deter India from attack. The civilian rulers also agreed with this view, as Mr. Abdul Sattar (former Pakistani foreign minister), Mr. Agha Shahi and Mr. Zulfiqar Ali Khan jointly authored an article on October 5, 1999 which states that "The exigency under which Pakistan may use nuclear weapons is spelt out as : Although the precise contingencies in which Pakistan may use nuclear weapons have not been articulated or even defined by the government, the assumption has been that if the enemy launches a war and undertakes a piercing attack to occupy large territories or communications junctions, the weapon of last resort would have to be invoked." The Pakistanis refused to accept the Indian proposal of signing a joint No-first Use Policy, as the felt that nuclear "First – Use" gave them the option of a pre-emptive nuclear strike, which could disrupt India's nuclear retaliatory capabilities and thus unsettle the Indian C&C system. A few red lines or thresholds under which nuclear weapons could be used were[15] :-

> ➤ Space Threshold. If India attacks Pakistan and conquers a large part of its territory;

- ➤ Military Threshold. India destroys a large part of Pakistan's land or air forces;

- ➤ Economic Threshold. India Proceeds to the economical strangulation of Pakistan;

- ➤ Stability Threshold. If India pushes Pakistan into political destabilisation or creates a large scale internal subversion in Pakistan.

Many analysts also believe that another red line that should not be violated is the Indus River Water Treaty (with the Indus water or its vital arteries) which forms the "lifeline" of Pakistan. Another red line is if any of the nuclear installations in Pakistan is attacked, or if there is a chemical or biological weapons attack against Pakistan, then it would be respond by massive retaliation. The economic threshold may also refer to a blockade of the Sindh province and the coastal cities of the Baluchistan province, which the Pakistanis think that if Pakistan navy is unable to safeguard effectively, then it can use its nuclear weapons.

Minimum Credible Nuclear Deterrence

In 1999 PM Nawaz Sharif had said that "Nuclear restraint, stabalisation and minimum credible deterrence constitute the basic elements of Pakistan's nuclear policy". "Minimal" numbers for credible deterrence in Pakistan depend on Rawalpindi's targeting strategy, which remains deliberately opaque. Pakistan believes in the concept of assured destruction capability, and the Minimum Credible Deterrence that has evolved as a result of this strategy and has four main objectives as stated by Mr. Durani[16]:-

- ➤ Deterrence of all forms of external aggression;

- ➤ Building an effective combination of conventional and strategic forces;

- ➤ Avoiding a pre-emptive strike through protection and the threat of nuclear retaliation; and

- ➤ Stablizing strategic deterrence in South Asia.

Challenges

The main purpose of nuclear weapons is for deterrence. From the doctrines of Pakistan and China we can see certain threats posed which act as challenges to the Indian stated doctrine: -

> **Tactical Nuclear Weapons**:- Pakistan has inducted 'tactical' nuclear weapons as part of its artillery arsenal to prevent any advancing Indian army division in the event of a war. The concept of using nuclear weapons as only means of deterrence is being challenged by Pakistan as it has stated the policy of first use and envisioned tactical nuclear weapons as weapons of fighting even a conventional war. This is a serious threat as the nuclear threshold is so low that Pakistan is willing to use them even in a conventional conflict scenario which could lead to escalation[17] .

> **Non-State Actors**: -Pakistan as discussed above believes in the concept of bleeding India through a hundred cuts for which it has used non-state actors. Pakistan has inducted 'tactical' nuclear weapons as part of its artillery and has plans to give it to field commanders making the possibility of theft or a rouge element aiding non-state actors very possible, and given Pakistan's support for non-state actors it is a major challenge[18].

> **Nuclear Terrorism**: -The possibility of using 'Dirty Bombs' or Radiological Dispersal Device that is using conventional explosive combined with some type of radiological material which will cause a large-scale disruption is a major challenge[19].

> **Cyber Warfare**: -This is an emerging threat area and is a challenge as other states and even non-state actors might try to obtain sensitive information to disrupt critical information infrastructure and control systems. India's civil nuclear programme must also be protected against cyber-attacks and cyber warfare can disrupt the command and control structure by corrupting the platforms which are required to launch and control missiles etc[20].

> China has been known to work with cyber warfare and has been accused of attempting to hack into government websites such as that

of the Indian National Security Council. This is an area which needs to be considered in the doctrine as it poses a serious challenge.

> **China-Pakistan Nexus**: - China has supplied Pakistan with advanced fighter jets(J-10), missiles(M11), tanks and has upgraded its submarine. China supported Pakistan in its nuclear programme by giving it the technology, fissile materials and technology for launch vehicles. China has also blocked India from entering the Nuclear Suppliers Group and has backed Pakistan's entry, though Pakistan is known to operate - proliferation network under Mr. A.Q. Khan and is alleged to have supplied North Korea fissile material. China has propped up Pakistan's capability to keep India occupied on two fronts and by giving Pakistan it's nuclear capability it has ensured that their proxy war by the use of terrorists against India continues[21].

> **China's Space Programme**: - The other major challenge is China carrying out various missile interception tests thus coming near to building a shield for China's air defence by intercepting incoming warheads such as ballistic missile in space. China's constellation of satellites is getting transformed from the limited ability to collect general strategic information, into a new era in which it will be able to support tactical operations[22].

Recommendations

In order to counter the challenges posed it is necessary to analyse the doctrine's features and try to fill gaps if they exist.

> **Tactical Nuclear Weapons**: -To counter the threat of tactical nuclear weapons there has been a call to review India's no first use policy. The first use policy of Pakistan and no first use by India means that India might have to withstand an attack before it responds. But a policy of first strike means having nuclear weapons ready which is escalatory in nature[23]. It would also mean massive changes in the force structure as a first strike requires a different command and control system which would mean that the current framework will have to be reworked. First strike is effective only if it can completely destroy the second-strike capability of the adversary, if not, then it would lead to retaliation which would have terrible consequences. Therefore, the NFU should continue but there should be efforts

to have better signaling so that the adversary understands India's nuclear capabilities[24].

➢ As China has a very big advantage with its larger Ballistic Missile Inventory, better strategic Missile strength and has a very secured method of storage of its nuclear weapons it would be infeasible for India to adopt a first use policy, moreover, the no first use policy had given India benefits which included the lifting of economic sanctions, and the removal of technology denial, civil nuclear cooperation agreements and accommodation in multilateral nuclear export control regimes. The policy of no first use also allows an opportunity to engage in conventional warfare below the nuclear threshold[25]. Hence, the 'No First Use' policy need not be changed, but India needs to signal its nuclear capabilities and its intent to use nuclear weapons if the contingency arises.

➢ **Non-State Actors and Nuclear Terrorism**: -To prevent non-state actors from gaining access to fissile material there must be a global effort to stop proliferation and gradual reduction in the nuclear arsenal. India's doctrine has stated that it is committed to global nuclear disarmament but will reduce its stockpile only if all other nations do. However, International Atomic Energy Agency (IAEA) has stated "Pakistan is seeking to convert its arsenal to plutonium weapons[26]. And hence it should be pressurized to sign important treaties.

➢ Pakistan's warheads are probably stored at eight sites and are disassembled. Those sites' security is one of the main concerns for the international community, especially due to political instability in the country". This would require serious consideration as the policy of Pakistan to increase its arsenal and designate tactical nuclear weapons to its field commanders increases the chance of non-state actors getting access to these nuclear weapons or material[27].

To deter Pakistan from supporting the non-state actors we need to reconsider our doctrines deterrence value:- "The strength of deterrence relies on convincing the opponent that punishment outweighs gains of aggression. But this punishment is a perception and the perception can be strengthened only through two things- Capability of the Deterrence and Certainty of Punishment" Hence India must consider adding a clause in the doctrine where in,- if the accountability of weapons which are being used by the non-state actors is proven and sufficient evidence has been gathered to point out the direct or indirect involvement of a state in aiding these elements, then it shall be considered as a nuclear first strike which would lead to an appropriate response.

There has been a call for reviewing the caveat of Massive Retaliation. According to Col G G Pamidi in targeting, India will have to hit counter value targets due to its policy of massive retaliation, to cause unacceptable damage.

It will have to have a large arsenal of nuclear weapons, and there will be a dilemma as to whether it warrants for a nuclear attack when it can be sorted by conventional attack. Hence keeping these factors in mind, it would be better to consider opting for a flexible response to deter the enemy from aiding nuclear terrorism and giving more options for the Indian establishment.

- Cyber Warfare: -To counter the threat of cyber warfare India needs to consider the cyber-attack on the Command and Control system should be considered as a First Strike or not. The "Stuxnet" episode of how Iran's nuclear programme was affected shows how dangerous cyber warfare can be is as it could lead to disastrous effects if the nuclear plants and command and control structures are targeted[28]. Hence India must add a clause in the doctrine to deter adversaries from targeting our nuclear programme.

- China-Pakistan Nexus: -The China Pakistan nexus as stated earlier is a cause of concern as Pakistan aided by China continues its proxy warfare and this can only be overcome be building friendly relations in the region. Also by building a credible deterrent by enhancing nuclear capabilities which the doctrine provides for. The issue here is that India needs to rapidly indigenise it's defence sector with private companies also taking an active part. Also, the government should adhere to timelines, when it comes to the deployment of nuclear weapons.

- China's Space Programme: India's doctrine must also include the space dimension as China has already in 2007 tested anti-satellite weapons by firing a ballistic missile to destroy a weather satellite. India will need to protect its assets in the space and the doctrine must consider an appropriate retaliation, if India's communication or positioning satellite were to be hit[29].

Hence, India must consider the feasibility of modifying the massive retaliation clause with a flexible response, to get more options and better deterrence. It must also consider adding its space programme to the doctrine to develop defensive capabilities of its space assets. It must also build friendly relations with neighbours and build indigenous capabilities and stick to timelines in deployment.

There must also be a revision as to include the realm of cyber warfare. For deterrence to be successful there must be more efficient signalling plan. Signalling could be based on an elaborate plan designed to showcase the preparedness of India's nuclear forces and the firmness of its political will. For example, information about regular meetings of both the political and the executive council of the NCA should be made public (without disclosing the agenda).India while increasing its capabilities must also use it's diplomacy to discuss nuclear confidence building measures (CBMs) and nuclear risk reduction measures (NRRMs) with both China and Pakistan, as ultimately the use of nuclear weapons is catastrophic and must be limited to deterrence purposes only, but in case of any contingency India must be able to respond effectively, as the ability to inflict pain is the ultimate deterrence.

Conclusion

India was forced to take up nuclear armament for the purpose of deterrence. India has viewed its nuclear capability as a political tool, but must now move to a slightly more practical view of showing its intent to use these weapons should the need arise. India is a responsible nuclear weapon state and has a commitment to global nuclear disarmament which itself shows that India's doctrine is largely successful but it needs to give emphasis on certain issues as discussed earlier and begin to effectively send out signals that India will primarily use nuclear weapons for deterrence, but should the situation arise it will not hesitate to use them.

Endnotes

1   Chengappa, Raj. 2000. *Weapons of Peace*, HarperCollins Publishers India, ISBN 81-7223-330-2.

2   Tellis, A. (2001). '*India's emerging nuclear posture*', 1st ed. Santa Monica, CA: Rand.

3   Ibid

4   Ibid

5   Colonel Pamidi, G G. 'Possibility of A Nuclear War in Asia - an Indian Perspective.', (2012). 1st ed. Delhi: Vij Books India Pvt Ltd.

6   Mea.gov.in. *Draft Report of National Security Advisory Board on Indian Nuclear Doctrine*. [online] Available at: http://mea.gov.in/in-focus-article.htm?18916/ Draft+Report+of+National+Security+Advisory+Board+on+Indian+Nuclear+D octrine [Accessed 5 May 2017].

7   Mea.gov.in. '*The Cabinet Committee on Security Reviews perationalization of India's Nuclear Doctrine*'. [online] Available at: http://mea.gov.in/press-releases.htm?dtl/20131/The_Cabinet_Committee_on_Security_Reviews_ perationalization_of_Indias_Nuclear_Doctrine [Accessed 5 May 2017].

8   Khanijo, R.(2014). '*The complexities and challenges of nuclear India.*', 1st ed. New Delhi: Vij Books India Pvt. Ltd.

9   Ibid

10   Ibid

11   Ibid

12   Zhang, H., James A. Winnefeld, J., Morell, M., Zhang, H., Lynn-Jones, S., Nye, J., Byman, D. and Zhang, H. (2017). *China's Underground Great Wall: Subterranean Ballistic Missiles | Belfer Center for Science and International Affairs*. [online] Belfercenter.org. Available at: http://www.belfercenter.org/publication/ chinas-underground-great-wall-subterranean-ballistic-missiles [Accessed 11 May 2017].

13   Khanijo, R, (2014). '*The complexities and challenges of nuclear India*', 1st ed. New Delhi: Vij Books India Pvt Ltd.

14   Ibid

15   Ibid

16   Ibid

17   Gurmeet Kanwal, Pakistan's Tactical Nuclear Warheads and India's Nuclear Doctrine, September 21, 2016, Institute for Defence Studies and Analyses.

18   Ibid

19   Ibid

20   Dr. Roshan Khanijo (2016), 'Does India Need to Review its Nuclear Doctrine?', No-4, United services Institution of India, Occasional Paper.

21   ManpreetSethi (2017), volume 5 March 2017, Global dialogue review.

22   Dr. Roshan Khanijo (2016), 'Does India Need to Review its Nuclear Doctrine?', No-4, United Services Institution of India, Occasional Paper.

23   RearAdmiral Raja Menon, 'Nuclear Strategy for India', Sage Publications,2000.

24   Khanijo, R, (2014). '*The complexities and challenges of nuclear India*', 1st ed. New Delhi: Vij Books India Pvt. Ltd.

25   Ibid.

26   Nuclear Doctrine and Strategies, NationalPolicies and InternationalSecurity, MarkFitzpatrick, Alexander Nikitin, Sergey Ozonobischev, The NATO Science for Peace and Security Programme, 20

27   Ibid

28   Zetter, K. (2017). *An Unprecedented Look at Stuxnet, the World's First Digital Weapon.* [online] WIRED. Available at: https://www.wired.com/2014/11/countdown-to-zero-day-stuxnet/ [Accessed 14 May 2017].

29   Dr. Roshan Khanijo (2016),'Does India Need to Review its Nuclear Doctrine?', No-4, United Services Institution of India, Occasional Paper.

Around The World

Geo Economics as a Strategy

Dr. Venugopal B. Menon and Mr. Paul Vargheze

Introduction

The basic study of geo-economics should first answer the question of the relevance of the topic. That is, why do we need to look in to strategy and why is geo political strategy being studied with so much interest. When we study the world around us we need to keep in mind certain constraints and parameters; such as the social behaviour which is specific to time or what we call as History, the place or stage where these behaviour act or Geography, and the limit to which we can understand the behaviour or Philosophy. The study of the world is also the study of human nature and his interests. The strategies are of importance when the human interests coincide and collide leading to persuasion and power relationship. Thus, Geo politics is the combined study of all the above and how they all act together. There cannot be politics without political realism and economic aspects of it lie at the core of politics. An individual, or a group of individuals or a nation which possesses economic wealth has resources and these resources are source of power. This explains why economics is the core of political strategy. Thus, in economic terms power is all about acquiring wealth and controlling the actions of others in the market.

Charles Darwin's Evolutionary theory has been adopted by many economists and social scientists around the globe to explain the behaviour of states. 'Survival of the fittest' best explains the rational behaviour of the states and its inhabitants. A state in order to achieve power tries to overpower the other states by taking over the markets and resources of the other state. This weakens the position of the counterpart and he becomes economically dependent and a sub servient of the former. Such situations lead to economic strategizing and alliances. Thus, evolutionary theory also in a way explains the significance of geo-politics (moreover geo-economics) as a subject.

Geo-economics as the word evidently indicates is the study of specific, cultural and tactical aspects of resources with the goal of achieving upper hand over other nation states. It is the amplification of geo-politics in the age of globalisation. In geo-economics, as in war, repulsive weapons dominate. Of these, R&D with government backing and taxpayer's money is the most noteworthy weapon. The R&D can take over the future and nations investing heavily in R&D will rule the world markets with technological superiority.

Emergence of the term Geo-Economics

The emergence of the idea can be dated back to the Peloponnesian Wars where Thucydides underlined that *"The war will not be decided in Attica, as some people think, but at the locations where Attica pulls out its resources"*. Years later the French economist François Quesnay proposed that agriculture was the lone root of the wealth of nations. He argued that the productive class of the population created the annual Wealth of Nation by cultivating the land.

The beginning of the 20th century also saw the use of the term, but it corresponded to economic geography. According to KonstadinosSfiris (a Greek economics professor in the 1920's), the first founder of geo-economy could be considered Karl Knies, with his 1835 work *"Die PolitischeOekonomievomStandpunkt der geschichtlichenMethode"*. Knies - who along with WilheinRocher and Bruno Hildebrant were the founders of the German historical school of economics- believed that the foundation of geo-economics' research lies in the strong connection between populations and the unique natural peculiarities of the areas in which they are living. The term has also been used by German scholars for the theoretical representation of the relationships between Geology and Practical Economy keeping in mind the mining economy that boomed in the country.

In 1946 in post-war Greece, Alexiades associated geo-economy with demography, pastoral farming and agriculture (traditional primary sector) in the frame of national territorial claims. In 1959 Mistradis talked about the geo-economics axis Mediterranean-Black Sea. He identified a geo-economics ring (belt) around the globe linked by tree major geo-economics axes i.e. Mediterranean Sea – Red Sea, Indian Ocean – Pacific Ocean and Pacific Ocean – Atlantic Ocean. In the 1960's Jacques Boudeville used the term geo-economy as an alternative to geopolitics, with which the term began to be associated to politics rather than geography and demography.

The formation of geo-economics as a branch of geopolitics is often attributed to Edward Luttwak, an American economist and consultant, and Pascal Lorot, a French economist and political scientists. Luttwak's claiming that *"both military power and classic diplomacy have lost their traditional importance in the central arena of world affairs"* gave geoeconomy a military dimension. With the advent of globalisation and the intermingling of nation-states it became closely knit. The mutual interdependence made it impossible to go for wars as they all would be badly affected in a case of such a scenario. This led to the idea of an economic war, thereby replacing the old political strategies and policies by the new geopolitical era.

A Contemporary Approach

Sir Halford Mackinder's Heartland theory and Nicholas Spykman'sRimland theory were the pillars of Geo Political strategy which later also became the basis of Truman Doctrine[1], Eisenhower doctrine[2] and Carter Doctrine[3]. But in this era of globalisation and economic interdependence the focus is no longer on Mainland and Rimland but Nareland (Natural Resources Land).

With the advent of globalisation and the era of information overload nations have started realising that war wouldn't be a viable option to gain power. Keeping this trend in mind, competitive nations have started shifting their resources towards science, education, production and trade. This may prevent nations from engaging in large-scale wars with one another and routing the money in research and development. Geo-economics and Geo-politics are closely knit words, but in the absence of an outright war geo-economics triumph over geo-politics.

After the Cold War era, the triads took over the reins- US, Europe and Japan. For them the strategy was five C's- Customers, Competitors, Company, Country and Currency- which thereby urged the New Multinational Enterprises (MNE's) to form their strategies accordingly. This thereby changed the role of the government, from protecting certain industries and certain clusters of people they reversed their plan of action to providing a stable access to the best and cheapest goods and services from anywhere in the world, thus a modern government's concern became jobs.

From the International Law's point of view, Article 1 of the Montevideo Convention (1933) stipulates that *"The State as a person of international law should possess the following qualifications: (a) a permanent population; (b) a defined territory; (c) government; and (d) capacity to enter into relations with other states"*. With the latest trend of globalisation and one globe, the perception of these four State characteristics has evolved respectively to Human Recourses, Markets - Consumers, Hierarchic Governance and Projection of Power.

With the growth and popularity of the term Geo-economics, lot of terms revolving around the it also began to be noticed. Most importantly SSE (State Scale Entities), which can be defined as any entity with State organization and international conduct, whose size and resources allow it to be capable of implementing independent "policy" actions that project market power and influence at a regional and global level. In geopolitics, the constituent unit of analysis is the nation-state while in geo-economics it is the SSE. The 21st century saw the evolution of SSE's to Digiti SSE's (Digiti SSEs are companies like Google, Facebook or Microsoft) and Digital Geo-economics. Also, Defence Geo-economics became a field of study with the formation of state mimicking SSE's (like terrorists' groups). One another term that came into mainstream strategic study was Hyper State Entities (HSE's) which comprise mainly international and regional Organisations, association of states and alliances.

Geo Economics and Developing Countries

With the advancement of technology in the field of nuclear energy and balance of power developed nations are unwilling to engage in military warfare. To compensate, these powers project their power by controlling the money flow through their control over multinational companies domiciled in developing nations. Economic sanctions and restrictions have become an integral part of the foreign policy of the developed nations to control the actions of the developing countries and to benefit from them. With economic sanctions, a developing country loses its bargaining power leading to slowing down of technological innovations and increasing poverty levels. This may lead to political upheaval and unrest further distorting the growth.

The world has moved on from Pax-Americana to a multipolar system in this age of geo-economics. This change in the balance has disturbed the growth and development of the dependent nations or developing nations as the rivalry among major powers have influence over the nature of trade deals, making them mutually competitive both politically and economically. The losers are global consumers, businesses and those countries in the periphery.

The interests of multinational companies and their parent countries saw a shift from strategic competition for access of resources to competition for inroads into new markets. The weight adjusted center of global GDP when studied showed Europe during the time of Industrial Revolution as the cartographic point. But with the passage of time there was a rapid reversion of this point towards Central Asia in the 21st century. The message being the weight is now shifting towards Asian countries and their markets. Large markets in countries like India, Brazil and other Asian, African and Latin American countries has attracted the developed countries to set up their camps. The developing countries in Asia, Africa and Latin American have a large young population as well as a burgeoning middle class that enjoys the increasing purchasing power. Once the developed economies set their camp, these countries become mere puppet economies, totally dependent on the developed nations. This makes the country politically, economically and socially vulnerable hampering their overall growth and development. This shift not only affects large market countries but also natural resource rich nations. The producers of natural resources will see their power eclipsing. The cheap qualified labour in countries like India and Brazil woo multinational co-operations towards them and shift the balance of trade and economy.

One another challenge that is being faced by the developing nations is the setting of rules and pathways for development. With the entrance of geo-economics and the idea of global governance, the idea of a developed nation is framed keeping in mind the European and American style of growth, which is a wrong trend. Each nation has its unique and distinct culture, thereby each nation's road to development will also be different. The infusion of Western economic ideas has set the tone of development in the Western terms, which has to be remodeled and redefined.

Conclusion

The old school political policies, war strategies and balance of power by arms race has been replaced by the new era of economic interdependence and intermingling where countries tend to form regional and international cooperation to stand their point. This age of globalisation is often compared to the industrial revolution which saw the change of phase of the globe, sometimes the era being referred to as the 4th industrial revolution. Regional powers have taken over the world stage, especially countries like Brazil, China and India who with their huge human resource have started dictating their rules to the world.

Geopolitical competition is reshaping the global economy and unravelling global power relationships and governance. In spite of the fact that wars happen across the globe, the battleground is in the economic front; economic sanctions are taking the place of military strikes, competing trade empires are replacing military amalgamations, resource wars are more common than the occupation of territory, and the manipulation of the price of resources such as oil is more substantial than customary arms races. The globe is now beholding what Edward Luttwak called the rise of geo-economics, a contest defined by the "grammar of commerce but the logic of war".

Geo-economics as a strategy was developed at a time when the industries were thriving on fossil fuels. Thus, geo politics and geo-economics were often used in connotation as a single topic, the world distribution of 'black gold' that is oil. The technological advancement, scarce hydrocarbon fuels and its negative impacts on the environment have altered and reinstated the term thereby widening its scope.

References

India-China Relations. (2016, January). Retrieved from Ministry of External Affairs:https://www.mea.gov.in/Portal/ForeignRelation/China_Jan_2016. pdf

Field, C. B. (2012). *Ipcc Managing The Risks Of Extreme Events And Disasters To Advance Climate Change Adaptation.* New York: Cambridge University Press.

Wuthnow, J. (2016, April 16). *Water War: This River could Sink China-India Relations.* Retrieved from The National Interest: http://nationalinterest. org/feature/water-war-river-could-sink-china-india-relations-15829? page=2

Endnotes

1   American Foreign Policy created to counter Soviet Geo-political expansion during the cold war. It was announced by American President Harry S Truman on March 12th, 1947 when he pledged to contain Soviet expansion in Greece and Turkey.

2   American Foreign Policy announced by President Eisenhower on January 5th, 1957, wherein any Middle Eastern country could request American economic assistance or aid from US military forces if it was being threatened by armed aggression.

3   American Foreign Policy announced by President Jimmy Carter on January 23rd, 1980, wherein US would use military force if necessary to defend the national interests in the Persian Gulf

Separatism and Struggle for Autonomy in Xinjiang

Dr. Sanchita Bhattacharya

Introduction

The restive region of Xinjiang has its unique features that are characteristic of the barren expanses of Central Asia. An immense territory of more than 1.6 million square kilometers, 2,000 kilometers long form east to west, and 1,600 Kilometers from north to south, Xinjiang has international border of 5,600 kilometers with Mongolia, Russia, Kazakhstan, Kyrgyzstan, Tajikistan, Afghanistan, Pakistan and India. [1] Xinjiang is divided between Muslims and Han Chinese immigrants. The largest single group is the Uyghurs, historically agriculturists, craftsmen and traders, who have a distinctive language and culture of their own. After centuries of Chinese rule, however, and inspired by Muslims of Central Asia, there is a consciousness of a separate Uyghur identity. This is mainly true in the *Altashir* region, which borders on Afghanistan and Pakistan and is home of majority Uyghur people of Xinjiang. [2]

The Uyghurs call the region as East Turkestan. Since October 2013, when China witnessed its first terrorist suicide car attack on Beijing's Tiananmen Square, for which the East Turkestan Islamic Movement (ETIM) claimed responsibility, the province has been haunted by a series of deadly assaults. Chinese administration has responded with its version of the 'war on terror' and the corroboration of a series of policies aimed at better assimilation of Uyghurs into the mainstream Chinese society. [3] The ongoing strife in the region has ramification not only for the country itself but also for the nearing region of Central Asia and Middle East.

Political History of Xinjiang

The continuing secessionist movements of Xinjiang needs to be analysed under the light of its long history of political disconnect with mainstream Chinese establishment. The separatists causing further terror incidents in the country have used the pretext of misconstrued history and political ambition of non-Uyghur Chinese in abusing the basic rights of the Uyghurs. The Xinjiang region was the homeland of various branches of Turkic people such as the Uyghurs, Kazaks, Kyrgyz, Tatars and Uzbeks. The Uyghurs comprised the single most numerous ethnic group in Xinjiang based on common Turkic ancestry and rich Uyghur language.[4]

The original inhabitants of Xinjiang were part of the great migration of Turkic speakers from what is known as Mongolia in the 9th century and the present-day Uyghurs claim descent from them. They adopted the Islamic religion during the 7th century. The Uyghurs began settling in the region in 840 A.D., following their expulsion from what is now known as Kyrgyzstan. In 1017, the Uyghurs would finally gain full control of the region; however, their empire would eventually fall to invading Mongols. Interestingly, in a move to secure its northwest borders, the Qing Dynasty annexed the region in 1759, and began calling the area Xinjiang (New Frontier) in 1768.[5] Chinese influence in the region goes back to at least the tenth century, but Chinese power was only consolidated in the eighteenth century.[6]

Even during the Qing rule, Chinese authority in Xinjiang was challenged for brief periods by successful rebellions led by Khoja Muslim leaders like Jahangir, Yousuf Katta Tora and Walli Khan Tora (in early nineteenth century) and Yakub Beg, all having come from Kokand. It was only in 1884 that Xinjiang was brought within the regular administrative organisation of Chinese empire and made into full-fledged province.[7] Xinjiang's relations with Beijing have been irritable ever since. The reason is simple: the native population of Xinjiang has no cultural, linguistic, ethnic, or religious connection with China which, in essence, is a "foreign" occupying power. In fact, the very name "Xinjiang" meaning "New Frontier", emphasizes the region's place at the periphery of the Han Chinese Empire.[8] Since the collapse of the Qing Dynasty in 1912, Xinjiang did enjoy varying degrees of self-rule and autonomy. Turkic rebels in Xinjiang declared independence in October 1933 and created the Islamic Republic of East Turkestan (also known as the Republic of Uyghuristan or the First East Turkistan Republic). The subsequent year, the Republic of China reabsorbed the region. In 1944, splinter groups within Xinjiang again declared independence, this time under the auspices of the Soviet Union, and created the Second East Turkistan Republic.[9] However, post 1949, the Chinese Communist Party got control of Xinjiang and the Han migration initiated in the year, 1950. On October 1, 1955, the Xinjiang Uyghur Autonomous Region (XUAR) was created.

Geography and Geo-strategy

The area of Xinjiang is divided into two separate units by the Tian Shan Mountain cutting it into the northern Dzungarian Basin and the southern Tarim Basin. The inhabitants of the northern area are Buddhist, while the southerners are of Turkish descent. The geo-strategic position made Xinjiang a crucial passageway for the Silk Route in the distant past and the stake in the "Great Game" between Russian, British and Chinese empires, now almost more sensitive amidst regional dispute. The crucial significance of Xinjiang has also been reinforced by the discovery of large oil deposits in its Tarim Basin.[10] More importantly, since the collapse of the Soviet Union, the vast energy supplies of the former Soviet Central Asian Republics (CARs) has become the focal point of geopolitical attention as regional and extra-regional states seek to secure access to new sources of oil. These factors combine to make the result of the separatist resistance in Xinjiang of growing international strategic significance and will influence progress in the region.[11]

Today is no different, as China must sustain control and stability within Xinjiang because the region once again holds substantial economic, strategic, and military importance for the country. With its close nearness to the Central Asian states, Xinjiang is vital to economic trade with the countries of Central Asia as well as to border security in the region. And because it contains vast natural resources, Xinjiang will play an important role in fueling China's future economy by providing energy resources to other parts of the country.[12] The region is important for China not only because of its geographical position but also its abundance of coal, crude oil, and gas. Of 145 minerals found in China, Xinjiang produces 118. The Altai mountain is rich in gold, mica and precious stones; the Kunlun mountain produce jade, crystal, asbestos and nonferrous metals.[13]

Xinjiang has 40 per cent of coal reserve, 22 per cent of petroleum reserve, and 28 per cent of gas reserve in the country. Further, the coal deposits in

Xinjiang are of higher quality compared to deposits in other provinces, as it contains less sulfur, while the oil deposits are more accessible since most of them are situated in shallow and middle strata oil-reservoir. Oil-gas fields in Xinjiang major gas-oil fields on the land, and are among the most productive ones.[14] The abundance of mineral resources and location advantage has upped the vigilance of Chinese authorities into the region and also resulted in various disadvantages for the local populace.

Why to Dissent?

The Uyghur are one of the recognised 55 ethnic minorities (*shaoshuminzu*) in China, and mostly inhabit the Xinjiang Uighur Autonomous Region.[15] The Uyghur rebelled several times during the 19th century, eventually gaining autonomy in 1877. Throughout most of the twentieth century, the Uyghur battled the Chinese government for independence, first with the Guomindang-led government (1928-1945), and then with the communist government (post-1949). For a brief period, 1945-49, the Uyghurs established an independent country called East Turkistan. In 1949, the communist government annexed the area, renamed it the Xinjiang Uyghur Autonomous Region in 1955, and granted the region's inhabitants some measure of self-rule.

The aspect of distrust has been catalysed at the same time by changes in the political context of the region. Indeed, the victory of the Afghan Mujahideen over the Red Army, and with the break-up of the Soviet Union, the independence of the Central Asian Republics (CARs) incited Uyghur separatism. Many of the militants have seen in the emergence of national states as homelands for the other large Turkic populations of Central Asia. Furthermore, by reason of the cultural and religious ties that the Uyghurs share with the rest of Central Asia, these events have given them hopes of drawing new support from beyond their own borders. This potentiality for destabilisation associated the swell of turmoil and unrest in Xinjiang.[16]

The development of energy industries leads to a rapidly growing economy in Xinjiang. But the local residents in Xinjiang, particularly, the Uyghurs, may not enjoy the benefits of oil and gas exploitation. Some activists claim that those involved with the development of energy wealth are mainly Han Chinese, rather than the Uyghurs, and the profits go mainly to Beijing. But the fact that the profits mainly go to Beijing cannot explain the anger of

Uyghurs. The problem does not lie in how much the central or state-owned companies gain from Xinjiang's natural abundance, but how meager Uyghurs receive in comparison to their Han neighbours in Xinjiang.[17]

The Han-Uyghur tension has taken a deadly shape in the form of contemporary terror activities of the region. The altered demographic landscape has led to a polarization of sentiments. The Han people, who identify themselves as Chinese citizens, feel no need to change the current situation and see the separatists as terrorists and religious extremists. The Uyghurs, who have lost their prior position of power in the province, feel increasingly endangered and distressed.[18] In 1949, Uyghurs made up the majority of the Xinjiang population, while Han Chinese accounted for only 6 percent. However, 2010 census shows that Han Chinese (41 percent) is now nearly equal to Uyghurs in number (43 percent). This demographic change has aggravated ethnic tensions. Uyghur feel that they have ever more been marginalised in XUAR, with competition with Han Chinese for jobs being marked by extensive biased and discriminatory recruitment and employment practices.[19]

There were disturbances in Aksu region in April 1980, which were suppressed by People's Liberation Army troops with great loss of life, a riot in Kashghar in the same year in which hundreds were injured and many demonstrations against ethnic and religious discrimination. In April 1990, the opposition to Chinese control reached a new level of strength when riots at Baren in the Kyrgyz region of southern Xinjiang called for a *jihad* against the Chinese and the founding of an independent Eastern Turkestani state. In May and June 1991 there were also armed insurrections in the cities of Bole and Dacheng in the northwestern part of Xinjiang. Bomb attacks on buses in the Xinjiang's capital Urumqi in February 1992 and there are reports of bombings in many other towns in Xinjiang in March the same year. In June 1993, a bomb exploded at government buildings in Kashghar. Later, in April 1995, there was strife in the area around the town of Yining.[20] The series of violent incidents finally got response in the form of Strike Hard policy of the Chinese State, which proved more detrimental to the local interests.

Strike Hardda fa Campaign

The campaign of 1996 was due to culmination of few events in the Central Asian region. The fall of Soviet Russia, followed by the creation of CARs and also rise of Uyghur nationalism resulted in such crackdown. At the start of the 1990s, the Chinese regime feared that the attainment of independence of the CARs, and also the spread of radical Islam in the region, would seriously destabilise Xinjiang if nothing was done. On the one hand, the accession to independence of other large Turkic populations of Central Asia was likely to legitimise and strengthen Uyghur separatism within China. On the other, the cultural links that bind the Uyghurs together with the people of the new Republics, allowed Beijing to dread that solidarity would build up between the Uyghur separatists and these states. During the same time as relations between the Chinese state and Uyghur society were becoming tense and disturbances, sometimes aggressive and fierce, were on the rise (the Baren insurrection in 1990, the disturbances of the summer and autumn of 1993 over the whole province, and the riots of July 7, 1995 in Khotan), the Chinese regime's grip was progressively tightened in the form of *da fa* Campaign.[21] The campaign's explicit goal was to "hit at enemy forces, purify society and educate the masses".[22]

At the global level, the Chechnyan crisis was also driving Chinese establishment for a rigid control over Xinjiang. The authorities were acutely aware of the parallels with the Chechen struggle for independence in Russia and gave the war in Chechnya as one of their reasons for clamping down so hard.[23]

In the month of April 1996, Strike Hard Campaign was initiated by the Chinese establishment. But the full force of the campaign was first felt in February 1997, when thousands of Uyghurs peacefully gathered in Yining, Xinjiang to demand equality, religious freedom, and greater political participation from China's central government. The Strike Hard policy was set into action: armed Chinese paramilitary police confronted both demonstrators and bystanders and attempted to break up the protest, in the process killing dozens and detaining hundreds of others. In the protest's aftermath, the Chinese government detained thousands more on doubt of taking part in the demonstration, and, in the aftermath, hundreds of Uyghur "separatists" were summarily executed.[24]

The campaign stopped after several years, however, it was re-launched in 2001 resulting in several executions, hundreds of arrests and prison sentences, and the deletion of a variety of illegal explosives, arms and ammunitions. The Chinese authorities maintained the campaign due to the sustained terrorist activities in the region.[25] Post 9/11 China accelerated its Strike Hard campaign with special force in Xinjiang-Uyghurs are predominantly Muslim-arguing that its long-running efforts to staunch Uyghur separatist inclinations aligned with the United States's worldwide "war on terror."[26] The 9/11 attacks brought Islamic terrorism under the spotlight, and by doing so, provided the Communist Part of China (CPC) with new expression to apply to its security policy in Xinjiang, articulated around US policy on 'War on Terror'. Since then, Uyghur activists have been systematically labelled as terrorists by the Chinese authorities.[27]

The Separatist Organisations

Beijing's policies towards the Uyghur minority in the second half of the twentieth century transformed a largely secular separatist movement into one rooted in religious fervor. Unlike today, in early Uyghur rebellions, religious identity played a nominal role in mobilizing the populace. Colonialism, rather than religious and cultural divisions, sparked the rebellions. In contrast, the contemporary uprising and violence movements have used Islam as a mobilizing force, sometimes even invoking the Holy War. Also, post 9/11 Xinjiang's separatist attacks have become ever more sophisticated and progressively more tied to religion, a sign that militants' cries for jihad are finding more public support.[28] The Chinese government, moreover, has methodically curtailed freedom of the press and basic liberties for Uyghurs. It has also controlled the information that comes out of the XUAR, particularly about the violent incidents. The absence of any political space or platform to articulate their legitimate grievances combined with the worsening of economic and political conditions in XUAR are marginalizing rising numbers of Uyghur youth and, in some instances, motivating their radicalization.[29] The separatist organisations, in a way are taking advantage of the grievances of Uyghur people to justify their violent and terror activities. Also, they are increasing the outreach of Uyghur cause in West Asian countries, especially Turkey.

China's repressive tactics in Xinjiang, such as banning certain religious names for Uyghur babies, restrictions on the length of men's beards, confines on observing Ramadan have further hardened Uyghur identity and increased Islamic radicalisation. This oppression is also a factor in the increasing Islamisation of what was previously a separatist insurgency.[30] Uyghur terror is founded on the claim of various terror groups to a separate state (which they call East Turkistan) or at the least, extensive autonomous authority.[31]

One of the most important factors behind the rise of separatist tendencies in Xinjiang is the Chinese policy of helping the Mujahideen against Soviet Russia. A number of Xinjiang Muslims are known to have fought alongside the Mujahideen in Afghanistan together with other dedicated revolutionaries from a number of Islamic states. China also helped these fighters in Afghanistan by pouring arms, training and some fighters into the anti-Soviet jihad in Afghanistan in the 1980s. Also, Chinese government trained and armed Uyghurs in conjunction with Pakistan as part of anti-Soviet policy.[32] China also set up camps in Xinjiang to train Uyghur fighters and had up to 300 instructors and advisors stationed in Pakistani camps in mid 1980s for training.[33] In a way Jihadism was initiated among the Uyghurs by Chinese establishment. Due to political and ideological rivalry, China decided to fight against the Soviet Union and eventually providing men and money for the cause of Afghan War.

Moreover, the growing menace of trans-national terror activities and their global outreaches have given an international dimension to even minutest of local dispute. The sense of depravity among the ethnic population of Xinjiang, as explained earlier is a threat for Chinese establishment and also for the region of Central Asia and Middle East, and also South-East Asia. We shall now discuss the various separatist organisations fighting for the Uyghur cause.

East Turkistan Islamic Movement (ETIM)

During the 1980s, Hizbul Islam Li-Turkistan, the first Islamist separatist movement in Xinjiang, was founded by Abdul Hakeem. One of his pupils was Hasan Mahsum, who left China in the early 1990s and settled n Afghanistan, where he established the East Turkistan Islamic Movement (ETIM). From 1995 to 1997, the ethnic movements in Xinjiang reached its peak, with increasingly frequent attacks by militants in Xinjiang.[34] It has been observed that the ETIM is best understood as an umbrella designation that covers a broad array of terrorist and separatist activities carried out by ethnic Uyghurs.[35]

According to China, the ETIM is one of the more extreme Uyghur groups. An indication that ETIM is a special concern for Chinese authorities came in December 2003 as the PRC Ministry of Public Security issued for the first time a most wanted list of people dubbed Eastern Turkistan terrorist comprising 11 names belonging to four separatist groups all based abroad. ETIM was prominent in the list.[36] Previously, ETIM-linked militants had mainly embattled Chinese law enforcement agencies in Xinjiang, but from 2013 onwards, a change in their strategy occurred with increase in ETIM led attacks targeting civilians.[37]

Some Chinese officials, along with Chinese and foreign analysts, claim that ETIM has evolved into a new organization—the Eastern Turkistan Islamic Party (ETIP)—which has claimed responsibility for several terrorist attacks that occurred in the PRC.[38]

Turkestan Islamic Party (TIP)

The TIP is considered as an offshoot of ETIM. It is also known as *KatibatTurkistani* (Turkistan Brigade). It has largely been known as an affiliate of Al Qaeda, receiving funds under the reign of Osama Bin Laden to orchestrate operations in Xinjiang province, and even reportedly getting training by jihadists in both Afghanistan and Pakistan.[39] The ideology of the Turkestan Islamic Party has undergone a number of significant changes resulting from rapprochement with Al Qaeda in Waziristan (2001-2010) and shifting collaboration with the ISIS in the name of Jabhat al-Nusra in Syria (2013-2016). In 2016, the TIP posted more than 30 videos and other propaganda material on the internet. The videos show that noteworthy changes have occurred in the ideological and strategic goals of the TIP since 2010. The position of the TIP against the Chinese authorities has become even more drastic. If previously the party's strategic objective was to conduct a terrorist struggle against the power structures of China and to separate Xinjiang from Beijing, today it sets a more global objective. TIP fighters call on the world's Muslims to join the jihad against Western countries in internet videos. Possibly most ominously for China, the TIP believes that Muslims may fight locally using various means instead of coming to Syria and Iraq to conduct a "holy war" against the "infidel" Western regimes.[40]

According to Uran Botobekov, an expert in Central Asian jihadist groups, there are approximately 2000 members of TIP in Syria, largely grouped in Idlib province. TIP appears to work well with locals in the territories where it is present and has readily cooperated with a number of non-Uighur jihadists in key battlefield operations in Latakia and Aleppo. Nonetheless, Uyghurs in TIP are not untarnished by some of the more extreme actions perpetrated by their fellow extremists and have desecrated churches, executed Christians, and participated in suicide bombings.[41] In spite of its growing military power in Syria, TIP does not appear to have the capabilities to carry out operations outside the Middle East independently. It is al-Nusra Front's resources, capabilities, and networks that have strengthened TIP's transnational reach.[42]

Islamic Movement of Uzbekistan (IMU)

It is probably the most important Islamic organization for persuading and engaging Uyghurs within the Central Asian Uyghur diaspora. IMU's roots go back to 1991 but it was formally created by Taliban in 1996, as an armed auxiliary to itself. The IMU obtained financial support and training in Al Qaeda camps, and operated in the Ferghana Valley. The IMU links most directly in Xinjiang with the Islamic Movement of Eastern Turkistan, providing military and financial assistance. The IMU changed its name to the Islamic Party of Turkistan (Hezb-e Islami Turkistan) in June 2001. The original goal of the IMU was to overthrow the Uzbek government and install an Islamic state in Uzbekistan. When the IMU changed its name to the Islamic Party of Turkistan, its aim expanded to creating an Islamic state for all of Central Asia and Xinjiang, which led to increased recruits of Uzbek, Uyghur, Chechen, Arab, and Pakistani operatives into the group. The IMU subsequently broadened its activities beyond Uzbekistan to attacks on surrounding countries.[43]

IMU also has a history of closely working with the Taliban. It contributed men and expertise to the Taliban in their fight against the Afghan government and international forces in return for receiving safe sanctuaries under Taliban territory. The two were also benefiting from the drug trade that IMU facilitated in Central Asia. The Taliban were not keen to support IMU's militant activities outside Afghanistan. [44] IMU has conducted terrorist attacks against civilian, government and foreign targets in Central Asia. The group's strategy includes hostage-taking (including foreigners), car bombing and firearms attack.

ISIS/Daesh Operating in Xinjiang

ISIS has expressed territorial aspirations toward Xinjiang. Like other countries, China is concerned that Chinese Muslim Uyghurs who enlist with ISIS will receive training in terrorist techniques, acquire terrorist skills, and expand their connections in international terrorist organizations. This is a serious threat to China's counterterrorism strategy, given that Beijing has been experiencing frequent terrorist attacks by its radical Muslim population. There have already been reports corroborating these apprehensions. The Chinese mainstream media, including newspapers, TV and a large number of websites, see the ISIS as an extreme religious-terrorist organization that threatens China's national security. According to media reports, Uighur militants from Xinjiang were training with ISIS to acquire skills in order to carry out terrorist attacks within the country.[45]

Incidentally, since the mid-2010s, ISIS has set its sights on Uyghur recruits. In recent years, a small number of Uyghur have undergone military training in ISIS camps. Registration documents leaked by an ISIS renegade in 2016 showed that 114 Chinese Uyghurs joined the group between mid-2013 and mid-2014.[46] Xinjiang furnished the highest number of foreign ISIS fighters from any one region of the world outside of Saudi Arabia and Tunisia, the study found.[47] Many were children; but some of the recruits were as old as 80; and all were uneducated and poor, suggesting that a significant proportion of these are whole families of Uyghurs who believed the group would provide refuge and support.[48]

Further, a report released by Washington based think tank New America examined the registration records of fighters who joined the group from mid-2013 to mid2014. Uighur fighters were illustrated as "older" and "poorer" than other fighters and more likely to join ISIS along with their family members. None of the recruits from China reported having a college level education. Chinese recruits bucked the trend of average ISIS recruits who are likely to join when they are single and around 26yearsold.[49]

The repercussions are already clear. On February 27, 2017, ISIS released a video specifically targeting China. In it, a Uyghur member pledges allegiance to the caliphate and threatens to flood the motherland with "rivers of blood," while heavily armed Uyghur children are shown training, giving speeches, and even executing an "informant", according to SITE Intelligence, the US agency that analyzed and translated the footage.[50]

The rise of ISIS poses a potential grave challenge to China's national security at both international and domestic levels. Consequently, the international community may be cheering China to commence serious efforts to deal with the ISIS by cooperating with other powers. China can benefit from gradually changing its long-held non-intervention policy, as its overseas interests continue to expand. In the end, a more active anti-terrorism policy would improve China's domestic security, overseas interests, and international image.

Anti-Terror Chinese Policy

China regards Xinjiang as an integral component of itself. It indomitably makes all efforts to avoid national dissolution and regards all separatist acts as 'splittism', an idea that is rooted in China's fear of the 'century of humiliation' inflicted upon by the West. This fear has fueled China's notion of nationalism today and in this scheme, Xinjiang's separatism has no place. In this context, the upsurge of the Uyghur movement from 1990s posed a serious threat to Chinese security. In Chinese perception, the movement had three features: separatist; Islamic fundamentalist and terrorist.[51]

With the rising wave of unrest in 1990s, the Chinese Government in 1996, signed the Shanghai Treaty with Russia, Kazakhstan, Tajikistan and Kyrgyzstan, using the pact to pressure Central Asian states to dissuade their respective ethnic Uyghur minorities from supporting separatism in Xinjiang and to pledge extradition of Uyghurs fleeing China.[52] The Chinese government has taken steps to fight both separatists and terrorists in its western province. In the wake of the 9/11 attacks in the U.S., China openly acknowledged the existence of domestic terrorism in its effort to collaborate with the U.S. and other countries in the global war on terrorism. In 2002, the Chinese government stated in an official release that the "East Turkestan" terrorist forces inside and outside Chinese territory, between 1990 and 2001, were responsible for over 200 terrorist attacks in Xinjiang, resulting in 162 deaths and more than 440 injuries.[53]

According to the U.S. State Department, Chinese authorities raided a suspected ETIM camp in January 2007, killing eighteen and arresting seventeen. Reportedly, China also monitors religious activity in the region to keep religious leaders from spreading separatist views.[54] Since taking office as China's top leader in November 2012, Xi Jinping has attached great importance to Xinjiang. To fight religious extremism, the CCP under his leadership held a high-profile "Second Xinjiang Work Forum" in May 2014, with the participation of all Politburo members and many other high-ranking officials. The meeting outlined China's guiding principles, basic requirements, and chief tasks in its efforts to attain the overall purpose of "social stability and long-term security" in Xinjiang.[55]

Since 2016, the authorities has introduced new security restrictions and also staged a series of mass rallies by the Paramilitary Police to show force and resolve. Moreover, there appears to be no loosening of the de-radicalization efforts. This conclusion is based on a Xinjiang CCP meeting of August 30, 2016. At this meeting, continuation of established principles and plan on Xinjiang were considered effected and therefore were to be continued.

While the Chinese government still pretends that large organized Islamic cells like ETIM are responsible for the acts of terrorism committed in Xinjiang or violence by Uyghurs more generally, evidence shows that violent actions in the outcome of China's new counterterrorism policy are generally spontaneous acts initiated by religious preachers and followers of "underground" Islamic schools. The Chinese counterterrorism policy articulated around the campaign of the 'War on Terror' might have been successful in fighting large-scale organizations such as ETIM, but failed to take into account the regional resistance to the CPC in Xinjiang. On the contrary, the harsh crackdown is giving more ground for individuals frustrated by religious and cultural repression to resort to violent action.[56]

Conclusions

The immediate threat of Uyghur militancy in China lies in the possibility that well organised and battle-hardened Uyghur militant groups like the TIP may form alliances with militant groups in the region causing more lethal attacks in future. With the presence of Afghanistan and Pakistan in the geographical vicinity, and the long association of terror groups active in this region, China need to be pragmatic in dealing with its internal disputes and not letting them take a much bigger image.

The Uyghur problem is growing worse, not better. In the mid-term, we therefore foresee the likely exacerbation and even escalation of the problem as political, social, cultural, economic, and international factors intensify the social pressures within Xinjiang. The Chinese policy also needs to be inclusive with respect to Uyghurs. The economic development and restricting of Uyghur dominated cities can never take the blame out of Chinese establishment's lack of empathy towards the different culture and ethos of Uyghur minority of Xinjiang.

Endnotes

1   Anwar Rahman (2005), Sinicization Beyond the Great Wall: China's Xinjiang Uighur Autonomous Region, Leicester: Troubador Publishing.

2   Michael Dillon (1997), "Ethnic, Religious and Political Conflict on China's Northwestern Borders: The Background to the Violence in Xinjiang", http://citeseerx.ist.psu.edu/viewdoc/download?doi=10.1.1.503.2817&rep=rep1&type=pdf

3   European Parliament (2014), "China: Assimilating or radicalising Uighurs?", http://www.europarl.europa.eu/EPRS/EPRS-AaG-538966-China-Assimilating-or-radicalising-Uighurs-FINAL.pdf

4   Abanti Bhattacharya (2003), "Conceptualising Uyghur Separatism in Chinese Nationalism", Strategic Analysis, 27(3): 357-381

5   Nicolas Becquelin (2000), "Xinjiang in the Nineties", The China Journal, 44: 65-90.

6   Michael Dillon (1997).

7   KulbhushanWarikoo (2000), "Muslim Separatism in Xinjiang", Himalayan and Central Asian Studies, 4 (3-4): 32- 55.

8   Sadia Fayaz (2012), "China's Xinjiang Problem and Pakistan", The Dialogue, VII (3): 235-254.

9   PreetiBhatacharji (2008), "Uighurs and China's Xinjiang Region", http://www.columbia.edu/cu/news/clips/2008/08/04/UighursTWPOST.pdf

10 Sadia Fayaz (2012).

11 Sadia Fayaz (2012).

12 Ming T. Wong (2003), "Xinjiang and China's National Security: Counter-Terrorism or Counter-Separatism?", http://www.dtic.mil/dtic/tr/fulltext/u2/a415744.pdf

13 Anwar Rahman (2005).

14 Weiwen Yin (2015), "The Natural Resource Curse in Xinjiang", Political Science Journal, 10 (1-2): 112-140.

15 Alessandro Rippa (2014), "From Uyghurs to Kashgaris (and back?): Migration and Cross-Border Interactions Between Xinjiang and Pakistan", http://www.ethnologie.uni-muenchen.de/forschung/publikationen/studien/11_rippa_uyghurs_kashgaris.pdf

16 RémiCastets (2003), "The Uyghurs in Xinjiang – The Malaise Grows", http://journals.openedition.org/chinaperspectives/648

17 Weiwan Yin (2015).

18 TeemuNaarajärvi (2012), "War on Terror with Chinese Characteristics?", http://www.sgr.fi/sust/sust264/sust264_naarajarvi.pdf

19 European Parliament (2014).

20 Michael Dillon (1997).

21 RémiCastets (2003).

22 Dana Carver Boehem (2009), "China's Failed War on Terror: Fanning the Flames of Uighur Separatist Violence", *Berkeley Journal of Middle Eastern & Islamic Law*, 2 (1): 61-124.

23 Michael Dillon (1997).

24 Dana Carver Boehem (2009)

25 Ming T. Wong (2003).

26 Dana Carver Boehem (2009).

27 Adrien Morin (2017), "Is China's Counterterrorism Policy in Xinjiang Working?", https://thediplomat.com/2017/02/is-chinas-counterterrorism-policy-in-xinjiang-working/

28 Dana Carver Boehem (2009).

29 KilicKanat (2014), "Repression in China and Its Consequences in Xinjiang", https://www.hudson.org/research/10480-repression-in-china-and-its-consequences-in-xinjiang

30 Colin P. Clarke and Paul RextonKan (2017), "Uighur Foreign Fighters: An Underexamined Jihadist Challenge", https://icct.nl/wp-content/uploads/2017/11/ClarkeKan-Uighur-Foreign-Fighters-An-Underexamined-Jihadist-Challenge-Nov-2017-1.pdf

31 YoramEvron (2007), "China's Anti-Terrorism Policy", *Strategic Assessment,* 10 (3): 76-83.

32 Sadia Fayaz (2012).

33 John K. Cooley (2002), *Unholy Wars: Afghanistan, America and International Terrorism,* London: Pluto Press.

34 Ely Karmon (2009), "Pakistan, the Radicalization of the Jihadist Movement and the Challenge to China", *Journal of Middle Eastern and Islamic Studies,* 3 (3): 14-28.

35 Xu Beina, Holly Fletcher and JayshreeBajoria (2014), "The East Turkestan Islamic Movement (ETIM)", http://www.cfr.org/china/east-turkestan-islamicmovement-etim/p9179.

36 DavideGiglio (2004), ""Separatism and The War On Terror In China's Xinjiang Uighur Autonomous Region", http://cdn.peaceopstraining.org/theses/giglio.pdf.

37 Zia Ur Rehman (2014), "ETIM's presence in Pakistan and China's growing pressure", https://www.files.ethz.ch/isn/183175/381280b226170116bb6f07dc969cb17d.pdf

38 Murray Scot Tanner and James Bellacqua (2016), "China's Response to Terrorism", https://www.uscc.gov/sites/default/files/Research/Chinas%20Response%20to%20Terrorism_CNA061616.pdf

39 KabirTaneja (2017), "Decoding China's New Threat from ISIS", http://www.orfonline.org/expert-speaks/decoding-chinas-new-threat-from-isis/

40 UranBotobekov (2016), "China's Nightmare: Xinjiang Jihadists Go Global", https://thediplomat.com/2016/08/chinas-nightmare-xinjiang-jihadists-go-global/

41 Colin P. Clarke and Paul RextonKan (2017).

42 NodirbekSoliev (2017), "The Rise of Uyghur Militancy in and Beyond Southeast Asia: An Assessment", http://www.css.ethz.ch/en/services/digital-library/articles/article.html/4696d1ab-5344-42ce-8696-3294dd481d41/pdf

43 DavideGiglio (2004)

44 HekmatullahAzemy (2016), "Challenges and Prospects for Daesh in Afghanistan and Its Relations with the Taliban", http://www.kas.de/wf/doc/kas_46739-1522-2-30.pdf?161028042843

45 Mordechai Chaziza (2017), "China's Middle East Policy: The ISIS Factor", *Middle East Policy Council*, XXIII (1).

46 Lindsey Kennedy and Nathan Paul (2017), "China created a new terrorist threat by repressing secessionist fervor in its western frontier", https://qz.com/993601/china-uyghur-terrorism/

47 Robbie Gramer (2017), "The Islamic State Pledged to Attack China Next. Here's Why.", http://foreignpolicy.com/2017/03/01/the-islamic-state-pledged-to-attack-china-next-heres-why/

48 Kennedy and Paul (2017).

49 Lydia Tomkiw (2016), "ISIS In China? Muslim Uighur Population Joining Islamic State In Syria, Iraq Amid Poor Economic Conditions", https://www.allthingscynthiamckinney.com/wpcontent/uploads/2017/09/ISIS-In-China-Muslim-Uighur-Population.pdf

50 Kenney and Paul (2017).

51 Abanti Bhattacharya (2003).

52 Xu Beina, Holly Fletcher and JayshreeBajoria (2014)

53 Zunyou Zhou (2017), "Chinese Strategy for De-radicalization", http://www.tandfonline.com/doi/full/10.1080/09546553.2017.1330199

54 PreetiBhattacharji (2008).

55 Zunyou Zhou (2017).

56 Adrien Morin (2017).

Egypt's Uncertain Future under President Al – Sisi's Rule

P. Arun Teja

Introduction

The uprising of 2011 which is widely known as *'Arab spring'* was not a sudden revolt, but a gradual resentment piled up against the repressive order of President Hosni Mubarak. Self-immolation of Mohammed Bouazizi, a street vendor on 17 February 2010 was the trigger point for the Tunisian revolution and the *'Arab spring'*, which led to the downfall of political regimes across the Arab region. Fleeing of Tunisia's president Zine El Abidin Ben Ali, President Abdullah Saleh of Yemen abdicating his powers after protracted negotiations with GCC nations, and the death of Colonel Gaddafi - ruler of Libya, are some of the notable events pushed by the Arab Spring.

The spillover effects of the latter events made people of Egypt to forego their fear and in response to the oppressive regime, raised their voices for freedom and dignity. The voices which were initially raised against the police brutality got converted into voice for freedom, asking President Hosni Mubarak to step down. The historic 18-day protest that began on 25 January 2011 which later came to be known as *'Tahrir square protests'* was successful in removing Mubarak from power. Mubarak announced his resignation officially on 11 February 2011.

The military council known as Supreme Council of Armed Forces (SCAF), which was convened only during great internal emergencies, announced it's taking over the command on the same day. SCAF was then headed by field Marshal Mohamed Hussein Tantawi who was defence minister under Mubarak and it constituted service heads and senior commanders of armed forces. SCAF has dissolved the parliament and suspended the constitution promising changes to the latter and holding free and fair elections. SCAF held referendum for the constitutional amendments on 19 March 2011 where it got accepted by 78% with a voter turnout of 46%.[1]

This referendum was backed by Muslim Brotherhood arguing that it would provide way for early elections. These amendments were welcomed as they restricted the term of president for 4 years, with 2 term limit, and cancellation of article 179, which civilians to be tried in military courts under counter terrorism provisions.[2] It has also made amendment to the constitution on 30 March 2011 which granted SCAF autonomy over the matters of armed forces and their budget.

Numerous parties emerged after the fall of Mubarak and during the parliamentary elections held in three rounds between 28 November 2011 and 11 January 2012, newly formed political wing of Muslim Brotherhood – Freedom and Justice Party formed on 30 April 2011, and salafist inspired Al - Nour party formed on 12 May 2011, under the leadership of Younes Makhioum have secured 47% and 24% of the parliamentary seats respectively.

But soon, this elected parliament was dissolved on the pretext of false electoral practices just before two days of second round of presidential elections i.e. on 14 June 2012. This has reduced the Power of Muslim Brotherhood in the parliament.

Actual political hold by Islamic party was achieved only after Mohammed Morsi, Islamist candidate of Muslim Brotherhood won the presidential elections by a thin margin against Mubarak's loyalist Mohammed Shafik held during 23 May 2012. SCAF being skeptic about giving power to Islamist parties on 13 June 2012 issued a decree, which authorizes the latter to arrest civilians and try them in military courts, which was contrary to the cancellation of article 179. Finally, on 16 June 2012, SCAF handed over the power to the democratically elected Muslim Brotherhood candidate, Mohamed Mursi.

But Muslim Brotherhood at the helm has taken a narrow approach to the governance emphasizing the prevalence of Islamic Law, ignoring secular nature of the nation. It created severe differences among the Nasserist military and Islamic parties. It has not only raised differences between military and Muslim Brotherhood, but also raised skepticism among the public. Mohammad Mursi has announced a new constitution on 21 November 2012, which provided president immense powers, placing the president above judiciary. The decree even prevented Supreme Constitutional Court, from dissolving the parliament. Morsi also failed to bring an inclusive coalition government which was considered necessary after the unexpected political development. These moves and Muslim Brotherhood's independent Islamic maneuvers have created animosity between the public and Muslim Brotherhood, where public was unwilling to sacrifice their secular outlook. It was widely opined that Muslim Brotherhood was immature as it acted independently without constructing an inclusive political coalition. "The Brotherhood had a degree of political stupidity," says Abdel Moneim Aboul Fotouh, a former Brotherhood big beast, who ran against Morsi in 2012, and was once considered the election's frontrunner.[3]

During Morsi's period, economic conditions of Egypt were deteriorating. Foreign currencies were depleting, inflation was on the rise, and tourism was collapsing. Spillover effect of political instability was one of the main reasons for the inability of Mursi to handle economic situation. There was little focus on the improvement of country's economy, the political isolation and nepotism, kept business class of the country far from acting in accordance with Muslim Brotherhood. This reduced the private investments within the country hindering the economic growth.

These political and economic situations led to anti Mursi protests. A group of young protesters calling themselves *"Tamarrod"* (Rebel) whose members included veterans of previous movements, such as Kefaya, Secularists, Socialists, Nasserites, Liberals etc raised slogans against Islamic rule. They demanded new elections and spearheaded a shrill campaign against the rule of Mohammed Mursi during June 2013.[4] On 29 June 2013, Defence Minister Al-Sisi met President Mursi to propose concessions which would appoint new prime minister and cabinet, but Mursi refused to relinquish his presidency. Looking at the growing density of protests, Al-Sisi issued an ultimatum on 1 July 2013, to Mohammed Mursi and asked to come up with political solution within 48 hours. Due to no improvement in the situation, on 3 July 2013 Al-Sisi removed President Mursi from power and appointed Adly Mansour, chief justice of Supreme Constitutional Court as acting president. The constitution was suspended again, which was a second time within a year. However, he promised a new draft constitution, and subsequently holding fresh parliamentary elections, followed by presidential election. There are speculations that military never accepted Muslim Brotherhood at the political helm and that it was just a cynical move by the latter to consolidate its own influence in the political establishment.[5]

Removal of Mursi followed huge protests by Muslim Brotherhood supporters. Sit-ins and street protests were heavily organized. Already wary army had ruthlessly silenced Pro Mursi supporters, crippling entire Islamic party, which stood as an opposition. Repressive measures were taken during the clearance of Rabaa al-Adaweya Square sit-ins on 14 August 2013, which killed more than 600 and wounded many more. Interim President Adly Mansour formed interim cabinet, without including Islamists, which further reduced their influence. He issued a decree (107/2013) on 24 November 2013, known as anti-protest legislation, which didn't allow public gathering of more than 10. The law speaks of an abstract use of force, which incentivizes police to take lethal steps to disperse the gatherings. These steps have completely crippled the Islamic parties in the country.

Defence Minister Al-Sisi in a television speech called for mandate to crush Islamic parties on the pretext of fighting terrorism. After toppling President Mursi's government, Al-Sisi resigned from the army on 23 September 2013 and announced his candidature for presidential elections. For the presidential elections which were conducted between 26 and 28 May 2014, Al-Sisi's campaign focused on development of agriculture, housing, education and impoverished areas and boost employment.[6] He promised Egyptians that they would see better living conditions within two years of him being in power. His popularity among public and with a feeble opposition, he was elected with a land slide victory securing 93.3 %[7] of votes. Although this is argued to be a rigged election, his popular support cannot go unnoticed. It became the responsibility of President Al-Sisi to bring back politico – economic stability to the country.

Al-Sisi's coming into power did not promote democracy in Egypt, but rather it moved towards authoritarianism. Political rights have been restricted, and inclusive development has become a little-known term. His repressive policies such as curbing the freedom of Press - by giving his assent to New Media Law, NGO law - which allows government intervention in their functioning, electoral law - permitting limited elections by listing, making protests illegal, and amending the labor laws to favour industries and curbs the rights of labor unions, makes his government appear moving towards an authoritarian regime.

His coming into power, based on economic progress, has met little success. Macroeconomic indicators have shown the amount of debt country carries, and the development indicators depicts that stagnation has remained unchanged since 2011.

Taking into account the present conditions of Egypt under President Al-Sisi, this paper analyses the Egyptian scenario in two parts: One part deals with the political scenario of President Al-Sisi, which focuses on the political condition of Egypt, the second part deals with the economic scenario of Egypt with the help of external and domestic economic indicators. With the scrutiny as mentioned in previous paras, paper analyses the dynamic conditions and predicts the immediate future of Egypt. Paper recommends necessary political and economic measures which might prove successful in the future.

Political Scenario

President Al-Sisi's coming into power has given military a greater strength and autonomy in political and economic sphere. President Al-Sisi's presence at the helm might portray that the state is under the influence of a single person, but military as an institution has major influence. Its control over the state can be recognized from list of incumbent governors of all the 27 governorates, out of which only 9 governors have civilian background.

Current extensive control of military over the country's political apparatus may resemble the Mubarak regime, where initially Mubarak appointed his military loyalists to important positions and secured political stability. Even on the economic front it might show the similarity, but with some changes- such as encouraging joint ventures between military and private industries.

Elections, Political Parties and The Parliament

The role of elected representatives elected in 2015 parliamentary elections, has become a mere play of puppets in a puppetry, as parliament doesn't represent the voice of people. The election law of Egypt, which was passed on 5 June 2014 by interim President Adly Mansour, provided most of the seats to independents which will be allowed to be dominated by businessmen and other wealthy individuals.[8] The ban imposed on Muslim Brotherhood and the boycott by other Islamic parties from participating in the 2015 elections, created a parliament with a little opposition, which further crippled the democracy. This paved the path for a scattered parliament, without effective representation of public voice.

Political parties rather than obtaining power to lead the country were focused more on gaining the support of the military leadership to avoid harsh consequences. One example of political parties looking for support from military is, parties and individual members joining the majority parliamentary bloc headed by Sameh Saif al-Yazel, a former intelligence officer favoring the policies of President Al-Sisi. It has almost gained the support of 2/3rd members of parliament.[9] New Wafd party and Free Egyptians party were the only one that distanced themselves from the coalition. Even though they are not part of the coalition, they are not anti Sisi either. Apart from this, it was observed that, to gain the allegiance and support of parties, present government intervenes in the internal matters of party creating a rift among party leaders. Naguib Sawiris, founder of Free Egyptian Party, was a hurdle to extend party's support to coalition. He denounced his power when the board of trustees of Free Egyptians Party got dissolved.[10] It is believed that two other parliamentarians were also expelled from the party as they opposed the parliamentary bloc.[11] These developments make us visualize that Egypt's parliament is allegedly moving towards authoritarianism.

Parliamentarian, Islmail Nasreddin, on 25th February 2017, proposed a constitutional amendment, to further extend president's tenure from 4 years to 6 years. [12]With a strong pro Sisi parliament, it would have greater chance of approving the constitutional amendment, and if approved, it would bring speculations of President Sisi unwilling to give away his power.

Civil Rights, are they Respected?

President Al-Sisi's government in the name of stability has taken repressive measures against opposition. Freedom of civil societies has been steadily slashed down. The current NGO law restricts civil societies from participating in political activities (Article 11) and strictly prohibits foreign funds (Article 17).[13] Vague legal terms used, such as *threat to the national unity, violating public order or morals* have incentivized authorities to crack down indiscriminately on the civil societies, curtailing their freedom. On 17 September 2016, Cairo

Criminal court froze the assets of three NGOs, and five human right activists, under the pretext of "pursuing acts harmful to national interests".[14] New draft NGO law[15] puts the functioning of NGOs and Civil Society Organizations (CSO) entirely under the control of government, including the appointment of board of directors. These measures have been severely criticized by international human rights organizations, and are pressurizing President Al-Sisi not to give his assent to the draft laws.

Trade and Labour Unions

The Trade Union draft law has also come under severe criticism as it allows government to intervene in the internal affairs of unions, leaving them with little autonomy. For example, government can request the removal of executive committee of trade union, if it provokes work stoppages or absenteeism in a public service or community services (article 72 (2)(b) of Trade Union act No. 35 of 1976, as amended by act no.12 of 1995)[16]. The draft law requires 100 workers at the facility to form a trade union committee, 30 thousand to form trade union and 300 thousand to form a trade union federation. Even if the trade union is formed, anti-protest legislation of 2013, would not allow workers to protest, which hinders the functioning of industry. These industries serve public demand, and hindering their functioning is considered to be a violation of article 7 of anti-protest legislation. Thus, the wavelengths of the workers' voice have been cut to its minimum, so that even if raised, it can't be heard. Not only public protests are banned, but also security forces are not allowed to protest. In the recent protest held by Police during January 2017, asking for a change in vacation system, 50 policemen have been charged with fines and 3 years imprisonment. This also included employment termination of 40 policemen.[17]

Media and its Freedom

In a meeting on 13 January 2016, cabinet approved new laws which impose fine of 10,000 – 30,000 Egyptian pounds and arrest- for publication, importation, promotion, transfer, trafficking, possession, distribution, rent or presentation of: drawings, symbols, posters, signs, publications, photos or other objects that symbolize terrorist entities within or outside the country.[18] This has curbed the freedom of press by restricting their access to political opposition.

According to the new law on terrorism adopted in 17 January 2016, journalists are obliged to report only official versions. Media is not allowed to cover the turmoil in Sinai region, which is an assault on the freedom of press. National Media Authority Law, which is a part of presidential decree on 11 April 2017, is seen to be restrictive of press freedom. It is likely to regulate not only the official, terrestrial broadcast media, but also satellite broadcasts and online video-streaming services.[19] Committee to protect journalists (CPJ) has ranked Egypt 161 according to the 2017 index where it ranked 159 in 2016. As a result of indiscriminate arrests of journalists across the country, Egypt is now considered to be one of the world's biggest prisons for journalists.[20]

Façade of Counter Terrorism

In the name of political stability, counter terrorism has been used, mainly to tackle political opposition in the country. Between January 2014 and January 2016, 71 percent of all counterterrorism operations on Egypt's mainland were aimed at the Brotherhood.[21] On 24 March 2014, Egyptian court sentenced 529 members of Muslim Brotherhood to death in a mass trial that lasted less than 2 days, merely on the charges of inciting and practicing violence. Minya court sentenced 180 defendants on the charges of committing violence against police.[22] Due to this, party affiliates throughout the country are either killed, arrested, or compelled to leave the country. Ideologically and organizationally fragmented Islamic group became susceptible for radicalization and easy targets for recruitment. Until 2014, terrorist attacks were restricted to North Sinai, but now they have entered inner parts of Egypt with concentration in greater Cairo. Number of homegrown terrorist groups emerged with their headquarters based in Cairo. Hizb ut- Tahrir, Revolutionary punishment, Al Gama'a al – Islamiyya, Soldier of Egypt are some of the groups which emerged recently in Cairo as a result of heavy crackdown on Muslim Brotherhood.

Bombing of the Italian consulate in Cairo, beheading of Sinai residents on the pretext of being informers, and downing of Russian Passenger Jet killing 224 people aboard, shows the growth of conflict between state and extremist groups.

Indiscriminate massive arrests as a part of counter terrorism have made prisons breeding grounds for youth radicalization. Prisons have become a place for radical youth, Muslim Brotherhood members, radical Islamists to share their common grievances. In addition to this, a decree passed by President and published in official gazette on 25 October 2015, gave unquestionable powers to jail authorities against prisoners. It increases solitary confinement from 15 to 30 days and allows prison authorities to put prisoner in solitary confinement for 15 days at their discretion.[23]

This provides a highway for major instability in the country's socio-political establishment, whatever may be the roots of Nasserism.

Tackling terrorism in the least appropriate way, would damage the country's political stability. It is unadvisable to indiscriminately target Muslim Brotherhood members as it leads to growth of extremist groups.

Economic Scenario

Egypt is in a critical period of economic crisis. The industrial monopoly and capital intensive investments offer a little sustainable economic growth. The current slowdown of economy is more visible in the huge current account deficits, rising inflation and unemployment, huge public debts, collapse of tourism industry and the falling oil revenue.

In the complex interdependent world, Egypt has been heavily entangled into the world market depending on the foreign credit to cover its expenditure. Foreign credit is mostly provided by the Gulf countries. Fearing the spread of democracy, GCC countries have stepped up their financial support to Egypt after the ouster of Mursi government in August 2013. Saudi Arabia, Kuwait, UAE pledged $12 billions of unconditional support to the Al – Sisi government. This financial aid is estimated to have reached up to $30 billion since 2013.[24] From decades, Egypt has not relied on IMF for the loans and was heavily supported by GCC countries. But Cairo's tepid support to Saudi led coalition strikes on Yemen and its divergence from Saudi policy on Syria, which supported Russian drafted UN resolution supporting Assad's regime, increased tensions between Saudi and Egypt. Egypt's independent stand in the regional politics has forced it to take the financial support of IMF. Egypt secured $12 billion[25] under extended fund facility (2016) from IMF which is a shift from dependence on GCC countries. The loan from IMF has installed confidence in the other financial donors which further brought $4[26] billion from UAE (2017).

One of the major revenue sectors - tourism industry collapsed drastically, after the downing of Russian plane by extremist groups over the Sinai Peninsula. Grounding of flights from London to Sharm El-Sheikh after this incident delivered a major blow to the industry. According to Foreign and Commonwealth office of Egypt, there is a 74% decrease in the tourist visit from UK in 2016, when compared to the previous year.[27] This had its spillover effect, due to which around 150 hotels have gone bankrupt owing to the fall in the tourism.[28] When compared to 2014 -15, the revenue of 2015-16 has dropped by 48.8%.

Tourism receipts of Egypt

Year	2011/12	2012/13	2013/14	2014/15	2015/16*
Tourism Income ($ US Bn)	9.419	9.752	5.073	7.37	3.768

Source: Arab Republic of Egypt. Ministry of Finance. The financial Monthly. (2017, January). Volume 12. No. 3

One hundred and forty-seven-year-old Suez Canal connecting Europe and Asian trade is one of the major pillars of the world trade. Canal can accommodate 61.2% of tanker fleet, 92.7% of bulk carrier fleet, 100% of container ships and other types.[29] After heavily decorated project of Al-Sisi opened a parallel Suez Canal in 2015, there isn't any significant increase in the Suez revenue. Surprisingly the total revenue has gone down. Ministry of Finance has attributed the decline in revenue was partially due to the slowdown in international trade and China's slowed economic growth. However, major investments into Suez Canal and development of Suez Canal economic zone would provide employment and increase the export capacity of Egypt. It is worth to be patient and observe how events would turnout, as the development of Suez infrastructure is a long-term project and cannot expect overnight results.

Suez Canal receipts of Egypt

Year	2011/12	2012/13	2013/14	2014/15	2015/16*
Total number of vessels	17664	16664	16744	17544	17252
Net Tonnage (million tons)	939	912	931	992	987
Receipts ($ US billion)	5.208	5.032	5.369	5.362	5.122

*Preliminary data

Source: Arab Republic of Egypt. Ministry of Finance. The financial Monthly. (2017, January). Volume 12 . No. 3

Apart from the increase in the current account deficits, foreign cash reserves are also dwindling due to the low oil prices. Even the remittances which Egypt gets from Gulf countries have dwindled, weighing pressure on the government Forex. These low remittances also affect the economic life of dependent families. Number of expatriate workers in the Gulf countries is about 6 million. Even if we assume that there are 3 members per family and they depend on remittances from Gulf workers, then the total population depending on remittances would amount to 18 million which is approximately 20% of the total population.

Recent economic package of *Saudi vision 2030* announced on 25 April 2016 has installed fear of being expelled from Saudi Arabia. There are speculations that Saudi Ministry of Finance would introduce a monthly fee on expatriate workers which would range from 100 riyals to 300 riyals. But due to the high exchange rate of Egyptian pound to Riyal, the monthly fee which is argued to be levied on expats would affect a little.[30]

Remittances received by Egypt

Country	2013	2014	2015	2016	2017
Rep of Egypt ($ US Million)	17,833	19,570	18,325	16,584	N/A

Source: World Bank staff calculation based on data from IMF Balance of Payments Statistics database and data releases from central banks, national statistical agencies, and World Bank country desks.

Complicating the economic situation, most of the state budget is spent on wages to its low efficient, heavily oversized[31] staff and for subsidies. 59.9% of the total expenditure according to 2015-16 general budget of Egypt goes into the latter's expenditure. Recently, Ministry of Planning Monitoring and Administrative Reform (MPMAR). has announced to increase the salary of civil savants[32] which weighs heavily on the government deficit. Encouraging private sector is one way to deal with the bulging government staff.

Expenditure on salaries to government employees and subsidies of Egypt

(US $ bn)	2011-12	2012-13	2013-14	2014-15	2015-16 (Budget sector)	2016-17 (Budget sector)
Total Expenditure	28.5	35.62	42.028	44.57	45.2	53.9
Wages and Salaries	6.8	8	10	11.1	11.8	12.65
Subsidies, Grants and Social benefits	11.3	14.74	16.48	15.6	11.1	11.4

Source: Arab Republic of Egypt. Ministry of Finance. The financial Monthly. (2017, January). Volume 12. No. 3

Government's Civil Service reform law, cuts in energy subsidies, and new social assistance programs like Takaful and Karama[33], further cash transfer program are believed to be necessary steps to reduce government expenditure.

Egypt was a net exporter of oil until 2006 and after, became a net importer of oil. This is because of the increase in the consumption and decrease in the production. Slump in the oil prices instead of aiding Egypt in adjusting their balance of payments has shown a contrary. Egypt's capacity to generate foreign currency indirectly and directly depends on oil. Nearly 40 of the Egypt's total merchandise exports include oil products.[34] This made the export revenues fall which had a higher impact relative to the reduction in the import cost. Owing to the low oil revenue, GCC countries also slashed their financial support on which Egypt stayed afloat.

Scrutinizing the government fiscal operations, government cash deficit is found to be constantly above 50% from 2011. This shows the country's heavy dependence on the foreign reserves to meet its domestic demand. Heavy spending on the subsidies and discouraging privatization would help a little to correct the mounting deficits.

Government overall cash deficit

Year	2011/12	2012/13	2013/14	2014/15	2015/16
Cash deficit (\$ US billion)	9.24	13.14	13.5		-
Percentage of total revenue (%)	56.1	67.81	53.5	57.6	-

Source: Arab Republic of Egypt. Ministry of finance. The financial Monthly. (2017, January). Volume 12. No. 3

With the public debt, more than 90% of its GDP, major policy changes are required to balance the government debt accounts. It is necessary for the state to reverse the economic downturn by addressing its short term fiscal deficits. In order to bring back the economy into healthy condition, necessary structural reforms must also be considered. Present government has taken responsibility by cutting down the corporate tax to 22.5% from 30% and sales tax to 5% from 10%, reduction of custom duties to 2%. On 19 August 2014, Al-Sisi passed an amendment to the building tax law No. 196/2008, which extends the property tax base to entire country including those under construction, whereas under the previous law, tax was levied only to properties within the cities.[35] The revenue from property tax has seen a substantial increase from \$0.72 billion in 2011-12 to \$1.54 billion in 2015-16. Value added Tax has been introduced in September 2016 which is presently stands at 14%. Egypt expects to raise 20 billion pounds from this tax in 2017[36].

According to new draft investment law, the total number of articles has been reduced to 56[37] from 115 making law investor friendly. Companies are allowed to have 20%[38] of foreign labor instead of 10% and companies in SEZ are allowed 25%[39] of foreign labor. According to the Egypt Investment Law which passed on 7 May 2017[40], industries are provided corporate impunity and insulation from legal accountability, primarily from criminal accountability. Under this, a company can't be held accountable for any activity of its employee and legal procedures will be initiated only against the person involved under any circumstances.

Another major reform is the labor law, which is now argued to be more inclined towards employers. For example, employer can remove an employee if the former believes that if he is embarking on competition with employer or if he aggressed against employer (Article 69 of labor law)[41]. Arbitrary contract termination is in the right of employer until and unless article 120[42] of labor law not breeched under which race, sex, social status, family obligations, pregnancy, religion or political views are viewed as insufficient grounds for termination.

These labor laws will encourage investments which brings capital into the economy whose trickledown effect may rise employment opportunities.

In order to increase the revenues from the exports, and due to the pressure from the international organizations, Egypt has liberalized its exchange rate on 3 November 2016 which currently stands at 18.08 LE per US$ in 2017 when compared 6.3 in 2013. This may increase exports but the current account deficits will not decrease as cost of imports increases. According to the data from CBE[43], Egypt is running under $18.6 billion current account deficit as per 2015-16.

Depreciation proved costly because 2/3rd of Egypt's imports are made of raw material and intermediate capital goods. Inflation has shot up to 30.8% measured in 2017 January. Head line inflation stands at 28.138% and food prizes inflation stands at 25.829%. Country in which 27.8%[44] of population lives below poverty - line, high rate of inflation puts severe pressure on the livelihood.

In order to control the inflation, monetary policy committee of Egypt has adopted tight monetary policy. It has increased the interest rates by 600[45] basis points, retail lending rates by 257 basis points and deposit rates by 398 bps. This reduces the money flow in the economy and increases the spending capacity of government with which it is expected to use wisely. Strong monetary policies are outmost necessary to bring down the inflation rates but crowding out effect must not be neglected which would slow down the investments.

Due to the lack of capital, government has also started planning to list state owned companies in the Egyptian Exchange (EGX). Minister of supply, Khaled Hanafy and Minister of Investment Ashraf Salman have collaborated to prepare an amendment to LAW no. 203 which bans offering state owned companies on EGX.[46]In 2015, Mr. Hanafy said, state is considering to list Food Industries Holding Company (FIHC) in Initial Public offering.[47] This allows state to distribute its economic power allowing private players to hold the reign. These disinvestments would provide capital but does not allow privatization as majority stake holders would still be the government. These steps are yet to be put on the ground and present government should not scrap its disinvestments as they have gained foreign credit to lift their expenditure.

These reforms attract investments but are heavily concentrated in the capital-intensive sector. In 2014-15 according to Central bank of Egypt statistics, 53.2% of foreign investments are into oil sectors and only 0.5% is into communication and information sector. In the Egypt investment forum which was convened in 15 March 2015, finance minister has announced that maximum investments are into the oil sector and not others. [48]

These heavy investments into the capital-intensive sector would boost countries economy but leads to a jobless growth. Encouraging heavy foreign investments without providing any level playing ground makes indigenous industries devoid of economies of scale and economies of experience. Egypt being a labor-intensive economy cannot afford investing heavily in the capital-intensive sector as it loses out its comparative advantage.

Sectoral wise distribution of Foreign Direct Investment into Egypt 2014 – 15

Main Invested Sectors	2014-2015 in %
Oil Sector	53.2
Finance	3.8
Real Estate	3.7
Manufacturing	3.4
Construction	1.5
Communication and Information	0.5

Source: Central Bank of Egypt, Statistical Bulletin December 2016

Even after the above steps, unemployment remains high. Unemployment stood at 12.014% in 2016 whereas world unemployment average stood at 5.743%.[49] When we look at the current employment statistics, most of the employment accounts for the low and semi-skilled sector which contribute a little to the knowledge economy.

Sector wise employment of Egypt

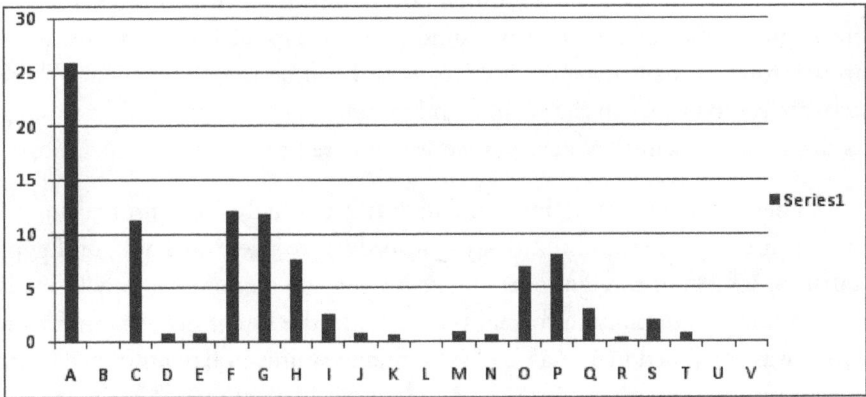

Note: Data regarding the chart is provided in the appendix.

The graph above shows the amount of labor employed in those sectors which contribute a little to knowledge economy. 25.8 % of labor is employed in Agriculture, hunting, forestry and cutting of wood trees and 12.1% in construction and building, 11.8% in motor cycle repair. Large chunk of workforce is found in informal sector and World Bank's Egyptian labor market report 2014 reasons that this is a result of stagnation[50] in the formal labor market. The informal sector equals to 65 – 70%[51] of formal sector and it is opined that in 2012 informal sector occupied 37.4%[52] of GDP. Total population of Egypt under age group 15-24 is 18213929 and the employees aged 15-24 according to the official data are 4395000. This means that only 24.1% of youth account for the formal employment and rest 75.9% are in the informal sector.

Out of total labor force registered during 2015, 19% has received university education and only 4.5% received vocational training. Gap between the education and employment opportunities is so huge that most of the unemployment is among the public who are educated above intermediate. According to Arab Human development report 2016, Youth of Egypt tend to migrate mostly due to the lack of economic opportunities.[53] Ministry level institutions looking after migration in Egypt shows the extent of outward movement of workforce.

As reported in ADHR report 2016, top two reasons for youth to give up education are either having no interest or failure in exams. Even within the provided education, scientific education enrollment is minimal. Suitable employment opportunities for technical graduates are also meager, which provides little incentive for students to pursue their higher education. In the dynamic technological world, technical skills must be upgraded constantly and for that providing required education and government investment in the development of human resources is very much necessary.

Military and the Economy

Since army has taken over the reins, it has enhanced its strength not only on the political front but also on the economic front. Approximately 40%[54]of the GDP is believed to be under the military control, but it's difficult to estimate a correct figure of its economic control. It has started diversifying its economic sources by entering into different sectors and engaging in joint ventures. Military hold over economy and polity has incentivized foreign investors to invest securely in Egypt. Foreign investors are more interested in collaborating with military as they provide security which no other state institution can provide.

For example, during the 2011 uprisings, Kharafi group announced expansion of its infrastructure investments by $80[55] million. This shows the extent of security provided by military and its ability to draw investors into the country.

Government's concentration can be seen in raising the capital and attracting the foreign investments without any focus on developmental policies. With a scrutiny, it can be observed that concerns of 2011 and 2013 are still not addressed. The measures taken by the present government appears to be less developmental oriented. Economic policies not emphasizing on the economic development along with resource development would temporarily reduce the economic imperfections but will not be sustained for long period.

What can be Done?

The major challenge of Egypt is of course first to overcome its short term fiscal deficit and then construct a path towards long term economic development while providing political stability. While the measures taken by President Al-Sisi government are not unadvisable, continuation would be unadvisable.

There must a shift in approach which would bring structural changes initially on economic front and then to the political front. Strong political will and stable government is necessary to take unpopular measures for the long term sustainable development.

Some of the measures that Egypt may want to undertake to get Egypt onto the development path:

1. Egypt's policy should be based on the development model emphasizing on resource development. For example, investing in education would build a strong base for the future generations and would create a path of sustained economic growth. To improve the knowledge economy, investments in vocational training, higher education and R&D is deemed as outmost necessary.

2. Focusing on its geographic advantage, steps must be taken to convert Sinai and Mediterranean ports into major transit hubs of the world. This would bring ever growing revenue for the country. But the investments needed for the latter cannot be borne by government solely. Therefore, private players must be encouraged which needs a strong State – Private Business relations.

3. Transparency in the governance must be improved so that every private business player can get access to all public tenders without any discrimination.

4. Tourism which is one of the vital sectors for revenue must be revived by improving the security conditions and bringing stability to Sinai Peninsula. For the latter, indiscriminate targeting of Muslim Brotherhood and other Islamic parties must be controlled. Local population of Sinai must be engaged by providing employment in the tourism sector which would bring down the membership of extremist organizations.

5. In the long term, improving exports must not be neglected. Accordingly, Egypt must exploit the economic niches of the market and constantly understand its dynamic comparative advantage. Investing in the renewable energy sector serves better for the latter as country's energy dependency is exponentially.

6. Indigenous industries must be encouraged which should be developed alongside with the education. MSME sector must be encouraged

which has a huge potential for employment generation and enough credit facilities are to be provided.

7. Without providing freedom to media and civil society organizations, an effective democracy would be difficult to build. Thus, NGO laws are advised to be in accordance with United Nations Human Rights Law and media must be allowed to report freely.

8. Steps must be taken to ensure economic, political and civil rights to the citizens, which ensures their liberty, which would make government rethink upon the laws already made such as Anti-terrorism law adopted on 17 January 2016, which is repressive and meant to curb the opposition and curtail the freedom of press.

Conclusion

Egypt's stability cannot be built on either political or economic factors. There should be a parallel development of both to stop Egypt from falling into the abyss of crisis. However, a strong effective government is necessary to implement unpopular measures on the economic front and present government proves to be arguably fit for the latter. It would appear that Egypt is moving in the correct direction by attracting foreign capital, but these are attributed as cynical measures. If continued with the same model, Egypt would fall into economic abyss deeply depending on the foreign countries. Their extensive debts will cause international financial institutions to formulate policies for Egypt.

On the political front, disempowering public from political rights may cause discontent and worsen the relation between government and citizens. This discontent may lead to apolitical actions such as riots, which promote individual goals or rather target individual policies. But these actions would not threaten the government. Egypt moving towards authoritarian rule might seem inevitable, but one must not stick to this notion, as authoritarianism is not inevitable.

After two revolutions, public might become wary about the results and are in need of political and economic stability. This makes 2018 presidential elections not a hard competitive one, as current President Al-Sisi has little opposition. The media, civil societies, political parties who stand at the opposition have been silenced, leaving little room for anti Sisi factions. There is a possibility that people would elect him back as the president, because they may believe that Egypt is on the path to recovery under his rule as the nationalistic fervor makes people believe in the military.

Previously it took 3 decades to overthrow an authoritative regime, and it is likely that it may take that long for another. Thus, it is hoped that the present government takes a sager path and provide more inclusive government.

Appendix:

A	25.8	Agriculture, Hunting, Forestry & Cutting of wood trees
B	0.1	Mining & quarrying
C	11.22	Manufactures
D	0.82	Electric, gas, steam, air condition supplies
E	0.75	Water support, drain, recycling
F	12.1	Constructions & Building
G	11.8	Whole and retail sale vehicles , motorcycles repairing
H	7.6	Transportation & storage
I	2.6	Food, residence services
J	0.8	Information, Telecommunications
K	0.6	Insurance & Financial Intermediation
L	0.1	Real estate, Renting
M	1	Specialized technical, scientific activities
N	0.7	Administrative Activities & Support Services
O	7	Public Administration ,defense, social solidarity
P	8	Education
Q	3	Health and Social Work
R	0.4	Amusement &Creation & Arts Activities
S	2	Other Services Activities
T	0.8	Services of home service for private households
U	0.1	International and Regional Agencies &Organizations
V	0	Activities not classification

Source: CAPMAS, "Statistical Year book: Labor", 2016, http://www.capmas.gov.eg/Pages/ShowPDF.aspx?page_id=http://41.33.20.197/di7web/ (accessed on 28 April 2017)

Endnotes

1   "The SCAF's Egypt (2011-2012)," *Fanack Chronicle*, last modified November 15, 2012, accessed May 17, 2017https://chronicle.fanack.com/egypt/history-past-to-present/the-scafs-egypt-2011-2012/

2   Dunne Michele and Mara Revkin, "Overview of Egypt's Constitutional Referendum," *Carnegie Endowment for International Peace*, March 16, 2011, accessed May 17, 2017, http://carnegieendowment.org/2011/03/16/overview-of-egypt-s-constitutional-referendum-pub-43095.

3   Kingsley Patrick, "How Mohamed Morsi, Egypt's first elected President, ended up on a death row?," *The Guardian*, June 01, 2015, accessed May 11, 2017, https://www.theguardian.com/world/2015/jun/01/mohamed-morsi-execution-death-sentence-egypt

4   Siddiqui Fazzur Rahman, "Five Years of Uprising: Egypt has Come Full Circle," *Indian Council of World Affairs*, April 1, 2016, accessed May 16, 2017, http://icwa.in/pdfs/IB/2014/FiveYearsofUprisingIB01042016.pdf.

5   "After**Egypt's military steps into politics, will politics step into the military?,**"*Heinrich-Böll-Stiftung*, February 2017, accessed May 9, 2017, https://tn.boell.org/sites/default/files/.

6   Springborg Robert, "Abdul fattah Al-Sisi: New Face of Egypt's Old Guard," *BBC News*, March 26, 2014, accessed May 11, 2017, http://www.bbc.com/news/world-middle-east-26188023.

7   Stephen Kalin and Maggie Fick, "Egypt's Sisi wins election, faces economic challenges," *Reuters*, May 29, 2014, accessed May 16, 2017,http://www.reuters.com/article/us-egypt-election-idUSKBN0E70D720140529

8   Mohamed Elmenshawy, "Egypt's New Parliamentary Election Law: Back to the Future," *Middle East Institute*, July 17, 2014, accessed May 17, 2017, http://www.mei.edu/content/at/egypts-new-parliamentary-election-law-back-future.

9   HALAWA OMAR, "Meet Egypt's New Parliamentary Majority Bloc: In Support of Egypt", *Atlantic Council*, January 11, 2016, accessed May 5, 2017, **http://www.atlanticcouncil.org/blogs/menasource/meet-egypt-s-new-parliamentary-majority-bloc-in-support-of-egypt.**

10 Mikhail George, "Is Egypt's main Opposition Party Switching Sides?," *Al Monitor*, January 13, 2017, accessed May 10, 2017, http://www.al-monitor.

com/pulse/originals/2017/01/egypt-free-egyptians-party-shift-pro-gpvernment-opposition.html.

11   Afify Heba, "Infighting Among the Free Egyptians: The leading Liberal Party is Downing in Internal Disputes, as another post 2011 party disintegrates," *Mada masr*, January 6, 2017, accessed May 4, 2017,   http://www.madamasr.com/en/2017/01/06/feature/politics/infighting-among-the-free-egyptians/.

12   Gomaa Ahmed, "Is Quest to Increase presidential terms really altruistic?," *Al Monitor*, March 10, 2017, accessed May 5, 2017 http://al-monitor.com/pulse/originals/2017/03/egypt-parliament-draft-law-presidential-term-renewal-sis-amp.html.

13   International Center for Not-for-Profit Law (ICNL), accessed April 23, 2017,http://www.icnl.org/research/library/files/Egypt/law84-2002-En.pdf.

14   "Egypt: Ruling Risks Eradicating Human Rights Work," *Human Rights Watch*, September 20, 2016, accessed May 152, 2017, **https://www.hrw.org/news/2016/09/20/egypt-ruling-risks-eradicating-human-rights-work.**

15   Najjar Farah, "Egypt's NGO law aims to 'erase civil society': The law is part of a wider crackdown on human rights groups, activists say.," *Al Jazeera*, February 16, 2017, accessed April 28, 2017,   http://www.aljazeera.com/indepth/features/2017/02/egypt-ngo-law-aims-erase-civil-society-170215121321442.html.

16   "Freedom of ASSOCIATION/Rights to Organise,"Survey of violations of Trade Union Rights, last modified Febraury 18, 2014, accessed April 12, 2017, https://survey.ituc-csi.org/Egypt.html#tabs-2.

17   "50 Policemen Sentenced for 3 Years for Striking,"*Mada Masr*, August 3, 2017, accessed August 3, 2017, https://www.madamasr.com/en/2017/08/03/news/u/50-policemen-sentenced-to-3-years-for-striking/.

18   Sayeed Abdul Raheem, "Egypt: The Suppression of Freedom of Expression , Legar Cover," *alarabi al jaded*, January 24, 2016, accessed May 16 2017, https://www.alaraby.co.uk/medianews/2016/1/24/%D9%85%D8%B5%D8%B1-%D9%82%D9%85%D8%B9-%D8%AD%D8%B1%D9%8A%D8%A9-%D8%A7%D9%84%D8%AA%D8%B9%D8%A8%D9%8A%D8%B1-%D8%A8%D8%BA%D8%B7%D8%A7%D8%A1-%D9%82%D8%A7%D9%86%D9%88%D9%86%D9%8A?utm_campaign=magnet&utm_source=article_page&utm_medium=related_articles.

19 Mansour Sherif, "Stifling the Public Sphere: Media and Civil Society in Egypt," *National Endowment for Democracy*, pp 11, 2015, accessed May 9, 2017, http://www.ned.org/wp-content/uploads/2015/10/Stifling-the-Public-Sphere-Media-Civil-Society-Egypt-Forum-NED.pdf

20 "One of the world's biggest prisons for journalists,"*Reports without Borders*, accessed May 7, 2017, https://rsf.org/en/egypt .

21 "Egypt's Failing <<War on Terror>>: Policy Brief Egypt 1 - Security," *Heinrich-Böll-Stiftung*, February 2017, accessed May 9, 2017, https://tn.boell.org/sites/default/files/policy-brief-egypt-1-security.pdf.

22 "Minya Court Sentences over 100 defendants to death," *Mada Masr*, June 21, 2014, accessed May 20, 2017, http://www.madamasr.com/en/2014/06/21/news/u/minya-court-sentences-over-100-defendants-to-death/.

23 Mada masr and Mai Shams El – Din, "Does Sisi's new Laws give Prison Administrators greater Powers?", *Mada Masr*, October 27, 2015, accessed May 17, 2017, http://www.madamasr.com/en/2015/10/27/feature/politics/do-sisis-new-laws-give-prison-administrators-greater-powers/.

24 Minty Imraan, "Escaping the Cycle of Debt: A Grand bargain for Egypt's creditors," *Al Jazeera Center for Studies*, January 26, 2017, accessed May 23, 2017, http://studies.aljazeera.net/mritems/Documents/2017/4/9/218781465d834451b245f474fd00594f_100.pdf

25 "Press Release NO. 16/501," International Monetary Fund, 2016, accessed April 22, 2017, http:/www.imf.org/en/News/Articles/2016/11/11/PR16501-Egypt-Executive-Board-Approves-12-billion-Extended-Arrangement,

26 Khan. T, "UAE allocates $4bn in assistance to Egypt," *The National*, April 22, 2017, accessed April 28, 2017, http:/www.thenational.ae/world/middle-east/uae-allocates-4bn-in-assistance-to-egypt.

27 Gardner Frank, "Egypt 'let down' by continued UK flight ban to Sharm," *BBC News*, April 27, 2017, accessed May 4, 2017, **http://www.bbc.com/news/uk-39729459.**

28 **Salah** Hisham, "2017 will not be the year tourism to Egypt improves: experts," *Daily News Egypt*, October 30, 2016, accessed April 29, 2017, **http://www.dailynewsegypt.com/2016/10/30/2017-will-not-year-tourism-egypt-improves-experts/.**

29 "Future Plans," Suez Canal Authority, 2015, accessed May 11, 2017, http://www.suezcanal.gov.eg/English/About/SuezCanal/Pages/FuturePlans.aspx.

30 Mostafa Amr, "Will Saudi Arabia expel Egyptian workforce?," *Al Monitor*, Febraury 12, 2017, accessed May 11, 2017, http://www.al-monitor.com/pulse/originals/2017/02/saudi-arabia-egypt-foreign-workforce-unemployment-tax-levy.html.

31 Adly Amr," Civil Service Reform in Egypt: Between Efficiency and Social Peace," *Carnegie Middle East Center*, March 16, 2016, accessed March 4, 2017, http://carnegie-mec.org/2016/03/27/civil-service-reform-in-egypt-between-efficiency-and-social-peace-pub-63442.

32 Al-Masry Al-Youm, "Egypt Cabinet to increase civil servants minimum wage," *Egypt Independent*, January 10, 2017, accessed May 8, 2017, http://www.egyptindependent.com//news/egypt-cabinet-increase-civil-servants-minimum-wage .

33 "Egypt Overview," World Bank, 2017, accessed May 8, 2017, http://www.worldbank.org/en/country/egypt/overview.

34 Adly Amr, "Egypt's Oil Dependency and Political Discontent," *Carnegie Middle East center*, August 2, 2016, accessed May 24, 2017, http://carnegie-mec.org/2016/08/02/egypt-s-oil-dependency-and-political-discontent-pub-64224.

35 Tadamun, March 31, 2015, accessed May 19, 2017, http://www.tadamun.co/2015/03/31/analysis-amendment-law-196-2008-property-tax/?lang=en#.WSO6xWmGPIU.

36 "Egypt sees value-added tax revenue up by 8 million pounds in 2017-2018," *Reuters*, March 28, 2017, accessed April 27, 2017, http://af.reuters.com/article/commoditiesNews/idAFL5N1H5162.

37 Shaimaa Al-Aees, "FEI number of Investment Law articles to 56 to facilitate investment process,"*Daily News Egypt*, 2017, accessed May 1, 2017, http:/www.dailynewsegypt.com/2017/04/19/fei-number-investment-law-foreign-direct-investment-process/. link removed

38 Talat Nayrouz, "Will new Law Attract More Foreign Investment to Egypt?," *Al Monitor*, January 13, 2017, accessed April 23, 2017, http:/www.almonitor.com/pulse/originals/2017/01/Egypt-new-investment-law-foreign-direct-investment.html.

39 "World Bank Disburses Another $1 Billion Loan To Egypt,"*Reuters*, March 20, 2017, accessed May 27, 2017, http://www.reuters.com/article/us-egypt-economy-loans-idUSKBN16R23O?il=0.

40 **Farouk** Ehab, "Egypt passes delayed investment law to smooth business, attract dollars," *Reuters*, May 7, 2017, accessed May 12, 2017, **http://www.reuters. com/article/us-egypt-investment-idUSKBN1830S7.**

41 "Employment Law Overview: Egypt," L&E Global, 2016, accessed April 20, 2017, http://knowledge.leglobal.org/wp-content/uploads/LEGlobal_Memo_ Egypt.pdf.

42 "Egyptian Labor Law," Maher MIlad Iskander & Co. Lawyers and Counselors, 2016, accessed April 20, 2017, http://mahermiladiskander.com/wp-content/ uploads/2016/04/Egyptian-Labour-Law.pdf.

43 CBE – Central bank of Egypt

44 "Demography," Central agency for public monetization and statistics, accessed May 3, 2017, http://www.capmas.gov.eg/Pages/ShowPDF.aspx?page_ id=http://41.33.20.197/di7web/.

45 Monetary Policy Committee, "Monetary Policy Report," Central bank of Egypt, 2017, accessed May 2, 2017, http://www.cbe.org.eg/en/MonetaryPolicy/ MonetaryPolicyReports/Monetary%20Policy%20Report%20March%202017. pdf.

46 AggourSara, " Ministry Of Supply Plans FIHC IPO:Studies on FIHC IPO and commodity exchange market to be finalised before year's end,"*Daily News Egypt*, February 9, 2016, accessed April 29, 2017, http://www.dailynewsegypt. com/2016/02/09/ministry-of-supply-plans-fihc-ipo/.

47 Egypt considers listing Food Industries Holding Company-minister," *Reuters*, February 22,2015, accessed April 23, 2017, **http://www.reuters.com/article/ egypt-supplies-ipo-idUSL5N0VW04W20150222.**

48 Anas Omair, "Egypt Investment Conference: Return of Crony Capitalism," *Daily Sabah*, March 15, 2015, accessed April 18, 2017, https://www.dailysabah.com/ op-ed/2015/03/15/Egypt-investment-conference-return-of-crony-capitalism.

49 World Bank, accessed May 24, 2017, http://data.worldbank.org/indicator/ SL.UEM.TOTL.ZS?locations=EG

50 "Egypt's Private Sector: A Driving Force For Job Creation,"*World Bank*, September 18, 2014, accessed May 7, 2017, http://www.worldbank.org/en/news/feature/2014/09/18/egypts-private-sector-a-driving-force-for-job-creation.

51 **Farid** Doaa , "Informal sector volume records around EGP 1.5tn: ECES," *Daily News Egypt*, September 23, 2014, accessed May 12, 2017, **http://www.dailynewsegypt.com/2014/09/23/informal-sector-volume-records-around-egp-1-5tn-eces/**)

52 Hany M.Elshamy, "Measuring the Informal Economy in Egypt," *International Journal of Business Management and Economic Research(IJBMER)*, Vol 6(2) {2015}:137-142, accessed May 12, 2017, http://www.ijbmer.com/docs/volumes/vol6issue2/ijbmer2015060202.pdf

53 "Arab Human Development Report 2016: Prospects for Human Development in a Changing Reality,"*UNDP* ,2016, accessed April 19 2017, http://www.arab-hdr.org/PreviousReports/2016/2016.aspx .

54 Casabon Christina, "Egypt's Military Economy. Open Democracy," *Open Democracy*, July 29, 2015, accessed April 28, 2017https://www.opendemocracy.net/arab-awakening/cristina-casab%C3%B3n/egypt%27s-military-economy.

55 Marshall Shana and Joshua Stacher, "Egypt's General and Transnational capital," *Middle East Research and Information Project*, Volume 42, MER 262, {Spring, 2012}, accessed April 26, 2017, http://www.merip.org/mer/mer262/egypts-generals-transnational-capital.

Countering China's Legal Warfare during Territorial Disputes: *Doklam and South China Sea*

Ms. Soundarya. J

Introduction

On 28 August 2017, as the news of "disengagement" between the Indian and Chinese troops in Doklam area (claimed by both China and Bhutan) came in, a 71-day tense stand-off between two nuclear armed countries came to a temporary end. This stand-off which came as a result of India stopping Chinese road construction in disputed area in Bhutan, and how it was dealt with, by India and Bhutan, offers insights for various stakeholders. The important one is how to deal with China's legal warfare along with psyche warfare. Chinese playbook for dealing with boundary and territorial disputes with other countries has been the same throughout-use the three-warfare strategy. The way it has been countered in Doklam is different from other cases; say the case of South China Sea. At the same time, the cases show the weakness of Chinese "legal" argument for territorial sovereignty in the disputed regions based on historical claims.

This essay attempts to show the nature of China's legal warfare in boundary and territorial disputes, how China uses legal warfare to "legitimize" its territorial claims, and how other countries can counter it through study of Doklam and South China Sea cases respectively.

The Larger Context: The Three Warfare Strategy

It is well known that the Chinese "Three Warfare" *(san zhan)* strategy refers to psychological, legal and media warfare. Scholars have always linked all three together, as they are interrelated and mutually reinforcing. While

Media warfare is about securing dominance over the venue for implementing psychological and legal warfare, psychological warfare is about providing underpinnings for media and legal warfare, and legal warfare is one of the key instruments of psychological and media warfare (Singh, 2013).

It is necessary to understand the larger political context of the 3Ws, because this 3Ws as a composite idea, is war by other means- if the object of war is to acquire resources, influence, and territory and project national will. It represents the Chinese commitment to expand areas of conflict from purely 'military' to 'the political' (Singh, 2013). By manipulating public opinion, legal systems and enemy or opposite party leaderships, China aims to wage a political warfare during a period of 'peace' to create conditions suitable for resolution of a conflict on favorable terms to China without resorting to war. While the "Three warfare" strategy appears to be interlinked, these three-warfare in their own right act as separate domains.

Psychological Warfare aims to disrupt or influence opponent's decision-making capabilities, degrade an adversary's will to fight or reduce their resolve and commitment towards the issue at stake. It uses diplomatic pressure, false narratives, rumours, to express displeasure, threaten or to assert its control. Chinese economy and access to market is particularly used as pressure point against countries (Halper, 2013).

Media Warfare seeks to create a Chinese narrative and make it the most prominent in the minds of masses and elites on a particular issue. It uses all instruments from films, TV programmes, to daily news, editorials, books, and even the social media and the internet

Legal Warfare/ Lawfare is aimed at providing 'legal' justification for China's actions and to make the adversary doubt about justification of their positions. Little is known of the origin of this 3Ws. While China officially released a set of code governing political warfare in 2003 and upgraded them in 2010, few suggest it goes back to Sun Tzu who laid emphasis on "winning without engaging in war." Some link the 3Ws to the "Unrestricted Warfare" concept first propounded two decades back by two senior PLA Air Force commanders. Altogether, 3Ws is about getting an upper hand for China and is about preparing enemy or opposite party to cede their ground without even needing to fight.

Lawfare in China

The term Lawfare was first used in the academia by Charles Dunloop to describe the strategy of "using or misusing law as a substitute for traditional military means to achieve an operational objective" (Deo, 2017). Lawfare, in the most basic sense means "arguing one's own side is obeying law and criticizing the other side for violating law and making arguments for one's own side in cases where there are violations of the law" (Yanrong, 2006). It can take several forms, the most obvious one being the use of legal norms to justify one's military or political actions as seen in South China Sea and Doklam issue. Another type is changing facts on ground to support legal claims and finally, using domestic laws to the disadvantage of other countries strategic objectives.

In China, the concept of legal warfare (*fulanzhan* or *fulanzhanzheng*) had generated wide range of debate and discussions which can be dated back to 1999 with the conceptualization of "Unrestricted Warfare" as warfare not limited by physical battlegrounds but an extended warfare across all sections of society. This was codified in December 2003, when the PRC promulgated the "Political Work Regulations of the Chinese People's Liberation Army"- a regulation specifying that the General Political Department (GDP) to implement "three warfare" strategy for political work purpose. In 2005, the Chinese's Central Military Commission ratified—and the former General Staff Department, General Political Department, General Logistics Department, and General Armaments Department, jointly promulgated—official guidelines (*gangyao,* literally "outline" or "essentials") for public opinion warfare, psychological warfare, and legal warfare, officially incorporating the concepts into the PLA's education, training, and preparation for military struggle. While these guidelines are not publically available, the open-source PLA literature on the three warfares, which dates back to the mid-2000s, constitutes a valuable resource for analysis and comparison (Kania, 2016). From Chinese viewpoint, political warfare, including legal warfare is seen as a form of combat (Cheng, Winning Without Fighting: Chinese Public Opinion Warfare and the Need for a Robust American Response, 2012). In 2015, the Lawfare was institutionalized when the Chinese Ministry of Foreign Affairs set up an international law committee in order to advance its interests through treaties and legal provisions (Deo, 2017).

Like conventional warfare, Lawfare is conducted in a combined manner along with the other two strategies, under a unified command organisation - most often. It includes the use of law to implement offensive actions, defensive actions, counterattacking actions and other form of combat, as well as used as a legal deterrent and for imposition of sanctions. Commonly used before outbreak of physical hostilities, to influence the domestic and foreign populations and leaders' perceptions, Lawfare aims to weaken the opposition party through pre-emptive legal strike.

This legal warfare or Lawfare in China is underlined by two major influences (Cheng, 2013.) : One, the Chinese view of rule of the law: *Rule of law* in China is more like *rule by law* i.e law is seen as an instrument of governance – a means through which authority can control the population, not a control extended over authority. Stemming from the Confucians and the legalist schools of thought, which influenced imperial China's understanding of law has been taken forward by the Communist Party of China under Mao. Even after Mao, Law in China remains to be an instrument which is applied to "masses" as opposed to the Party.

Two, Chinese perception that other states already employ Lawfare – Chinese believe that countries like the USA already employ legal warfare, noting the US obtaining UN authorization before the first Gulf War, and justifying its action in Kosovo with the support from NATO. This had resulted in extensive study of legal warfare of other countries by Chinese scholars and policymakers alike. For instance, studying the Second Gulf War, one of the scholar who is a part of PLA, explains that the US was able to manipulate international law to portray Iraq as the violator of law, but at the same time Iraqis had waged a successful legal campaign against the US during the Second Gulf War by preventing the US from obtaining a UN approval for the invasion. However, Iraq's legal advantage did not translate into a political or legal advantage for them. Such detailed studies done by Chinese scholars under the aegis of their government shows the extent of seriousness China attaches to legal warfare as part of 3Ws strategy.[1]

Lawfare in Territorial Boundary Disputes

The Case of South China Sea

China's aggressive attempt to claim land in South China Sea, by building artificial islands in the disputed areas and at the same time threatening opposition party during the negotiations and preventing them from going on with any lawful activities in the entire region, through 3Ws as well physical presence (such as preventing Vietnam's and other countries such as the Philippines oil exploration projects along with other country from taking place, preventing their fishing vessels to enter the zone by verbally threatening and ordering the other country vessel to leave the area, sending Chinese own oil rigs, and fishing vessels and even military vessels and equipment to the disputed territories such as Scarborough Showl/Mischief Reef) is considered to be an attempt to pre-empt any legal claims by other countries on South China Sea. Apart from land reclamation, China also passed a series of domestic legislations aimed at legitimizing the 9-dash line which encompasses vast swathes of South China Sea. China went as far as to distribute the maps in United Nations meeting once and the United States Office of Secretary of Defense in its 2010 went on to say, in its annual military report on China that Beijing "appears to be making concerted efforts through enacting domestic legislation inconsistent with international law, misreading the negotiations and text of UNCLOS and overlooking decades of state practice" in order to solidify its claims (Deo, 2017).

Taking on China's Legal Warfare: The Imperfect Case of South China Sea

This legal warfare by China in South China Sea was fought head on by the Philippines, when it filed a case under UNCLOS against China's aggressive assertion of its claim in South China Sea on historical basis. The tribunal constituted under the Permanent Court of Arbitration in Hague, to adjudicate on this, decisively ruled against China. The Significant conclusions that emerged from the 500-odd page verdict are:

> ➤ China has no legitimate claim to exercise "sovereign rights" within its nine-dash-line in the South China Sea.

> ➤ The maritime region around Mischief Reef and Second Thomas Shoal are within the Exclusive Economic Zone of the Philippines, granting it the sole right to exploitation of natural resources.

> ➤ China has a positive obligation not to impede Filipino fishing vessels from exercising their EEZ rights, and to prevent Chinese fishermen from exploiting the same resources.

> ➤ China's island building activities and conduct in the Mischief Reef — not the Second Thomas Shoal — constitute a violation of its obligations under the UN Convention on the Law of the Sea (UNCLOS) to preserve the marine ecosystem and settle maritime disputes peacefully.

> ➤ The UN Convention on the Law of the Sea enjoys absolute primacy as the arbiter of maritime disputes. (Sukumar, 2016)

The legal basis of China's claim on South China Sea was quashed through this judgment and shows the weakness of Chinese legal argument in this case, and also how Beijing can be argued against and won. However, South China Sea is a case of imperfect warfare by the Philippines. It is one thing that China called this verdict "null and void" as it refused to participate in the adjudication from the beginning, in spite of being a signatory to UNCLOS. It is another thing that China continued its activities with much more vigour in South China Sea immediately after the verdict. At the same time, Beijing unleashed a 3Ws against the Philippines and the international community supporting the Philippines. Supplemented with a diplomatic onslaught, this resulted in the Philippines succumbing to the Chinese pressure, as expected out of it by Beijing, and also achieved some success in undermining the coalescence of consensus in support of the ruling (Kania, 2016).

China's continuous aggressive posture and Lawfare against the disputing countries in South China Sea despite losing international arbitration saw some South China Sea littoral states (the Philippines, Malaysia, Indonesia exception being Vietnam) concede to China and agree to settle it bilaterally than multilaterally through ASEAN, invariably allowing China to dictate the terms favourable for itself. In fact, China has succeeded in dividing the ASEAN countries on this matter, which was clearly visible when all countries except Vietnam voted for a Chinese dictated Code of Conduct in South China Sea, to be followed by all SCS littoral states this year.

The case of South China Sea shows that while China's Lawfare can be countered legally and even be won, it requires continuous political will to not succumb to China's Lawfare strategy supplemented with the other two strategies given China's money, muscle and might.

The Case of Doklam: Another Model in Making to Deal with China's Lawfare?

The Doklam issue saw the 3Ws strategies being used against India in full swing given the Chinese media reportage, a full-scale diplomatic offensive by the Chinese side which used Lawfare extensively. Here again, China used a century old 1890 Treaty between British India and China as the legal basis to support its road construction activity in Doklam plateau. China went on to release a 15-page position paper during the stand-off to validate its actions (in line with using domestic legislations to support legal claims strategy) and the subsequent confrontation with the Bhutanese and the Indian army respectively[2].

China claims that Doklam, according to the 1890 Treaty has been delineated as part of China, formally reaffirmed several times (selectively quoting Nehru's letter to Zhou En Lai while leaving the contradicting other parts) and that China has sovereign rights over it which legitimizes its road construction activities in the area. This subsequently makes India's intervention to stop the road building activity illegal.

However, if one looks closely, this argument actually doesn't have any legal grounds. The1890 Treaty, first of all is a contradiction in itself because the first and second article of the treaty go against each other. While the first article says Doklam, the tri-junction point between India, China, and Bhutan will mark the boundary between India and Tibet, the second article says the boundary will be based on watershed principle by which Mount Gimpochen will mark the boundary line between India and Tibet. This leads to a question of which article holds good.

However, this question need not be addressed because subsequently as the countries attained independence, and established themselves, all three countries have established bilateral mechanisms and have signed separate treaties to settle the disputed boundaries. The most important treaties to be seen are the 1988 and 1998 China- Bhutan agreement and 2012 India-China agreement (which Shiv Shanker Menon, former. Ambassador said are the guidelines agreed upon by India and China to settle boundary issues) on boundary disputes. Close readings of these agreements reveal that Doklam area is still disputed and Bhutan and China have agreed to settle the dispute bilaterally, while pledging to not unilaterally change the status quo on ground by any means. At the same time, since it is a tri-junction point, it has been agreed between India and China that such tri-junctions in boundaries will be settled after consultation with all three countries, rather than bilaterally between Bhutan and China.

Going by this, it is seen how the 1890 treaty which China bases its argument on is completely irrelevant and immaterial to the current proceedings. However, China continues to insist on the legality of this agreement. At the same time, it shows how China's road building activity is actually actions to pre-empt legal claims by changing status quo on ground.

China's argument that India unilaterally intervened and violated Chinese sovereignty also holds no ground. As seen above, the area is still disputed and hence there is no Chinese sovereignty to violate. Second, Bhutan issued a demarche[3] to China to stop its road building activity and refrain from changing status quo, which did not get any response from China, resulting in Bhutan informing India about the Chinese actions and soliciting its help to stop Chinese construction activities. This was based on a 2007 friendship agreement signed between Bhutan and India that stated if any action threatens national security of the other country, both the countries will consult each other and act accordingly. Given the location of Doklam plateau right next the strategically important Siliguri corridor or Chicken neck which connects to the Northeast India, Bhutan informed India and at the same time asked India to stop the construction activities. On this account, India intervened by sending in its troops to the disputed region and stopping the Chinese troops from undertaking any construction activities. [4] This resulted in a tense eyeball-to-eyeball confrontation between two nuclear powers.

While China released daily statements and a 15-page white paper to legitimize its actions with a media blitzkrieg, Bhutan and India resorted to issuing a demarche and two diplomatic statements detailing the treaties and agreements signed between them and China, respectively, showing that Chinese legal arguments hold no ground. At the same time, Bhutan and India, together denied China any opportunity, to change the status quo on ground by the military stand-off which if not done would have resulted in favour of China.

India created a stalemate by physically denying China any opportunity to change the status-quo and prevented China from creating facts on grounds to support its legal claims. Given that China wanted to win a war without having bullets fired, and India and Bhutan both denied this opportunity to

China, by standing up to it militarily, this military standoff thus temporarily came to an end, due to internal and external factors influencing both the countries situation.

This Lawfare of China was not fought in any courts, as it happened in South China Sea, but rather physically on ground with military standoffs, and the same in media. However, the opposing parties refused to succumb to Chinese pressure and called Beijing's bluff off, effectively winning the Lawfare by bringing the Chinese back to the diplomatic table. This is a temporary win given the troops are still there in the region and China has still not stopped clamouring about its legal arguments. However, if the political will to not succumb to China's 3Ws strategy as shown now is carried on, the win will be permanent. Thus, Doklam offers a new playbook to counter Chinese Lawfare. The South China Sea littoral states, may take a page from this new playbook, deny Beijing the objectives it wants to achieve, and translate their legal advantage into political advantage to win against China.

References

India-China Relations. (2016, January). Retrieved from Ministry of External Affairs: https://www.mea.gov.in/Portal/ForeignRelation/China_Jan_2016.pdf

Field, C. B. (2012). *IPCC MANAGING THE RISKS OF EXTREME EVENTS AND DISASTERS TO ADVANCE CLIMATE CHANGE ADAPTATION.* New York: Cambridge University Press.

Wuthnow, J. (2016, April 16). *Water War: This River could Sink China-India Relations.* Retrieved from The National Interest: http://nationalinterest.org/feature/water-war-river-could-sink-china-india-relations-15829?page=2

Nambiar, M. (2015). A Decade of Disaster Risk Management in India. *Economic and Political Weekly.*

Singh, A. (2013). China's 'Three Warfares' and India. *Journal of Defense Studies.*

Halper, S. (2013). *China: The Three Warfares.* Cambridge: University of Cambridge.

Deo, A. (2017, July 7). *Standoff on the Doklam Plateau: Another instance of Chinese warfare.* Retrieved July 11, 2017, from Observer Research Foundation,: http://

www.orfonline.org/expert-speaks/standoff-doklam-plateau-another-instance-chinese-lawfare/

Yanrong, H. (2006). *Legal Warfare: Military Legal Work's High Ground: An Interview with Chinese Politics and Law University Military Legal Research Center Special Researcher Xun Dandong.* Legal Daily (PRC).

Kania, E. (2016). The PLA's Strategic Thinking on Three Warfares. *China Brief.*

Cheng, D. (2012). *Winning Without Fighting: Chinese Public Opinion Warfare and the Need for a Robust American Response.* Heritage Foundation.

Cheng, D. (2013.). *Winning Without Fighting: The Chinese Psychological Warfare Challenge.* Heritage Foundation.

Sukumar, A. M. (2016, July 12). *The Wire.* Retrieved July 16, 2017, from South China Sea Case: A Guide to the Verdict: https://thewire.in/51045/the-hague-verdict-is-a-big-victory-for-the-philippines-but-not-for-the-south-china-sea-dispute/

Endnotes

1   For more, see ZongWenshen, Legal Warfare: Discussion of 100 Examples and Solutions (Beijing, PRC: PLA Publishing House, 2004)

2   See Ministry of Foreign Affairs of People's Republic of China, Position Paper on Doklam, http://in.china-embassy.org/eng/embassy_news/P020170802545119276265.pdf

3   See Ministry of Foreign Affairs, Royal Government of Bhutan, Press Statement, June 29, 2017 http://www.mfa.gov.bt/?p=4799 Accessed on June 30, 2017

4   See Ministry of External Affairs, India, Press release on Recent Developments in Doklam Area, June 30, 2017,http://mea.gov.in/press-releases.htm?dtl/28572/Recent+Developments+in+Doklam+Area Accessed on July 1, 2017

Changing World and the Threat

Creating World and Other Poems

The Impact of Climate Change on Natural Disasters in India

Ms. Bhavya A G

Introduction

Climate change is among the many non-traditional security threats which impacts India, and is also a global challenge. It represents one of the biggest challenges to mankind. Global climate change affects almost every aspect of human existence. The steady environmental degradation has taken a huge toll on the existence of life on Earth. It has altered the ecosystem that has led to extinction of distinct flora and fauna. The World Bank in 2016 has estimated that 12.6 million deaths annually are due to climate change.[1] It has already shown impact on food, water, and energy security, demography, health and economy of a nation. One of the major impact of climate change is the increasing occurrences of natural disasters with increasing complexity and destructive capacity. In the past, natural disasters were linked to climate change, on a short-term natural variability but with climate change manifesting at an unprecedented rate, the two forces can cause high level of destruction. Climate change, "refers to a change in the state of the climate that can be identified (e.g. using statistical tests) by changes in the mean and/ or the variability of its properties, and that persists for an extended period, typically decades or longer."[2]

The South Asian region faces daunting climate related problems due to rising temperatures, low lying lands, and higher precipitation levels. The region is also highly vulnerable to natural disasters. The worst affected countries due to natural disasters were reported to be India, Bangladesh and Pakistan. These forces also can have potential impact on the people, as South Asia consists of ¼ of world population. Recent occurrences of natural disasters in India are evidences of the dangerous impact of climate change. Examples: In 2013-14 India witnessed several major natural disasters-Uttarakhand floods (2013), Orissa cyclone (2013), floods in Andhra Pradesh (2013, 2014), and droughts in Maharashtra.[3]

The melting of Himalayan ice caps, rising sea levels, increase in temperature have affected all aspects of life. In India, nearly 59% per cent of the landmass is prone to earthquakes of moderate to very high intensity; over 40 million hectares (12%) of land is prone to floods and river erosion; close to 5,700 kms, out of the 7,516 kms long coastline is prone to cyclones and tsunamis; 68% of cultivable area is vulnerable to droughts; and, the hilly areas are at risk from landslides and avalanches.[4] A large volume of population, high density of the population, low lying coastal areas and an economy closely tied to the natural resource base, intensifies India's vulnerability. As it is not possible to have an exact assessment of the estimate of damage due to climate change, it is important for India to be aware of the associated risks so as to think through its strategies carefully on the national as well as global level.

For India, tackling climate change and the associated risks of natural disasters becomes important as India is a growing power and in case of extreme events, valuable resources would go into handling these events, impeding growth. This paper attempts to study the increased threats of natural disasters in India due to adverse effects of climate change and its impact on India's growth profile.

Linking Climate Change and Natural Disasters

Definitions of the concepts:

Natural Hazards: "Natural process or phenomenon that may cause loss of life, injury or other health impacts, property damage, loss of livelihoods and services, social and economic disruption or environmental damage."[5]

Natural Disaster: "A serious disruption of the functioning of a community or a society involving widespread human, material, economic or environmental losses and impacts, which exceeds the ability of the affected community or society to cope using its own resources."[6]

Natural hazards are balancing templates on Earth. These geo-physical events occur periodically to maintain equilibrium between external and internal environment.[7] Natural hazards are part of the natural climate system and have occurred, even before the onset of human civilization. However, in human habitation, natural hazards lead to natural disasters. While natural variability continues to play a key role in climatological disasters, climate change has shifted the odds and changed the natural limits, making certain types of disasters much more frequent and more intense.[8] When climate change increases the frequency and magnitude of certain natural hazards, it leads to natural disasters. The *Centre for Research on the Epidemiology of Disasters* (CRED) Report of 2007 states," there is increasingly conclusive evidence which confirms that global climate change will have an impact on the occurrence and magnitude of extreme events. These impacts are envisaged to increase human vulnerability to natural disasters, thus emphasising the need for improved measures of preparedness in every part of the world".[9] The *Intergovernmental Panel on Climate Change* (IPCC) AR4 indicated that, "increased confidence that some weather events and extremes will become more frequent, more widespread and/or more intense during the 21st century and the impacts due to altered frequencies and intensities of extreme weather, climate, and sea level events are very likely to change."[10] These reports are based on the observation of past and present trends of natural disasters. The increasing events of natural disasters had led researchers to probe deeper and establish a link between climate changes and increasing events of natural disasters. There is evidence from observational data that weather and climate extremes have changed since 1950 due to the human impact on the climate system.[11] Heat waves have increased over Europe, Australia, and Asia. A hottest day that used to occur once every 20 years is likely to occur once every other year by the end of the twenty-first century in most areas around the globe. WHO in 2016 reported that globally, the number of reported weather-related natural disasters has more than tripled since the 1960s. Every year, these disasters result in over 60 000 deaths, mainly in developing countries.[12]

Natural hazards occurred in the past and are going to occur in the future, however, the environment under which they will occur is changing increasingly and this will have significant impact on the frequency and intensity of the hazards resulting in disasters.

The Impact of Climate Change in India

Climate change is likely to adversely affect the occurrence and destructive force of the following natural disasters:

1) **Cyclones, Storm Surges, Coastal Flooding**

Coastal lines have been focus of variety of activities such as fishing, recreation, and settlements. UNEP has reported that nearly 40 million Indians will be at risk from rising sea levels by 2050, with people in Mumbai and Kolkata having the maximum exposure to coastal flooding. The sea levels could rise by 18 to 59 cm by 2099. Since 1870, global sea level has risen by about 20 cm at an average rate of 1.7 mm/year. But in recent decades, the rate has risen sharply to 2.5 mm/year. Between 1901 and 2007, it registered a mean temperature rise of 1.62°C. The sea levels around the coastal cities are rising by 2.4 mm every year.[13] The IPCC has projected that sea level rise could result in flooding of the habitats of millions of people especially along the coastlines. Almost 60% of the sea level rise will be in South Asia. (The seas will be 40cms higher than present by the end of 21st century). Sea level rise is expected along the coast from Pakistan through India, Sri Lanka, Bangladesh and Myanmar from change in world's climate and their impact. The sea level rise not only inundates land but also increases the salinization impact of waves and storm surges. Ocean acidification leads to warming of oceans. Warmer oceans expand giving more rise to sea level problems. Warming oceans absorb less and less carbon-di-oxide and this will lead to more rise in the temperature. The projected rise in sea level due to greenhouse warming may affect the storm surges in the Bay of Bengal and consequently the coastal flooding. The combined effects of sea level rise and storm surges are extremely dangerous to the population around Bay of Bengal. Council of Scientific and Industrial Research (CSIR) showed an increased occurrence of cyclones in Bay of Bengal under climate change. The risk to the Eastern coast of India could be aggravated due to increase in sea level. The resource depletion and environmental stress can lead to large scale migration in the Sunderban Island. The island is also prone to recurrent coastal flooding, embankment failure, severe cyclones and storm surges. The embankments built to protect from flooding have worn out with time, and the river beds raised by siltation, this has created conditions for total wash out during cyclone and storm surges. The warming of the oceans also causes changes in the strength of tropical cyclones, storms, typhoons, and hurricanes. The rising seas have started affecting the fishing communities in India. Not only they face the problems of land inundation, but also losses to their livelihood, as the number of fishes are decreasing. Therefore, ultimately it would damage coastal infrastructure, aquaculture and coastal tourism, due to erosion of the sandy beaches. The diverse impact is expected as a result of sea level rise which includes increased flooding of low lying coastal area, land loss and population displacement, loss of yield and employment resulting from inundation and salinization. However, the extent of vulnerability depends not just on the physical exposure to sea level rise, (and the population affected), but also on the extent of economic activity of the areas and capacity to cope with impacts. The extended deep-depression in the mountain regions are increasing the strength of cyclonic winds, making them lethal day by day.

2) Droughts

Climate change will result in many parts of the country suffering from recurrent droughts and battling water scarcity, while others reel from floods. The change in India's climate is most likely to manifest through disruptions in the monsoon cycle. Such changes will include longer dry periods in most parts of Gangetic plains, the forested central uplands, and the Himalayan region and in Western India, affecting the availability of water in those areas. The 2010 assessment report by the Ministry of Environmental and Forest Affairs (MoFA), suggests that the Himalayan region will experience moderate to extreme severity drought from 2030 onwards. The changes in the pattern, intensity and frequency of rainfall will have significant impact on floods. Climatic changes could result in more frequent high-intensity rainfall. UNFCC has projected that Kutch, Saurashtra regions are likely to face acute scarcity of water, as are the river basins of Mahi, the Pennar, the Sabarmati and the Tapti.[14] Climate change related melting of the glaciers could seriously affect half a billion people in the Himalaya, Hindu-Kush region who depend on glacial melt to meet their water needs. Himalayan glaciers have lost about 10 percent of their volume in the past four decades. The rate has doubled since the 1970s. Majority of the glaciers are retreating (melting) at varying rates from 5-20 meter per year. Dokriani glacier in Bhagirathi basin is retreating between 15 and 20 meters per year since 1995 whereas Chorabari glacier in the Alaknanda basin is retreating 9-11 meter per year (2003-2014).[15] The increasing rate of the glacial melt suggests that the Ganga, Indus, Brahmaputra and other rivers that crisscross the northern plains may become seasonal rivers in the near future as a consequence of climate change. This will affect the river dependent economies. This is also projected to drastically cut down water availability downstream plains of UP and Bihar. Such glacial melting could lead to floods, acute shortage of drinking water, threats from water borne diseases. Glacial melt and low rainfall will play havoc with the mountain environment, successive droughts will disrupt and perhaps in the end destroy the country's agriculture, and the forest will often change beyond recognition.

3) Floods

The Himalayas, Western Ghats, coastal areas and north east are likely to experience floods exceeding the existing magnitude by 10-30%. The glacial melting in the Himalayan Mountains could lead to sudden flash floods causing damage to life and property of people. The river Godavari, Brahmani and Mahanadi, will have severe flood conditions. The lakes in Nepal and Bhutan are filling rapidly with water due to the melting of glaciers and surrounding snow areas. A dangerous situation may be created because once the high-altitude lakes reach their peak levels, they could burst banks. The quantity of water involved could be so vast, that it could spread to hundreds of kilometers along the valley affecting people's lives and property.

4) Landslides

Landslides can affect large areas of the country every year during monsoons. They can also be caused by earthquakes. The areas that suffer from landslide hazards are located in the hilly tracts of the Himalayas, Northeast India, Nilgiris, Eastern Ghats and Western Ghats. With the melting of the glaciers in the Hindukush-Karakorum Himalaya region, and the foreseeable increase in heavy rain events, and the incidences of landslides are likely to increase. The erratic rainfall as a result of climate change further increases the incidents of landslides.

Impact of These Disasters

Natural disasters directly impact economy, infrastructure, health and sanitation, food and water resources, thus impacting lives of people. Hence it is one of the single largest concerns of developing nations. The burden of the natural disasters falls heavily on the developing nations. The disaster risks are related to the economic development of these nations. The poorest of the communities are most at risk as they tend to live in risk-prone areas such as floodplains or unstable slopes. The limited assets also increase the chances such as they live in poorly built houses, are dependent on climate sensitive sectors such as agriculture, have limited ability to cope with disasters and limited access to technology and emergency services. The migrations for these people are difficult as they are entirely dependent on coastal resources for their livelihood.

India is already battling high population and rapidly increasing urbanization. The population of India is forecast to be around 1.4 thousand million by 2020.[16] The urban population is growing faster than the rural population. The coastal megacities of Chennai, Calcutta and Mumbai lie generally only a few meters above sea level.[17] The high population pressure combined with increasing cyclone intensity and sea-level rise will put millions of people and their livelihood at risk of being hit by storm and flood disasters.

With rapid development of coastal areas, industrialization and urbanization, more populations are becoming vulnerable to climate-associated calamities and many have no choice but to move to safer places. It is estimated that approximately 142 million people may inhabit coastal India in 2050 and India's total number of flood zone refugees alone could be anywhere between 20 and 60 million, with 30 million as a conservative figure.[18]

The geophysical changes due to climate change and natural disasters will lead to soil erosion and increase in vector borne diseases. The variation in temperature and erratic monsoon, the soil erosion due to floods and sea level rise will create food and water scarcity leading to malnutrition and under nutrition. It will also affect the livelihood of people dependent on subsistence sectors. These adverse impacts on human security would bear on national security as well. The climate change impact can also affect agro based industries, urban and rural infrastructure and tourism. Agricultural output and the lives of people dependent on agriculture is largely to be affected during to cyclones, floods, droughts or erratic rainfall.[19] There could be more hunger, more law and order problems, overcrowding of cities as a result of food and water scarcity. Due to inadequate public health systems and low adaptation capacity, there would be greater strain on governments' resources. Climate change could create chronic economic problems including unemployment. Unemployed youth could take to militancy, terrorism and organised crime. It could create fresh conflicts due to environmental reasons and also aggravate the existing conflicts.

The financial setbacks that disasters could inflict can be ruinous, in contrast to its developed counterparts, as disasters, disrupt short term financial and economic management by diverting resources for relief programmes. These disruptions would necessitate realignment in spending plans, adjustments in economic targets and changes in economic policy and have negative long-term consequences for economic growth, development and poverty reduction.

India could also face bilateral problems with neighbouring countries due to climate changes and increased risk of disasters. For instance, a large number of environmental refugees could come to India from Bangladesh thereby altering the demographic balance in the Indian states. Environmental Refugees are those groups of people who have had to leave their habitat either temporarily or permanently because of the potential environmental hazards of disruption in their life supporting ecosystems.[20]

Migrations could also take place from Sri Lanka, Maldives and Nepal. With the increased risk of natural disasters migrants might be the direct cause of tensions between India and neighbors.[21] Conflicts due to river-sharing could arise between India and China, India and Bangladesh, India and Pakistan. Tensions between Sri Lanka and India could also ensue over fishing zones considering the rising sea levels.

The frequency and intensity of natural disasters including cyclones, floods and famines could increase greater strain on the armed forces in disaster management. The border security forces will have to deal with increased migration flows from the neighbouring countries. Increasing incidents of disasters could increase the pressure for Indian military forces to participate in increasing humanitarian assistance, disaster relief and evacuation operations. This had manifested in the Tsunami of 2004, Cyclones in Bangladesh of 2008, and Cyclone in Myanmar 2008.[22] The recurrent deployment of the forces to assist disaster relief will require realignment in force structuring, equipment standards, operating procedures, and training principles. The armed forces may also be compelled to change their war-fighting doctrines and operations in light of climate change. The meltdown of the Himalayan glaciers has its own military implications such as disruption of the communication networks. Rapid melting of snow would cause flash floods downstream which would make movement of troops difficult.

India has signed bi-lateral maritime agreements with Maldives, Sri Lanka, Indonesia, Thailand, and Myanmar and three tri-lateral agreements with Sri Lanka and the Maldives; Indonesia and Thailand; Myanmar and Thailand.[23] As a result, the maritime boundary with the countries with the exception of Pakistan has been settled. The contention with Pakistan is on the Sir Creek area. The rise in sea levels leading to inundation would alter the baseline points which could give rise to new tensions. Climate change induced shifts in the marine ecosystems would alter fishing zones and coastal navigation zones.

Maintaining access and containing instability in the mineral and other resource rich areas is likely to increase in importance, alongside wider developmental and stabilisation roles. Military intervention may be required to protect the integrity of sites where resources are located, and to secure investments.

Around 95 per cent of India's trading by volume and 70 per cent by value is done through maritime transport.[24] Rise in sea level and the increased threat of storm surges and cyclones would have severe implications on shipping operations. Naval operations such as weapon firing, maintenance of schedules and crew can be affected due to extreme weather events.

Defence spending may reduce because of the increasing disasters. Governments may increasingly modify the priority that is afforded to defence, in the light of the increased imperatives for disaster risk reduction, and other changes in the dynamics of security. If there is failure to achieve self-sustaining development progress following major disasters, it will most likely pose instability risks, with impacts on neighbours and the international system. The scale and intensification of these risks is likely to elicit military responses as national interests would be threatened. (Nambiar, 2015)

Recommendations

A nations' ability to prevent, mitigate, respond and recover from catastrophic events is increasingly being recognised as a prime driver for national security and strategic growth.[25] However, much would depend upon how India manages environmental, political and demographic challenges and importantly the emerging challenge of climate change and the unexpected shocks to the economy due to increasing threat of natural disasters. The exposure and experience from past disasters has brought disaster risk reduction and effective disaster management into forefront. The level of intensity and degree of loss raise the question regarding effectiveness and preparedness of disaster risk management in India. India's high poverty level and increasing rate of urbanization intensifies India's vulnerability to the impact of natural hazards and climate change. In the 12th Five Year plan the GOI estimated that 1 trillion will be required to bridge the gap over the next two decades.[26]

In India, disaster management is under the National Disaster Management Authority (NDMA). Under the NDMA, SDMA at the state level and DDMA at the district level. The effectiveness of the Disaster management framework was put to test during the Orissa cyclone of 2013. The low loss of lives despite the severity of the cyclones was successful on the part of government the state and central level. However, not all states are equally prepared which was the case during the Uttarakhand floods which, makes it imperative on all states to strengthen their disaster reduction and management mechanisms at state as well as district levels.

> The framework also has to integrate the local bodies at the rural and urban level which though recognised are not sufficiently utilized. Government policies usually focus on mitigating disasters. However, an effective policy will have to involve mitigation and adaptation.

> Adaptation is a neglected aspect both in disaster risk reduction and climate change talks. Adaptation in the forms of poverty reduction, progressive economic development, shifting of economic activities from primary sectors into less prone economic activities, effective mechanisms to cope with urbanization, better access of technology in risk prone areas.

> Building codes and regulations have to be adhered to during construction.

> Pro-active community participation-example: training local masons, distributing resilient building construction plans, shelters managed by the community.

> Involve in long term risk financing plans with the help of community or partnerships, and providing incentives are some of the recommendations which should be done on a priority basis.

Endnotes

1   An Estimated 12.6 Million Deaths Each Year Are Attributable to Unhealthy Environments". *World Health Organization*.N.p., 2017.

2   *Some major disasters in India*. (n.d.). Retrieved from National Disaster Management Authority: http://www.ndma.gov.in/en/disaster-data-statistics. html

3   *Glossary of terms*. (n.d.). Retrieved from IPCC: www.ipcc.ch/ipccreports

4   *Disaster Vulnerability Profile*. (n.d.). Retrieved from National Disaster Management Authority: http://www.ndma.gov.in/en/vulnerability-profile.html

5   Sandra Banholzer, J. K. (2014). The Impact of Climate Change on Natural Disasters. In Z. Singh, *Reducing Disaster: Early Warning Systems for Climate Change* (pp. 25). Illionos : Springer.

6   Sandra Banholzer, J. K. (2014). The Impact of Climate Change on Natural Disasters. In Z. Singh, *Reducing Disaster: Early Warning Systems for Climate Change* (pp. 25). Illionos : Springer.

7   Mishra, A. (2014). An Assessment of Climate Change-Natural Disaster Linkage in Indian Context . *Geology and Geosciences*, 2.

8   Ibid, p.2

9   Chauhan, S. (2009). Climate Change, Natural Disasters and India. In IDSA, *Security Implications of Climate Change for India* (pp. 74). New Delhi: Academic Foundation.

10 Ibib, p 74

11 Field, C. B. (2012). *IPCC MANAGING THE RISKS OF EXTREME EVENTS AND DISASTERS TO ADVANCE CLIMATE CHANGE ADAPTATION*. New York: Cambridge University Press.

12 Ibid

13 Climate Change and Health". *World Health Organization*.N.p., 2017.

14 Pandve, H. T. (2010, January). Climate change and coastal mega cities of India. *Indian Journal of Occupational and Environmental Medicine*, 22-23. Retrieved from NCBI.

15 Chauhan, S. (2009). Climate Change, Natural Disasters and India. In IDSA, *Security Implications of Climate Change for India* (pp. 77). New Delhi: Academic Foundation.

16 Population Estimates and Projections | Data". *Data.worldbank.org*.

17   Glaciers Melting At 5 To 20 Meter Rate Annually, Says Government".(2016). *The Indian Express*.

18 Chauhan, S. (2009). Climate Change, Natural Disasters and India. In IDSA, *Security Implications of Climate Change for India* (pp. 85). New Delhi: Academic Foundation.

19 Dasgupta, P. (2012). Economics and Adaptation to Climate Change. In IDSA, *Security Implications of Climate Change* (pp. 105-126). New Delhi: Academic Foundation.

20 Mohan, I. (2002). *Environmental Problems in 21st Century.* New delhi: Anmol Publications.

21 Uttam Kumar Sinha, S. D. (2012). Impact on India's Bilateral Relations with Neighbouring Countries. In IDSA, *Security Implications of Climate Change* (pp. 127-141). New Delhi: Academic Foundation.

22 Sunil Chauhan, P. G. (2012). Impact on Warfighting Capability of the Indian Military. In IDSA, *Security Implications of Climate Change for India* (pp. 142-158). New delhi: Academic Foundation.

23 Uttam Kumar Sinha, S. D. (2012). Impact on India's Bilateral Relations with Neighbouring Countries. In IDSA, *Security Implications of Climate Change* (pp. 127-141). New Delhi: Academic Foundation.

24 India, and Shipping India. "Ports In India: Market Size, Investments, Economic Development, Govt Initiatives | IBEF". *Ibef.org*.

25 Chauhan, S. (2009). Climate Change, Natural Disasters and India. In IDSA, *Security Implications of Climate Change for India* (pp. 90). New Delhi: Academic Foundation

26 Nambiar, M. (2015). A Decade of Disaster Risk Management in India. *Economic and Political Weekly*.

ISIS and India

Mr. Shantanu Roy-Chaudhury

The so-called Islamic State of Iraq and Syria (ISIS)/Daesh rose from sectarian tensions in Iraq and the civil war in Syria. The terrorist organisation follows the fundamentalist Wahhabi and Salafist strain of Sunni Islam. According to this ideology, Muslims must strive to spread and implement Islam in all areas of life by liberating the lands of Islam from other cultures (especially Western culture) through jihad (holy war), which is perceived as the personal duty of every Muslim.[1] The group declares itself to be a caliphate and claims religious, political, and military authority over all Muslims all over the world.[2] The rise of ISIS in such a short span has been alarmingly quick. Unlike other terrorist organisations in the area, they were able to successfully capture and hold on to land under their leader Abu Bakr al-Baghdadi. ISIS is not just any ordinary terrorist organisation.

There was a notion that the crisis in Iraq and Syria would not have an impact on India due to the fact that India is geographically far away. However, ISIS released a list of countries they intended to go to war with in order to secure an Islamic World Dominion. According to them, Muslim rights were being violated in these countries. India features in this list and thus, ISIS has made threats against India; along with the fact that India was also part of the imagined Khorasan territory of the ancient caliphate which ISIS was seeking to recreate. India has the third largest Muslim population in the world, the majority of them Sunni, and therefore seemed to be a fertile recruitment ground for the organisation. The subcontinents main threat would stem from successful ISIS recruitment, lone wolf attacks, and attacks claimed by the group carried out by local militias.

Though ISIS vowed to wipe out the Shia Muslim and Hindu populations in the country, till date only a single attack has taken place with direct links to the organisation. An attack that injured ten passengers after a bomb went off in a train in Madhya Pradesh was the first successful terrorist strike by ISIS in the country.[3] We also see that only a handful of people have been successfully recruited by ISIS in the country, fewer than 90, according to reports. And within India, only 103 people have been arrested for ISIS related links or on suspicion of such ties, an inconsequential number in relative terms.[4] A report by the UN Security Council stated that there were more than 25,000 foreign fighters currently involved in jihadi conflicts. In comparison, Tunisia had the most foreign fighters in ISIS with around 6,500 members.[5] Overall, we can see that the terrorist organisation has been unsuccessful in India.

There are many reasons why ISIS has failed to gain a stronghold in India after more than two years of trying. Although India has its fair share of terrorist organisations within or across its borders, ISIS was not able to successfully penetrate the country and recruit many people. Some of this has to do with preparedness. India is neither inexperienced nor unaccustomed to dealing with terrorism, both at home and abroad. According to the Global Terrorism Index 2016, India ranked as the 8th most affected country by terrorist attacks.[6] Although India's loopholes in combating terrorism were exposed during the November 2008 Mumbai attacks, the country has in recent years taken important steps to improve its prevention and response capacity.

The government has initiated a series of steps to check the spread of ISIS, including the launch of a counter-radicalisation and de-radicalisation strategy. The government set up a 'war room' with a 24/7 center designed to continuously monitor social media. People with suspected links to ISIS were put under surveillance and were being observed by the authorities. Officials of Ministries of Home and Telecommunication and agencies like the Intelligence Bureau (IB), National Technical Research Organisation (NTRO) and Computer Emergency Response Team-India (CERTIn) also deliberated on immediate measures to combat the growing use of cyber space for spreading communal hatred.[7] Since ISIS has been highly successful in gaining followers through online recruitment, it was imperative that the government gave these measures a priority. The online recruitment policy is also not guaranteed to work in India as internet literacy is quite low among the lower middle classes and the poorer sections of the society.

Another major reason for ISIS' failure to penetrate India was the Indian Muslims reluctance to resort to extremism. This is grounded in India's historic roots of harmony, tolerance, mysticism and diversity.[8] In addition to strong family values, India has a very strong cultural and national identity that cuts across religious beliefs, which has played an important role in preventing radicalization.[9] Moreover, the majority of Muslims in India have historically also followed the Sufi strain of Islam, which is liberal and spiritual unlike the radical Wahhabi and Salafist strains followed by members of ISIS. Nearly 70,000 Indian Muslim clerics also signed a fatwa against ISIS and other terror groups, stating that they were not Islamic organisations. The head of the Dargah Aala Hazrat shrine at Ajmer, Rajasthan, where the fatwa was issued, stated that it was written in the Quran that killing one innocent person was equivalent to killing all of humanity.[10]

Politics also helps. In India, the Muslim community has traditionally been decently represented in the political sphere at different levels of administration and governance, thus they are not inclined towards joining a global caliphate and are ideologically and historically against it. Indian Prime Minister Modi also addressed a four-day conference of Sufi scholars in March 2016. This conference in New Delhi was attended by scholars from 20 countries and was held to promote tolerance as a counterpoint to the rise in terrorism and extremism. The Prime Minister's presence was seen as an outreach to Muslims and a bid to ease concerns that his Bharatiya Janata Party (BJP) is pursuing a Hindu revivalist agenda.[11]

India's liberal democracy and foreign policy also plays an important part in the positive relationship the community has with the government. Though India has been asked to play a more active role in the Middle East, the government has chosen not to join the U.S. - led coalition against ISIS. Apart from having enough internal and closer external problems to worry about, if India were to join the coalition, it could lead to the country's enormous diaspora of around seven million people being targeted by the terrorist organisation in the Middle East. There could also be a backlash in the form of heightened propaganda and radicalisation within India, resulting in an attack by ISIS. The decision to bomb ISIS could also face criticism from the Muslim community in India. Air strikes in the Middle East are not without casualties, and the destruction of life and holy places could be condemned by the community. The government also does not want to take drastic action which could instigate Shia-Sunni tensions within the country.

Sending troops to the Middle East might cause resentment among Indian Muslims and provide an opportunity to become a breeding ground for the various terrorist organisations.[12]

Yet another factor that prevents Indians from going to Syria and fighting for ISIS is how radicalised people from the subcontinent are viewed by the terrorist organisation. The fact that Indians are used as soldiers' ready to be sacrificed, which attributes to their high casualties along with other South Asians does not have a wide appeal. They are viewed as inferior to their Arab and western counterparts, and also receive worse salaries and accommodations. The belief that ISIS has mainly made Indian fighters carry out suicide attacks also deters ISIS sympathisers in India from going to fight for them. Though there is the potential risk of fighters returning to India to carry out attacks, most of those who have returned have been disillusioned after realizing that jihad was not as glamorous as it was made out to be, and that it was not what they had signed up for.

To prevent further radicalisation the government is also trying to reach out to vulnerable populations. Indian security agencies have studied other countries' practices in dealing with radicalised Muslim youth. The Home Ministry has favoured the Austrian model, which includes a counselling hotline run by non-profit groups instead of the police, and is in the process of implementing it. With the emphasis on counselling and not punishment, the idea is to provide professional help to 'de-radicalize' radicalized youngsters.[13] It is also important to educate those youth who do not have anything to do and might become disoriented and radicalized. The Ministry of Minority Affairs has been asked to implement various welfare and employment-oriented schemes, especially in the vulnerable pockets of the country for this sole reason.[14] Though poverty is not an indication of radicalization in India, steps need to be taken to reduce economic disparities between communities, to prevent poverty becoming a factor.

The country also needs to pay special attention to sensitive areas like Kashmir and the North East. The rise of ISIS may give a fillip to the jihadi forces in Kashmir and cross border terrorism as there have been previous linkages between the group and Pakistani terrorists.[15] The North East with its insurgencies could also become a breeding ground for terrorism as ISIS has been known to rely on local groups for help. Adequate care and importance needs to be given to developing and integrating these regions into the country, in a more significant way. In accordance with this, security at the borders needs to be increased. Cross border attacks like Pathankot and Uri are unnerving, and the prevention of terrorists crossing into India needs to become a priority.

In the event that an attack does manage to take place, we have seen from the November 2008 terror attacks in Mumbai that response time of the security forces plays an imperative role in tackling the situation. This called for specialised police teams being formed, trained, and organised in every state to act as first-responders without having to rely on national forces like the National Security Guard.[16]

Lately, the ISIS threat to India is diminishing. With ISIS loosing major ground due to the coalition air strikes, and its stronghold of Raqqa being taken back by the Syrian Democratic Forces, the organization has lost much of its power and reach. Due to foreign intervention, by November 2017, the Syrian Government managed to recapture Palmyra and Aleppo, establishing full control over the cities. With help, the Syrian army also successfully captured 400 towns, and 10,000 square kilometers of territory. This successful intervention has completely changed the dynamics in Syria as ISIS no longer has majority control over big cities and is proving to be less of a threat globally. 60,000 ISIS fighters have died since 2014, and its administration is no more.[17] Its impressive flow of propaganda which was imperative in gaining support has also ceased. However, in its retreat from Iraq and Syria, the terrorist organisation seems to be setting up and relocating its sanctuary to Afghanistan.[18] Due to the instability in the country, and the high level of terrorist activity, Afghanistan seems ideal for ISIS. Numerous attacks claimed by ISIS have taken place within Afghanistan, with the US military stating there are 600-800 ISIS fighters in the country.[19] ISIS doesn't seem to have been entirely defeated and has simply relocated. Due to their overall decline in the last year or two, the risk of extremists returning to their respective countries is higher than those leaving it and joining ISIS.

Lone Wolf Attacks

'Lone Wolf' attacks are now a greater threat than a direct confrontation with ISIS. Security forces have been strengthened and warned about the possibility of 'lone wolf' attacks taking place within the country. According to a senior intelligence official, "our biggest concern as of now is a 'lone wolf' type strike.

If a person decides to get a weapon and go on a killing spree or plant explosives somewhere without involving others, chances of detection are minimal."[20] These attacks are carried out by individuals, or small groups of people who do not have to have a direct link or funding from the terror group. These attacks usually do not have extensive planning and are extremely difficult for intelligence agencies to track and prevent. Lone wolf attacks like the Boston marathon bombing and the attacks in Paris are aimed at crowded areas with the purpose of inflicting as many casualties as possible. These attacks succeed in instilling fear into the people as they can happen anywhere at any point of time. ISIS has attempted to extend its region of terrorism by propagating its sympathizers in western countries to carry out these types of attacks. India remains highly vulnerable to these types of attacks. The countries heavy concentration of people in public areas offers a large number of potential targets.[21]

Conclusion

Although ISIS is not as major a threat at it used to be a few years ago, the terrorist organisation cannot completely be written off. As seen earlier, although defeated in Iraq and Syria, they now seem to have relocated to Afghanistan. India and the west however, should not treat the triumph in Iraq and Syria as a victory, as foreign fighters will now be looking at returning home, and ideologies, especially those inspired by religion, are hard to destroy. Thus, precautions need to be taken, especially against 'lone wolf' attacks which are unpredictable and a much greater threat to India than a 'mass casualty' attack directly by ISIS. On the positive side, the vast majorities of Indian Muslims have condemned ISIS, their actions, and ideologies, and have realised that it is threat to world peace.

Endnotes

1   The Meir Amit Intelligence and Terrorism Information Center – November 2014, ISIS: Portrait of a Jihadi Terrorist Organization, http://www.crethiplethi. com/isis-s-ideology-and-vision-and-their-implementation/islamic-countries/ syria-islamic-countries/2015/

2   RadwanMortada, 30th June 2014, what does ISIS' declaration of a caliphate mean? al-akbhar English, http://english.al-akhbar.com/node/20378

3   Hugh Tomlinson, 9th March 2017, Isis launches first strike on India with train attack, The Times, https://www.thetimes.co.uk/article/isis-launches-first-strike-on-india-with-train-attack-8kch9l06r

4   Ministry of Home Affairs, 20th December 2017

5   Jason Burke, 26th May 2016, Islamist fighters drawn from half the world's countries, says UN, The Guardian, http://www.theguardian.com/world/2015/ may/26/islamist-fighters-drawn-from-half-the-worlds-countries-says-un

6   Global Terrorism Index 2016, Institute for Economics & Peace, http:// economicsandpeace.org/wp-content/uploads/2016/11/Global-Terrorism-Index-2016.2.pdf

7   Abhishek Bhalla, 24th December 2015, India wants 24x7 war room to tackle cyber threat from ISIS, Mail Today, http://indiatoday.intoday.in/story/ government-plans-social-media-scanning-centre-to-take-on-isis/1/554878.html

8   Abhinav Pandya, 29th December 2015, Why ISIS Can't Make Much Headway with Muslims In India, The Huffington Post, http://www.huffingtonpost.in/ abhinav-pandya/why-isis-cant-make-much-h_b_8824410.html

9   RachitRanjan, MunshiZubaerHaque, 15th August 2015, Tackling the ISIS: Towards a Robust Indian Anti-Terrorism Policy, http://www.indrastra. com/2015/08/FEATURED-Tackling-ISIS-Indian-Anti-Terror-Policy-by-Rachit-Ranjan-and-Munshi-Zubaer-Haque.html

10   Caroline Mortimer, 11th December 2015, 70,000 Indian Muslim clerics issue fatwa against ISIS, the Taliban, al-Qaeda and other terror groups, Independent UK, http://www.independent.co.uk/news/world/asia/70000-indian-muslim-clerics -issue-fatwa-against-isis-the-taliban-al-qaida-and-other-terror-groups- a6768191. html

11 AnjanaPasricha, 17th March 2016, Indian PM Praises Islam at Sufi Conference, Voice of America, http://www.voanews.com/content/indian-prime-minister-praises-islam-sufi-conference/3242329.html

12 DevanikSaha, 14th January 2015, five reason why India should not join war on ISIS, daily O, http://www.dailyo.in/politics/five-reasons-why-india-should-not-join-war-on-isis-narendra-modi-barack-obama-pakistan/story/1/1504.html

13 Ronald Meinardus, 6th March 2015, Deaf Ears: India and the "Islamic State", The Globalist, http://www.theglobalist.com/deaf-ears-india-and-the-islamic-state/

14 May 9th, 2016, India Monitoring Social Networks To Combat ISIS Threat, NDTV, http://www.ndtv.com/india-news/india-monitoring-social-networks-to-combat-isis-threat-1404218

15 Chandra Mauli Singh, Proclamation of caliphate by ISIS: Challenges for India, http://www.academia.edu/7767788/Proclamation_of_caliphate_by_ISIS_Challenges_for_India

16 Ibid.

17 Jason Burke, 21st October 2017, The Guardian, https://www.theguardian.com/world/2017/oct/21/isis-caliphate-islamic-state-raqqa-iraq-islamist

18 Dan Falvey, 12th December 2017, ISIS could be preparing to form new home in Afghanistan after losing war in Iraq and Syria, Express, https://www.express.co.uk/news/world/891155/isis-news-terrorism-syria-iraq-afghanistan-new-home-extremist-terror-attack

19 Steve Almasy, 14th April 2017, ISIS in Afghanistan: A battle against increased threats, CNN, https://edition.cnn.com/2017/04/13/middleeast/isis-afghanistan/index.html

20 Abhishek Bhalla, 14th June 2016, Orlando-style lone wolf attack worries intelligence agencies, Mail Today, http://indiatoday.intoday.in/story/spectre-of-orlando-style-lone-wolf-attacks-worries-intel/1/691235.html

21 Vivek Chadha, 10th December 2015, Lone Wolf Attacks: An Assessment in the Indian Context, Policy Brief, IDSA, http://www.idsa.in/policybrief/lone-wolf-attacks_vchaddha_101215

The Need for Global Cyber Laws

Mr. Aditya G.S

Introduction and the Need for Laws

The world is getting digitalized and the services of internet have reached common people to a great extent. Adding to it, a large amount of information in the contemporary world is being stored in the form of data, either in a computer or in some other electronic form. Thus, taking an advantage of it, many countries would extract, espionage or misuse, the available information of a country thus, preparing itself for a cyber-attack. A cyber-attack is an attack conducted through cyberspace. These attacks may target either the public or national and corporate organizations. Whenever, a nation state tries to penetrate into another nation's computer network in order to damage it, it is called as Cyber Warfare[1]. This Cyber war is no longer a fiction, it has already begun[2]. Nations are hacking into other networks and infrastructures laying down logic bombs and trap doors, in peacetime.

This war which is fought in cyber space has no geographical boundaries or territories. Cyberspace is neutral and vast. The US department of defence defines that "cyberspace is a domain characterized by the use of computers and other electronic devices to store, modify and exchange data via networked systems and associated physical infrastructures"[3]. These attacks happening through cyberspace happens in various kinds and categories. However, the attackers are broadly divided into 3 categories and they are: cyber criminals, non-state actors and state sponsored attackers. The attacks are used mainly for financial and data theft, revenge, prestige, promotion of political cause, and the individual or group of individuals who use this, are called cyber criminals. However, when a state sponsors citizens or cyber criminals to carry out espionage and conduct covert operations for politics and state operations, they are called as non -state actors and when a nation state itself conducts cyber-attacks as a part of national policy it is called as cyber war and these types of attackers are called as state sponsored attackers[4].

A cyber-attack is not just a criminal activity, but in most of the cases it affects the sovereignty and the conditions in which a country performs its usual functions, such as:

a. Sovereignty and Politics of a Nation:

A sovereignty of a state guarantees a nation state the right to control and exercise jurisdiction over its territory without any interference from other nation states[5]. Thus, whenever a nation state's systems are attacked by other states, it can be considered as interference in the usual working of the nation and the nation's systems; which can be termed as a violation of a nation's sovereignty. This similar type of instances can be seen in the various cases of 21st century, for example: After the event called Bronze night in Estonia, Russians launched a cyber-attack on Estonia denying its people to access government sites, news websites, and electronic services through DDOS (distributed denial of service)[6].

Russians also launched a series of cyber-attacks on Georgia. This attack through DDOS had brought down Georgian banking sector, mobiles, Media, government sites and credit card system. This attack when tracked was found out to be linked with Russian intelligence[7]. Many such instances can be drawn all throughout the world even when China stole personal data of CIA agents through US websites[8]. Also, Israel aerial bombing on construction sites of Syria stating it to be a part of Syria's nuclear plan. These attacks were conducted by hacking the computed aerial defence system of Syria. This cyber-attack was conducted by using a trap door or Trojan horse which made the Israeli planes undetectable[9]. Cyber-attacks have also played a major role in politics, regime change and changes in government this can be through hacking a candidate's mail for example: US claiming Russia to be responsible for hacking Hillary Clinton's mail or USA sending mails to Iraqi troops through secret Iraqi network and asking them to run away from the fields and disguise as civilians to remain safe during second Iraqi war which ultimately aimed at a regime change[10].

b. Economy of a Nation:

These days personal finances, national infrastructure, amenities, public and private services are managed through computer network. These opening create new vulnerabilities and increase in risk of cyber-attacks such as economic espionage, cybercrime and state sponsored exploits. In 2014, MacAfee and centre for strategic and international study estimated that cybercrime on a whole has cost the global economy up to $445 billion. Countries such as Estonia, Germany, U.S.A, Japan, Malaysia, Switzerland, Netherlands and Singapore are concerned due to high risks in cyber-attacks[11]. The economic and financial activities of governments are also disrupted by cyber-attacks in many cases, for example: The US office of personal management and Japanese pension service were also disrupted by cyber-attacks[12].

According to EOS (Executive Opinion Surveys) data, In Europe the extent of concern about cyber-attacks is lower when compared to North America and East Asia. However, it is one of the major concerns only in countries such as Germany, Estonia, Netherlands and Switzerland. In North America, USA and Canada's one of the biggest concerns in doing businesses are cyber-attacks. USA ranks second globally, for online business to consumer transactions thus, making it most vulnerable to cyber-attack. In East Asia and Pacific Asia cyber-attacks are considered to be 3rd biggest risk for doing business. At the global level amongst the major concerns for doing business, cyber-attack holds 6th position. Cyber-attacks are considered among top 3 risks in 18 countries. These risks of cyber-attacks will be a major concern for investors, who will further hesitate to take risks by investing and setting up business in these regions.

Cyber-attack doesn't only pose a challenge for doing business and investments, they also are playing a major role in affecting the finance and functioning of an economy by crashing down[13] servers of the stock exchanges such as London stock exchange and New York stock exchange. In many instances, hackers have also stolen money from banks and credit cards one such example can be seen wherein an amount of over $80 million was stolen from Bangladesh's central bank. This attack was carried through malwares and hacking. However, the criminals escaped without even getting traced[14].

c. Other Effects

Cyber-attacks can also play a devastative role in destroying the infrastructure of a country. This maybe done either through spreading virus or shutting down servers which are critical for day to day activities such as shutting down the systems or servers which show the navigation for transports, shutting down the servers for medical equipment and machinery, shutting down the computers and systems which controls purification of water, electricity for houses, streets and industries etc. Cyber-attacks may also delete or alter data related to religious and cultural issues, stockpile and existence of chemicals, necessities, food, goods etc.

A Cyber-attack also locates and receives information of people by hacking or tracking them. Cyber-attacks may also harm an individual through extracting or destroying their data.

The Need for Global Cyber Laws

Dealing with a cyber-attack can be classified into two broad categories, and they are technical ways and legal ways. Technical way is generally through software development where as a Legal way is done through legislations. Cyberspace has no geographical boundaries and no one can claim sovereignty over it. Thus, a person can commit a cybercrime even after new software development by finding its vulnerabilities and remain elusive as he maybe in some other country. Collection of cyber forensic evidence as per universally acceptable protocols often requires collaboration from multiple agencies in several countries and this is difficult to coordinate and execute. A cybercriminal often doesn't get arrested because of jurisdictional, legal and sovereignty implications which must be abided by all the nations. A major problem lies where in countries differ by laws. Thus, a country considering an event as a crime may not be a crime in some other country. These types of complexities are making it necessary to have cyber laws which are applicable to all the countries as a whole so that the criminal never escapes without being punished.

Prevailing Conditions

There are no cyber laws that are applicable to all the countries of the world. Since, there is no law that specifically prevents a cyber-attack many countries do feel that they can conduct a cyber-attack on the other countries, and in order to prevent cyber-attacks many countries have individually designed cyber laws since the start of the century. In early 2000s it was seen that only over 50 nations had some kind of updated legislations, drafts and updated statutes to protect themselves from cyber-attacks[15].

However, 33 of these countries had no updated laws to counter a cyber-attack. Whereas, 9 countries had enacted laws against five or fewer cybercrimes and around 10 countries had updated laws regarding 6 to 10 types of cyber-attacks.

These 10 countries which were substantially and fully updated, included Australia, Canada, Estonia, Mauritius, India, Turkey, Peru, Philippines, USA and Japan. Whereas over 9 countries such as China, Brazil, Chile, Malaysia, Czech Republic, Denmark, Poland, Spain and United Kingdom had partially updated cyber laws and over 33 countries such as Albania, Bulgaria, Cuba, New Zealand, Zimbabwe, Nigeria, Nicaragua, Morocco, South Africa, Dominican Republic, Fiji, Ethiopia, Egypt, France, Iran, Italy, Jordan, Kazakhstan, Latvia, Sudan, Vietnam etc had non-updated laws. However, out of these non-updated countries over 13 countries had the updating progress underway and they were Latvia, Albania, Cuba, Gambia, Iran, Kazakhstan, Malta, Morocco, New Zealand, Sudan, Vietnam, Zambia and Lesotho[16].

These legislations had definitely helped in deterrence of cyber-attacks but they only prevented its citizens from conducting or being victim of cyber-attacks conducted within the nation. Attacks from other territories or nation states were only defendable to some extent and these criminals were never caught due to problems such as lack of jurisdictions and respecting of sovereignty of other nations. Thus, it was realized that international cooperation among the nations was required to overcome this problem. Since then some measures have been taken on regional and global levels of cyber-attacks and some of these were as follows:

1. **Budapest Convention:**

This convention on cybercrime was initiated in 2001 by the council of Europe. This convention has clearly defined the meaning of service providers, computer data and systems in order to prevent any further confusion. This convention also ensured that every party of the convention must design its domestic laws on illegal access, illegal interception, data and system interference, computer related frauds, misuse of devices, child pornography, infringements of copyrights and infringements of related rights. Article 11 of this Convention makes it mandatory for its parties to implement criminal offences on individuals who intentionally violate article 2-10. The violation of these articles may also lead to punishments such as deprivation of liberty or even monetary sanctions. This convention also ensured that the parties get enough power and authority to collect, to store, to use and safeguard the data. Article 23 of this convention also specifies the maximum extent of international cooperations to be made possible on criminal matters such as collection of evidences and investigations. This convention also ensures extradition of cyber criminals among its parties[17]. This convention is one of the benchmark conventions on cybercrime but it is only a regional convention restricted to European council and few other voluntary members such as Argentina, Australia, Canada, Chile, Colombia, Costa Rica, Dominican Republic, Ghana, Israel, Japan, Mauritius, Mexico, Morocco, Panama, Paraguay, Peru, Philippines, Senegal, Sri Lanka, USA, Tonga and South Africa[18]. However, this convention fails to specify the consequences of its member launching a cyber-attack on one of its fellow members. This convention has also laid down a lot of rules and functions specifying on how and what kind of domestic laws its members must implement, rather than establishing uniform laws for all the members of this convention.

2. **Tallinn Manual:**

Tallinn is a city located in Estonia. In 2009 an international military organisation called NATO cyber defence centre for excellence, invited an international group of independent experts to produce a manual on law governing cyber warfare. This manual consists of over 95 rules and doesn't speak of any nation's position regarding cyber laws. These are just views of the international experts. The rules in this manual are broad and the experts have also not created any new laws for this manual, they have represented a text which is accurately replication of customary international laws. These laws are not abiding and no government or organization has implemented it till date. Tallinn manual at first defines what sovereignty is and how a cyber-attack can affect the sovereignty of a nation along with defining cyber-attacks and cyber terrorism. Then, the manual also describes about jurisdiction of a state over an attacker, devices, victim and equipment located in a nation state's territory or in some other territory. This manual also makes sure of a nation state's control over a cyber infrastructure that exists in its territory and at the same time it prevents the state from using it to harm people in one's own or other countries. This manual also permits the countries to resort to countermeasures through cyber-attacks in retaliation for a cyber-attack. It also permits cyber-attacks by a nation whenever it is in a war, provided the attack must be only to weaken the military of the enemies. However, the citizens even in the worst case must suffer minimal damage. The manual protects civilians from unnecessary suffering and starvation during cyber-attacks. This manual also ensures that a country can cause a cyber-attack for self- defence if it is evident that the country will be facing a severe cyber or kinetic attack. This manual also guides about treatment of cyber warriors after defeating or getting captured. It ensures citizens and their objects for a minimal damage during cyber-attacks. It also prevents the nation states from cyber attacking on daily needs and basic necessities such as transportation of food, medicines, medical machinery, destroying systems which generate electricity, purifies water etc. The manual briefs how to conduct a collective self defence against a cyber-attack and what actions can be taken against a state by the international organizations if it violates cyber laws. It also puts the blame on the commanders and other superiors who are responsible for instigating or knowing about a cyber-attack and committing a war crime. This manual provides rules to safeguard neutral actors such as UNO, Red Cross society, UN personnel and also how neutral states must be protected during cyber warfare and what will be the consequences of attacking these neutral bodies or states. One of the important things that this manual state is prohibiting nations from destroying the data related to diplomatic archives and the culture of people[19]. Tallinn manual is one of the recent manual on cyber-attacks. This manual is one of the benchmark for governing cyber laws all throughout the world. This manual focuses on cyber warfare and what kind of laws can be implemented during a cyber war. However, it is very important to realize that this cannot be done without the existence of global cyber laws, and this manual in no way explains how to get these cyber laws into existence. The manual also doesn't explain about cybercrimes and importance of international cooperation in designing laws to establish strong cyber security legislations among all the countries and the need for extradition of cybercriminals.

3. UNO and Cyber Laws

The United Nations organisation is one of the key answers for most of the modern-day problems. One such problem of today is 'Cyber Security' which in order to be solved must definitely go through the United Nations organisation so that the norms regarding cyber-attacks can be introduced. Issues like Cyber war and cybercrimes have already been introduced in the general assembly over 15 years ago but not even once have these been introduced in the Security Council. However, the general assembly of UN can only recommend changes and only the Security Council can make decisions which have to be followed by the member nations. International telecommunications union is an independent body of UN bureaucracy which is acting independently as norms entrepreneur under article 57 of the UN charter and is playing a major role in designing norms on cyber-attacks and crimes.

Regarding cyber war, in the year 1998, the Russian government introduced a resolution in the first committee regarding computer related crimes. This Russian draft of 1998 for the first time mentioned military potential for information and communication technology. This resolution was adopted in the assembly without vote but however USA and European states suspicious of the treaty did not push for an international treaty. Russia wanted to develop international law for preventing use of information technologies for purposes incompatible with missions of ensuring international stability and security. However, the debates in general assembly ended with USA opposing Russia's proposal for cyber arms control treaty. However, in the year 2005 this draft was passed for voting by the member nations and U.S again vetoed against such a resolution. After, rejecting the draft in 2006, it got sponsored by Russia, China, Armenia, Belarus, Kazakhstan, Myanmar, Kyrgyzstan, Tajikistan and Uzbekistan. However, American opposition on the draft continued and the sponsorships of other nations making the issue complicated, forced the secretary general to conclude that due to the complexities no consensus can be reached on final report. However, in 2010 the Obama administration presented a position paper and called for various parties to come together and to reach on a consensus on information security as a major threat in the 21st century. The threat was considered a risk to international peace and security. It requested for furthermore talks among the countries to deal with national and international infrastructures along with finding possibilities to elaborate common terms and definitions relevant to the UNO. Recently, Russia, China, Tajikistan and Uzbekistan have sent a letter to UN secretary general which included a draft for International code of conduct for international security.

Whereas regarding cybercrimes in the year 2000 a draft resolution terming it as combating the criminal misuse of information technologies which was introduced by USA and other 38 members in 2001 a follow up resolution was again passed by 81 countries along with USA and this draft resolution was adopted without a vote. In 2002, cyber-crime related issues were moved from general assembly to commission on crime prevention and criminal justice. In the year 2002 USA again introduced a new draft called creation of global culture of cyber security to discuss macro-economic policy questions: science and technology for development this draft was again re introduced in 2005 and 2010 with some resolutions by USA and co-sponsored by 39 other countries[20].

Here, it can be seen that the norms which are being introduced in UNO are proceeding very slowly and are generally being changed and influenced by domestic and international policies and politics of the member nations. The member nations have not yet reached on a consensus, which is a major drawback in order to implement and introduce these laws.

Introducing and Implementing the Cyber Laws

The contemporary world is witnessing various changes in the politics and policies of the nations. The nations and nationals trying to be more self-centred, has left the international organizations in doubt, whether cooperation among these nations is possible to solve the problems. However, the climate change agreement in Paris has proved that the negotiations and cooperation among the countries is possible and the nations are ready to set aside their personal aims and goals and come together in order to tackle the major threats and problems that the world will be facing or is facing.

The cyber laws in order to be implemented on the global basis must be discussed with all the countries in the prior case. These negotiations are for sure exhaustive and member nations will try to gain something for themselves with these new laws being introduced. However, most of the poor and developing nations would agree to the cyber laws on a universal basis as these countries are lacking the technologies and legislations to counter cyber-attacks and these laws will further ensure that they won't get affected from cyber-attacks conducted by criminals and nations who in most of the cases remain un-punished. The developed nations which are highly dependent on internet, digitalization and systems for their day to day activities would also agree to be a part of these negotiations, as they are facing major threats from cyber criminals and attackers from all corners of the world. After, the negotiations, the next step would be discussion of all the countries which has agreed to take part in the negotiations, these talks and discussions happens at different platforms. However, United Nations General Assembly would be a more preferred platform as it includes all the countries as member nations and these norms cannot be violated once Security Council ratifies it. The general assembly then passes the draft for convention on cybercrimes if more than half of the member states vote for establishment of a convention. This convention must be backed and assisted by UNO. At the same time the Security Council must ratify the conventions, as cyber-attack is more concerned with international peace and national stability. The Security Council must also make it mandatory for all the member states of the UNO to take part in the convention and fund them. Once ratified then all the member nations must abide these laws. However, if any country failing to do so will have to face the sanctions imposed by the members of the convention.

Private firms and IT related mammoths such as Google, windows; Android, IOS, etc. play a major role in today's globalized global economy. Thus, being a more vulnerable target for cyber-attacks. These private bodies in no country have the authority and power to punish the cyber criminals. As a result, often these sectors invest a huge amount of capital to tackle, defend and deter against the cyber-attacks. But however, these investments make no sense if a cyber-attack turns out to be successful and the criminal is not arrested due to jurisdictional, legal and technical problems. Thus, it becomes necessary for these firms to align with their respective governments and agree to be the part of the convention in order to seek protection. Similarly, the members will also be beneficial as they can sign a mutual technical assistance programmes with these firms. Ultimately making it a win-win situation, both for the private bodies and the members of the convention.

The funds contribution to maintain and establish the convention from member states will differ from nation to nation according to the economic conditions of the members. Added, to it the money collected from firms, sanctions, fines and penalties will also be used in administration and maintenance of the convention after deducting the amount of compensation for the affected countries or firms.

This convention in the first case will include the issues broadly related to cyber-attacks such as cyber war and cybercrimes and these aspects must not be separated from each other. This convention just like Budapest convention must make it mandatory for countries to design laws regarding cybercrimes on a domestic level so that all the issues regarding cyber-attacks doesn't have to be tackled in an international level or platforms.

Cyber Criminals

The domestic laws of a country will be applicable only on its own citizens who commit a cybercrime or cyber-attack on a system which is physically located within the same country's territory. However, if the attacker or system doesn't belong to the same country then these laws may not be applicable and the attacker will be charged for breaching sovereignty of a nation. This type of attacks on some other country's systems or citizens would be dealt with a series of laws that will be standard for all the countries recognised by the United Nations. These laws must include the kind of punishment given to the criminal depending on the type of crime committed along with specifications of kind and period of punishment for the criminal. This convention must also ensure of international cooperation by member states through providing evidences and investigation assistance. This convention also must talk of extradition programme through an application if the attacker is a citizen of a country but is in asylum or located in some other country. This convention must also permit for the court which will provides with fair and free trial for the citizens charged with a cyber-attack or cybercrime on some other nation's systems or citizens. This court must also look after the cases and applications of extradition of the criminals among the member nations so that it will not be misused.

State Sponsored Cyber Attacks

This convention would also specify that no nation state would directly or indirectly indulge itself in a cyber-attack on some other country's system or citizen either through financial, material or technical assistance until and unless they find themselves in a kinetic war with some other nation states. The convention must also set guidelines to the country while conducting a cyber-attack and must make Tallinn Manual as the legal source to be followed by all the countries during a kinetic war. However, this convention must also mention that no country would be retaliating a cyber-attack of a country with a kinetic attack. Any country directly or indirectly indulging in a cyber-attack when there is no kinetic war should be tried through international court of justice and if proved guilty would face sanctions as to ever the Security Council suggests. These sanctions would differ from fines to trade and financial sanctions, as per the damage made by a nation on some other member state.

Cyber Terrorists and State Sponsored Cyber Attacks

This convention must also specify that if a convict who if proved in the court of being indirectly or directly assisted by a nation state for cyber-attack on other nation would be charged guilty of breaching a country's sovereignty and at the same time the sponsored country must also be punished with sanctions as specified by the security council.

Conclusion

Cyber-attacks are one of the major threats to the world in the contemporary age these attacks cannot only be stopped through new software or strict laws of a nation. These laws even if implemented only by one or only some countries would be of no great use. Cyber-attacks can be tackled by global cyber laws implemented by global consensus. These measures, legislations and convention suggested above may prevent cyber war and crimes to a huge extent; however, it is all dependent on nations and its policies. All the countries need to cooperate and step aside the differences so that these laws can be created. However, the chances of one country breaching other country's sovereignty, and the fear of a country destroying another country's economy through cyber, infrastructure and politics will continue to be high.

Endnotes

1   Col Sanjeev Relia, Cyber warfare its implications on national security, Vij Books India Pvt. Limited, 2015, (19),

2   Richard A. Clarke, Robert K. Kanke, Cyber War, Harper Collin publishers, 2010, (31)

3   Col Sanjeev Relia, Cyber warfare its implications on national security, Vij Books India Pvt. Limited,2015, (06)

4   Ibid (33)

5   International group of experts by the invitation from NATO cooperative cyber defence center of excellence. (2013). Tallinn manual. Cambridge, United Kingdom: Cambridge university press.

6   Richard A. Clarke, Robert K. Kanke,(2010) Cyber War, p 13-16, Harper Collin publishers,.

7   Ibid 18-21

8   Ibid 58

9   Ibid 02-08

10 Ibid 10

11 World economic forum. (2016). The global risks report 2016 – 11th edition. retrieved from https://www.weforum.org/reports/the-global-risks-reprort-2016

12 World economic forum. (2016). The global risks reports 2016 – 11th edition. retrieved from https://www.weforum.org/reports/the-global-risks-report-2016

13 Mohamed Jaber (2016, June 05). Hackers attack the stock exchange. Daily mail online. Retrieved from www.dailymail.co.uk/news/article-3625656/Hackers-attack-Stock-Exchange-Cyber

14 Kandelwal Swati, (2016, March 14). Here's how Hackers stole $80 million from Bangladesh bank. The hacker news. Retrieved from thehackernews.com/2016/03/bank-hacking-malware.html?m=1

15 MC Connell international (December 2000) cyber crime... and punishment? Archaic laws threaten global information. Retrieved from www.mcconnellinternational.com

16 MC Connell international (December 2000) cyber crime... and punishment? Archaic laws threaten global information. Retrieved from www.mcconnellinternational.com

17 Council of Europe (2001), Convention on cybercrime. Budapest, Hungary: Author.

18 (ND) retrieved from Council of Europe portal https://www.coe.int/en/web/conventions/full-list/-/conventions/treaty/185/signatures

19 International group of experts by the invitation from NATO cooperative cyber defence center of excellence. (2013). Tallinn manual. Cambridge, United Kingdom: Cambridge university press.

20 Maurer, Tim. Cyber norm emergence at the United Nations - An analysis of the activities at the UN regarding cyber security, Harvard Kennedy school, Belfer Center for science and International affairs September 2011.

Index

www.ingramcontent.com/pod-product-compliance
Lightning Source LLC
Chambersburg PA
CBHW031549260326
41914CB00002B/342